COMMUNITY POLICING

CLARENDON STUDIES IN CRIMINOLOGY

Published under the auspices of the Institute of Criminology, University of Cambridge, the Mannheim Centre, London School of Economics, and the Centre for Criminological Research, University of Oxford

GENERAL EDITOR: ROGER HOOD (University of Oxford)

EDITORS: ANTHONY BOTTOMS and TREVOR BENNETT
(University of Cambridge)

DAVID DOWNES and PAUL ROCK
(London School of Economics)

NICOLA LACEY and ANDREW SANDERS
(University of Oxford)

Other titles in this series:

Prison Systems: A Comparative Study of Accountability in England, France, Germany, and The Netherlands

JON VAGG

Reporting Crime: The Media Politics of Criminal Justice

PHILIP SCHLESINGER & HOWARD TUMBER

Grendon: A Study of a Therapeutic Prison

ELAINE GENDERS and ELAINE PLAYER

The State of Our Prisons

ROY D. KING AND KATHLEEN MCDERMOTT

Community Policing

Nigel Fielding

CLARENDON PRESS · OXFORD
1995

Oxford University Press, Walton Street, Oxford OX2 6DP
Oxford New York
Athens Auckland Bangkok Bombay
Calcutta Cape Town Dar es Salaam Delhi
Florence Hong Kong Istanbul Karachi
Kuala Lumpur Madras Madrid Melbourne
Mexico City Nairobi Paris Singapore
Taipei Tokyo Toronto
and associated companies in
Berlin Ibadan

Oxford is a trade mark of Oxford University Press

Published in the United States
by Oxford University Press Inc., New York

British Library Cataloguing in Publication Data
Data available

Library of Congress Cataloging in Publication Data
Fielding, Nigel.
Community policing / Nigel Fielding.
p. cm.
Includes bibliographical references.
1. Community policing—Great Britain. I. Title.
HV7936.C83F53 1995 363.2'3—dc20 95–33041
ISBN 0–19–826027–X

1 3 5 7 9 10 8 6 4 2

Printed in Great Britain
on acid-free paper by
Biddles Ltd., Guildford and King's Lynn

General Editor's Introduction

Community Policing is the fifth volume to be published since *Clarendon Studies in Criminology* was launched in 1994, as successor to *Cambridge Studies in Criminology*.

Clarendon Studies in Criminology, which is published under the auspices of the Cambridge Institute of Criminology, the Mannheim Centre for Criminology and Criminal Justice at the London School of Economics and the Oxford Centre for Criminological Research, provides a forum for outstanding work in all aspects of criminology, criminal justice, penology, and the wider field of deviant behaviour. It welcomes works of theory and synthesis as well as reports of empirical inquiries and aims to be international in its scope.

Community Policing, the first book on the police to appear in this series, deals with a subject which has been widely debated but so far little researched. Nigel Fielding's ethnographic study is the first attempt to discover what 'the local bobby on the beat' actually does. Through the skilful and sensitive use of faithfully reported examples, drawn from over 1,200 observations of police–public encounters and informal interviews with a wide range of officers in Inner London and Surrey, Nigel Fielding has provided telling insights into how community constables go about their day-to-day tasks in policing communities where there is often a good deal of ambivalence about, and sometimes outbreaks of overt hostility to, police intervention.

While recognizing that no locally based studies can pretend to answer all the issues raised by the complex and often rather vague concept of community policing, Professor Fielding clearly demonstrates that there is much that community constables can do to help in the prevention of crime, the provision of social services, and in bringing offenders to book. Moreover, he suggests that they may, by carefully sifting information gathered through personal knowledge, be better placed than other police officers to negotiate with citizens in order to reduce conflict and ultimately enhance the legitimacy accorded to police actions.

Nigel Fielding's evidence, and his challenging discussion of its wider implications for the politics, organization and practices of policing, will undoubtedly be of value to academics involved in police studies and criminology as well as to those responsible within the police for shaping the direction that the service takes. The editors are delighted to welcome this fascinating study to the *Series*.

Roger Hood
August 1995

Preface and Acknowledgements

In an earlier book, a study of police training, I wrote that those who would improve policing must learn more about 'how officers identify specific achievements as desirable, recognize certain skills as related to those achievements and therefore worth refining, and set about practising and improving these skills in their work' (Fielding 1988b: ix). Such an approach may seem apt in addressing police training but is not perhaps so obvious when applied to routine policing. Here research has tended to highlight the obduracy of police officers in the face of new approaches to delivering police services, the strength and self-serving nature of the occupational culture, and the confusion of purposes engendered by the breadth of the police mandate. Yet I would make a case that, if we are genuinely concerned with competence in police practice—how it is construed and what can be done to promote it—we have little option but to regard police officers as active learners.

It may seem perverse to take this view when one cannot help but be conscious of the many faults and failings of police officers and the police organization. But to deny that police seek to develop and refine occupationally-relevant skills is to ignore the lessons of organizational theory, occupational psychology and the sociology of work. One does not, in fact, have to imbibe the academic literature to see that police are thoughtful about their work in these ways. Whether we call it 'ethnographic methods' or 'hanging around with the police', a little exposure to police talk soon reveals an interest, indeed, a preoccupation with, competence. It also reveals a preoccupation with the obstacles the organizations put in its way, and a sophisticated appreciation that 'competence' in this, of all occupations, is supremely 'situational' and highly susceptible to one's viewpoint.

Thus, when I came to study long-term beat assignment in London and Surrey I sought to introduce rather broader themes than might be associated with the evaluation of one particular community policing programme. It seemed essential to discover how community constables constructed their brief, whether they actively interpreted it and how consistently it was applied. The community policing programme I researched was avowedly directed to crime control as well as social service, and I wanted to see by what means and with what degree of autonomy the community police went about cultivating contacts, gathering information and acting upon it. I wanted to know the tricks of the trade, the criteria of success, and whether supervision and management helped or hindered. These seemed useful dimensions to add to the existing literature, which tells us much about the policy side of evaluation without quite conveying what it is that community police actually do. Thus, this book is organized around activities identified by community police as key elements in working their 'permanent' beat, and which I have attempted to bring alive by narrative description of incidents which I observed.

I feel some hesitancy in employing the first person singular in this preface. This book largely draws on data collected by myself, but the overall project was a collaboration with Charles Kemp and Clive Norris. Their acute ethnographic insight, remarkable stamina in the field, and phenomenal industry in documenting and contributing to the analysis of the data made work a constant pleasure. Great dedication and high skills of organization were displayed by Alwyn Whitehead, our project secretary. At Oxford University Press, Richard Hart and John Whelan, and series editor Roger Hood, were kindly, courteous and patient with yet another author for whom his books are his babies. The anonymous readers of the manuscript provided immensely valuable guidance for which I am grateful indeed, as I am to the Economic and Social Research Council for funding the research, and the Police Foundation for facilitating much more than research access. But my utmost thanks go to the police officers who, with grace and humour, let me catch glimpses of their working world.

Contents

1

Negotiating Order

Studies of community policing have been preoccupied with one thing—does it work. Generally the answers have been gloomy.[1] But seldom has anyone paused to examine what community policing is. Indeed, it has several meanings.[2] On the police and policy-making side, community policing offers 'political' benefits and is readily embraced for reasons having little to do with the reality of police practice. The recent proliferation of schemes based on community policing—'sector policing', 'area policing', 'total geographic policing'—attests to its enduring appeal, as does the recurrent finding that people want 'more bobbies on the beat'. But on the academic side, community policing is sceptically regarded precisely because other audiences are too uncritical of it and because research suggests it is less effective than is claimed. For those inclined towards radical social and political change, community policing is easily seen as mere tinkering or as a disguised part of a repressive political apparatus.

Is there something distinctive about community policing? How do community police actually carry out their work? How does it compare to conventional patrol styles and systems? Why does it still appeal both to police and public? Perhaps there is something missing from the policy-related literature on community policing. Perhaps, too, police and policymakers have too quickly embraced community policing for its occasional successes rather than its routine reality. This book takes a different tack, by looking closely at the work, spelling out the tactics, looking at the negotiations, with the public and within the force. We need to know the phenomenon before we evaluate it.

A key concern is whether there is anything distinctive in decision-making by community police. Assumptions about decision-making based on management theory and the cost-benefit perspective of *homo economicus* produce models with limited explanatory value.

[1] Brown and Iles (1985); Bennett (1992a).   [2] Weatheritt (1983).

'Prescriptive decision-making models do not take into account organizational structure, nor the temporal aspects of the process of decision-making . . . the sources of practice and the traditions which guide and constrain decision-making in organizational contexts.'[3] Models of decision-making based on quantitative data about police actions[4] have limited value in explaining decisions like making arrests, and are even less useful in explaining informal actions. But qualitative approaches which examine officers' values and occupational culture as a basis for inferences about likely actions have not offered compelling evidence that these explain their decisions and behaviour.[5] Further, the explanatory value of situational variables (e.g., citizen attributes, specifics of the incident) is modest and mostly limited to the arrest decision.[6] As an alternative, Worden and Brandl advocate the 'collection and evaluation of decision-makers' verbal reports of the cognitive steps taken to make choices', so as to trace the process whereby information is received and manipulated to produce decisions.[7] In sympathy with this approach this book draws on field observation and accounts in interviews and police documents to examine decision-making by community police as they go about their difficult task in the inner city.

To some, the key to police action is simply whether it is lawful. Certainly the law provides a resource which influences officers' actions, and indeed the law governing police practice has been strengthened, notably by the Police and Criminal Evidence Act 1984. But police are the arbiters of law in their encounters with the public, and their construction of the law often remains the one on which the public rely in negotiating incidents. We cannot rely on the law to tell us what officers do, and why. If we want to understand why the police act as they do we need to bring into account both the 'temporal aspects', a term including the situational dynamics which mean no two incidents are exactly alike, and the influence of the 'organizational structure' on their decisions.

Organizations are broadly regulated by their socially-accepted role, which warrants action within the boundaries thought necessary for its pursuit. The 'charter' of the police organization emphasizes both the duty to uphold the law, to control crime, and to ensure the maintenance of civil order. In inner city policing, and especially long-term assignment to one beat, these equally-stressed elements of the

[3] Manning (1983) at 50.   [4] For example, Black (1971).
[5] Worden and Brandl (1990) at 288.   [6] Worden (1989).   [7] See n. 5.

charter highlight the exercise of police *discretion*. This fundamental concept obliges officers to act as arbiters of competing interests and interpreters of the law.[8] This is because the law is written with discrete events in mind, namely, particular occasions of law-breaking, whereas officers applying the law over the course of long-term contact with community members see events as part of a sustained sequence. Sometimes one 'side' prevails, sometimes another, but both groups will still be there tomorrow. The law does not lay down any 'balancing factors' that are meaningful in these terms. Incidentally, this is not to say that community policing is all discretion; one theme of this book is that community constables play a significant, unsung part in law enforcement. _____

Neither should we discount the oppressive side of a greater emphasis on communal, informal law enforcement. Policing in some Asian countries has long operated on such a close integration of police and community that it is seen as a distinctive policing type.[9] Some commentators have looked East with envy to see how such conditions could be promoted here. Yet the system whose neighbourhood police stations seem so benign and oriented to social service violates UN human rights conventions. Suspects in Japan routinely remain in police custody for long periods rather than being remanded; in 1991 the Tokyo High Court ordered the release of a man police held in solitary confinement for 70 days, but it remains legal to hold suspects for 23 days without charges, and indefinite periods awaiting trial. Where the community sees it as a duty to apply social control itself, by berating suspects to confess and then offering support, it is hardly surprising that Japanese police insist that station custody and interrogations are necessary to maintain their extremely high conviction rate (*Guardian*, 24 April, 1991).

A Socio-legal Perspective on Community Policing

Police discretion poses compelling problems of selective enforcement or non-enforcement, for example, in the case of racial harassment. Here it must be recognized that selective enforcement is but the other side of discretion and it is usually folly to write law that allows for no exceptions or denies scope for interpretation 'on the ground'. The solution to complaints of selective enforcement or non-enforcement

---

[8] McCabe and Wallington (1988).   [9] Bayley (1982).

is not to abolish discretion but to build channels of public consultation and accountability.

The exercise of discretion is an enduring concern because the legal position and powers of the office of constable are hardly matters of clarity. Some hold the constable's authority to be of a peculiarly personal nature.[10] At the extreme, the 1962 Royal Commission asserted that the constable's authority as defined by the courts, 'is original, not delegated, and is exercised at his own discretion by virtue of his office'; indeed, constables were neither Crown servants nor servants of police authorities.[11] It is doubtful whether legal doctrine in reported cases does support this assertion and it may be more reasonable to say that a constable's status derives from the common law which 'defines his or her powers, immunities, privileges, rights and duties insofar as his or her discretionary power exists to investigate crime, make arrests and bring suspects before justices of the peace'.[12] There the constable needs no prior approval from a higher body. In the exercise of discretion the constable's authority *is* original, not delegated, but the law determines its bounds and can be changed.

Statutes conferring discretionary powers on constables include Section 1 of the Police and Criminal Evidence Act, giving a power to search vehicles if there are reasonable grounds to suspect they contain stolen or prohibited items, and Section 24, giving powers to arrest without warrant if grounds exist to suspect guilt of an arrestable offence (or the intention to commit one). Lustgarten observes that 'the factual condition precedent is his knowledge of certain events and of the behaviour of the person searched or arrested . . . [T]hose facts must be . . . reasonably suspected to be true, by the constable—and by no one else, including a superior officer'.[13] Similarly, the Public Order Act 1986 permits officers to proceed on the basis of their own judgment; no member of the public need be present as in previous public order law.[14] In the operation of such powers, sociologists of law tell us that 'due process is for crime control'.[15]

Experience teaches the alert constable that the law is less a hindrance than a resource.[16] '[L]oosely-worded, ambiguous statutes did not create the problem for the practical police officer that some writers who have attempted a literal interpretation of the legislation have

---

[10] Marshall (1965).   [11] Royal Commission on the Police (1962), *Final Report.*
[12] Hogarth (1982) at 113.   [13] Lustgarten (1986) at 13.
[14] Crisp and Newburn (1991).   [15] McBarnet (1981).   [16] Fielding (1988b).

suggested. The interpretational latitude provided by such legal instruments enabled the police officer . . . not only to refrain from making arrests but to make an arrest and then invoke the *resource charge* to provide legal legitimation.'[17] Further, the consent of people ignorant of the law can easily be managed. It is doubtful that most people are aware that, short of arrest, they can refuse to accompany officers to the station. 'It is by no means clear whether "I went along only because I thought I had to, but I wasn't forced" constitutes consent, legally or philosophically.'[18]

But there are other themes in the office of constable pertinent to community policing. The office has both a Saxon and Norman heritage. The Saxon root provided the notion of locality, that all community members had an obligation for the good behaviour of their neighbours. The 'tything man' was head of each ten family unit and had to produce wrongdoers for trial and see that order was maintained. Tensions arising from collective responsibility and the problem of community definition and role can be traced to this. The Normans provided the notion of independence which promoted the pre-eminence of order maintenance over law enforcement by associating the Norman constable with royal authority, having responsibility for the King's Peace 'by hue and cry and other means'.[19]

However, the constable's role was eclipsed by the Justices of the Peace Act of 1361. The JPs were directly appointed by the sovereign, had broader responsibilities and powers, higher social status and often presided over the 'leet court' appointing the constable. Constables became their executive agents. Even through the formative nineteenth century the police were seen with indifference or disdain by the middle and upper class, being incorporated into a pre-existing local government hierarchy. 'Urban ratepayers saw their police forces unproblematically and precisely as servants, paid to protect property and keep the streets clean.'[20]

While the changing ties between dominant social classes and police remind us that the institution has not always played the same role, the fundamental source of the ambivalence which endures in policing remains the common law tradition itself. Its essence is the gradual evolution of law, whose source is the 'distillation and continual restatement of legal doctrine through the decisions of the courts',[21]

[17] Chatterton (1981) at 26.   [18] Lustgarten (1986) at 134.
[19] Critchley (1978) at 5.   [20] Steedman (1984) at 7.
[21] Cotterrell (1989) at 21.

modified but not supplanted by the modern preference for legislative drafting of statutes. Perhaps the germ of the centrality of discretion to policing is the idea that common law is better characterized as a set of principles than a system of rules. Thus, 'to represent it as a systematic structure of rules is to distort it; it is to represent as static what is essentially dynamic and constantly shifting'.[22] While this doctrine is conducive to common law jurisprudence, it is not an unalloyed blessing to the police. The absence of clear rules regulating decisions excites public suspicion that the police are abusing their authority. Williams argues that the imposition of rules on routine practice, such as action at domestic disputes, 'might be made attractive to the police . . . [by] includ[ing] within the rules guidance on choosing alternatives to arrest'.[23]

It is, then, no coincidence that a concern with officers' decision-making brings us to themes of ambivalence and lack of administrative guidance in the exercise of discretion. It is consistent with the 'judicial empiricism' Pound saw in the common law, a pragmatic, case by case decision-making guided by judicial precedents.[24] Our historical preference, it seems, has been for broad guidelines which underlie but only loosely direct individual decisions. The sometime quirkiness and independence of our judiciary are of a piece with the original authority in the office of constable. Rather than a 'system', legal theorists see common law as a set of maxims, broad notions resistant to systematization. The judge is an extrusion of the immanent wisdom of law which has gone before; law is 'the repository of the experience of the community over the ages',[25] a neo-*volkisch* common-sense wisdom encouraging police to see their role as arbitrating competing interests to find the correct path. This is often the middle path because it is least likely to provoke either side to withdraw legitimacy from the process, and the most likely to prompt each to continue within that process to seek its interest, rather than demand a new process.

This attentiveness to what will reconcile competing interests and maintain the community speaks to the status of the law's officers as well. Thus, under common law, 'the authority of the judge is not as a political decision-maker (certainly not as delegate of the King or parliament) but as representative of the community'.[26] The point is

22 Postema (1986) at 10.   23 Williams (1984) at 129.
24 Pound (1921) at 182.   25 Postema (1986) at 25.
26 Cotterrell (1989) at 27.

that custom is not itself changeless. Since custom may change over time so can law, as an expression of that custom. But 'the mechanisms of change are in society (or the community)'.[27] To avoid law becoming ossified the judge is seen as spokesperson of the community,[28] just as the police officer's exercise of discretion is to be informed by a grasp of local normative standards.

The modern legislative state has eroded the ambit of common law, but what remains clearly addresses a need. As Cotterrell puts it, 'the idea of judicial authority rooted in community remains perhaps the strongest, most vibrant, contribution of common law thought'.[29] Thus, 'community' is a fundamental influence on common law. But common law's image of community is of a 'broad consensus and an already constituted social unity'.[30] Such a notion of community cannot have been readily sustained even in the circumscribed polity of early times. An important influence in bringing to common law a sociological sense of community was Sir Henry Maine, who saw that the prevailing trend was away from legal rights and duties based on the status of individuals and towards transactions based on contractual relationships or, in his famous phrase, 'the movement of the progressive societies has hitherto been a movement *from Status to Contract*'.[31]

The common law tradition, then, came to appreciate that society was not the close-knit community associated with common law's idealized past. After Maine, the running was increasingly made by those who emphasized statutory law-making, and consequently saw law's inspiration in political power rather than in community.[32] But, for its parallel to the debate over community policing, we should note Cotterrell's valediction: 'Despite much ambiguity . . . the theory of common law . . . emphasise[s] the vital importance of maintaining law's link with community life. By implication [it] pose[s] a warning against the arrogance of legislators who treat law as no more than an affair of efficient rules organised as an instrument of coercion.'[33] Here are the roots of discretion.

Police in Community

Banton gave an early warning of the danger in seeing 'the police' and 'the community' as simple, undifferentiated categories.[34]

---

[27] *Ibid.* at 28.
[30] Postema (1986) at 19.
[32] Cotterrell (1989) at 49–51.

[28] *Ibid.* at 30.
[31] Maine (1861).
[33] *Ibid.* at 51.

[29] *Ibid.* at 32.

[34] Banton (1974).

Complaining about the phrase 'police-community relations', he commented that 'the pitfall . . . is the tendency to represent the two categories as homogenous ("all the same") and mutually exclusive ("as if no one could belong to both at the same time")'.[35] Instead he proposed a 'three level' model, with level one as 'the community', level two, 'police and public', and level three, ' "the bosses" and "the men" '.[36] Thus, the 'two sides' at level two are not mutually exclusive, joining up at level one, 'for police officers also belong to the community and play many roles in which they are not differentiated from non-policemen'.[37]

Banton also emphasized discretion, which was not only critical to understanding what officers did but affected job satisfaction, 'for few things made them more discontented than orders which limited their freedom to exercise discretion'.[38] When Banton sought the origins of discretion he found them in police training, the (contemporary) decisions of the courts and participation in society.[39] In other words, the community did influence the exercise of discretion, and this was from direct experience, as officers interacted with others, out of uniform, and learned how police action was regarded. Officers also resented discipline codes which limited public contact lest conflicts of loyalty arose.

The more a policeman is hindered from participating in the community the less he will understand public sentiment, the less well he will exercise his discretion, therefore the more are [people] likely to be irritated by his behaviour, the more will they treat him differently in social contacts, the more isolated will the police become. As their sympathy for members of the public declines further, hostility towards them increases, they become further isolated, and so on.[40]

The relationship of police and public is, then, influenced by police participation in the community. Obstacles to integration, such as section houses and the phenomenon of the commuter constable, can be damaging, although cultural isolation—flight into a social 'police ghetto'—is at least as dangerous as physical isolation. The kind of check on police behaviour Banton envisaged is shown by his observation of different approaches by black and white American police. 'Black officers stressed that they had to meet in the community some of the citizens they dealt with as policemen, and that if their behav-

---

[35] Banton (1974) at 164.   [36] Ibid.   [37] Ibid.
[38] Ibid. at 165.   [39] Banton (1964).   [40] Banton (1974) at 165–6.

iour was not correct this possibility would act as a check upon them.'[41] Banton had concluded, in 1974, that 'in a city like London police officers cannot easily participate in a shared community'.

Banton also recognized the limitation of his attempt to replace 'two sides' with 'three levels', because it assumed a single community at level one. Plainly his research on American and British city policing repudiates that, and his 1974 paper differentiates the police relationship with 'Asians' and 'West Indians', along with class and other differences. 'The policeman's personal participation is in a society which is . . . divided and this affects his conception of his duties. There are also divisions between the generations and between groups with different aspirations.'[42] It is possible to read Banton as suggesting that the best course through these conflicts is for police to apply the law enforcement brief with real impartiality by, for example, making strenuous efforts against corporate crime as well as street crime,[43] or combating racial harassment as well as monitoring groups of black youths. For Banton, the real meaning of 'crime prevention' is the extension of law enforcement to the Establishment. 'The police . . . should have both the expertise and the political muscle to put pressure onto local authorities and private companies to see that they allow for the long-term criminogenic consequences of their policies as well as calculating the votes they can retain or the profits they can make.'[44] This is a fascinating idea, and readers should not kid themselves that many in the force would not relish it. But policing has not followed this course.

But neither does community policing require officers to passively reflect the demands of the community, as Waddington's response to the same issue suggests. Suppose, he suggests, that a 'homogenous, white, respectable working class "community" with stable communal values, is subjected to an influx of New Commonwealth immigrants with alien values'.[45] If community policing is taken seriously, 'surely the indigenous, white community should be able to require local police to enforce laws selectively against immigrants in defence of their pre-existing "communal values"'. To make his point that community policing will not automatically tend to humane values, Waddington contrasts the tolerance being asked of police in respect of blacks smoking cannabis with the prospect of enforcing racist 'communal values'. But to do this he has to discount the

---

[41] *Ibid.* at 167.   [42] *Ibid.* at 170.   [43] *Ibid.* at 170– 1.
[44] Banton (1974).   [45] Waddington (1982).

preparedness of police to act as arbiters, a role they may not relish but have always proven willing to undertake.[46] Police are not so bound by community demands that they comply automatically. It is not just that the sum of police actions can be presented as impartial and thus for the overall good of the greatest number. What is significant is the active construction Banton places on crime prevention. It is seen as investigative information gathering, and allied to the crime-controlling efforts of relief policing. Banton cites the community involvement branches of Scottish police.[47] When Banton wrote that 'if [the officer's] role is defined in these terms [crime prevention at the service of all sections of society] it will resolve the major problem in the way police approach community relations',[48] he was pointing the police away from mistaken efforts to jolly along one section of the community—ethnic minorities—so as to 'keep the lid on' the polity, and towards the mission central to their mandate.

Police and Culture

Generally the internal prestige of a segment of the police organization is enhanced the more directly its mission is associated with crime control. Community policing in the research divisions (described in chapter 3) was no exception to the widely-remarked problems of integration between sections of the police.[49] This obstructs any section pursuing a facilitative role vis-à-vis other sections. Manning notes that 'the police have come to believe that their survival depends upon their capacity to control crime'.[50] Even though their most successful relations with other agencies are often where they bear 'service' roles,[51] most officers believe that crime control is pre-eminent. A survey of London police found that 77 per cent thought the most important source of public satisfaction was the detection, prosecution and arrest of offenders, whereas only 54 per cent identified helping on non-crime matters.[52]

However, the British Crime Survey found that 'consumer contact', at 41 per cent of contacts, was over twice as frequent as 'adversarial contact', numerous studies show that only about a third of calls to police are crime-related,[53] and a third of crime-related incidents turn

---

[46] Fielding (1991).
[48] Banton (1974) at 171.
[50] Manning (1982a) at 56.
[52] Irving et al. (1989).
[47] Banton (1974) at 171; see also Schaffer (1980).
[49] Manning (1977); Reuss-Ianni (1982).
[51] Packer (1968).
[53] Punch and Naylor (1973); Comrie and Kings (1975); Hough (1980); and Ekblom and Heal (1982).

out to be false alarms.[54] The centrality of crime control to the organization's daily business is, statistically, something of a myth. However, no one would pretend that this means the police should cease regarding themselves as the premier law enforcement agency. The issue it does pose is why social service is relatively devalued.

It may be thought that what officers think will have little to do with the way they work. But officers embrace, adhere to, and refine working styles based on their understanding of the police role. In Chatterton's analysis it is not enough to take account of the officer's training, technical abilities or grasp of law. While some arrests are chiefly competency-related, others relate mainly to style: the officer's working personality and fundamental orientations, including conceptions about the role and its satisfactions. This informs 'his approach to situations, his search procedure, what he looks for and how he assesses what he finds. From [this] . . . the police officer works out what *ideally* he would like to achieve at an incident.'[55] Such occupational perspectives guide choices and reflect assumptions about the organization, its environment and sanctioned practices. Much of this is shared, but differently valorized. One of the dangerous advantages of community policing is the distance its officers are carried from customary occupational perspectives. It is dangerous because they may become critics as well as insiders. As we will see, community constables do bear renegade sympathies.

Assignment to a section of which many police are sceptical is not the only way the commitment of officers to core perspectives may be called in doubt. The promotion and transfer system challenges commitment. Orientation to crime control, differences of style and perspective, the value accorded to experience of practical police work, and ambition, provide enduring themes of police culture. From the outside the occupational culture may seem solidary, but from the inside it is marked by deep and intensely-felt divisions.[56] The problematic status of community policing, and of the officers who do it, reflects essential divisions as deep as those that mark the community itself.

Differentiating the Community

Tonnies argued that, in modern urban life, the community has given way to the association, a group merely organized for the purpose of

[54] Hough (1980) at 11.   [55] Chatterton (1981) at 3.   [56] Fielding (1989).

particular interests, and hence unable to claim the inclusiveness and affiliation featured in community ties.[57] In such circumstances community policing must capitalize on the most compelling shared interests. Crime control affords police their best 'in' to marshal a mutual community of interest. To do this the police need good information, the essence of any claim community policing can make to the support of either the community or other officers.[58] If, instead, the police are to embark on a mission to promote community sentiment,[59] their role will have to be both intrusive and sectarian. They will have to initiate the engineering of groups they regard as suitable to represent the community. This is more likely to register with home owners rather than tenants, commercial interests rather than the unemployed, the elderly rather than youth, whites rather than ethnic minorities. Unless they want to represent within themselves the deviant, the marginal and the dispossessed, there is no prospect of police embodying what Alderson called 'the face of the community'.[60]

The community police we researched remained preoccupied with controlling crime, in relation to which they invoked the importance of gathering and collating crime-relevant information, particularly on 'beat crime', crimes not rated major but which provide the bulk of recorded offences. Crime is a close-to-home activity; a high percentage of all types of crime occur within four miles of the criminal's residence, and much within one to two miles.[61] Comparing two urban neighbourhoods in Ohio, Baker and Donnelly found that 70 per cent of all crimes resulting in arrest were committed by residents.[62] The neighbourhoods were similar in population, household size and composition, but one was mainly black and the other mainly white. Public order and traffic offences committed by residents within their communities differed little, but in the 'black' neighbourhood fewer personal offences were committed by residents while its residents committed a higher proportion of local property crimes, reflecting the lower incentive for outside property criminals to cross into poor neighbourhoods. Youth crime was less mobile than adult crime. When youths did travel to offend, it was not far. For the black neighbourhood, 26 per cent of youth arrests were for crimes in the nearby downtown area and 21 per cent in adjacent neighbourhoods. Almost two thirds of residents arrested for personal crimes commit-

[57] Tonnies (1955).   [58] Fielding (1991).   [59] Azarya (1985).
[60] Alderson (1975).   [61] Turner (1969).   [62] Baker and Donnelly (1986).

ted their offences in the area. Most neighbourhood crime was committed by people living within about a mile of the crime site, and most of those who went out of the neighbourhood to commit crime did not wander more than a mile.[63]

In getting to grips with the very 'locality' of local crime the police have to differentiate the community's population. There is powerful evidence that when black skin and youthful appearance combine, police are much more likely to stop, question and search.[64] But to fulfil its mission, community policing needs a finer-grained vision of the relevant dimensions of community. Social divisions are a good deal more complex than simple conflicts of race or class. Brewer notes that 'wider ethnic divisions can be refracted by differences of class, generation and region within each group'.[65] There may also be political and ideological fragmentation, and the divisions are not always immutable, for 'alliances can emerge which demonstrate ethno-political identity to be contextual and flexible'.

Far from an undifferentiated, threatening mass, both 'ethnic minorities' and 'offenders', as social categories, must be divided into sub-categories. For instance, if we take the category 'Afro-caribbean' it is obvious that, in the first generation, this could be divided by colonial origin. But 'there are varieties of background within Jamaica as diverse as those between Cardiff and Caernarvon. The parish of origin . . . might provide some measure of a person's orientation along a rural/urban dimension.'[66] There are, of course, different social classes in Jamaica, divisions of skin colour (the 'marry bright' legacy of white rule), religion, family type.

These divisions apply primarily to first generation immigrants, but the point is that police are used to making fine social distinctions within the category 'white', and any effort at community involvement should acquaint them with appropriate bases of differentiation. In 1974, Wood differentiated five West Indian 'life styles'. 'Mainstreamers' were conformists wanting integration, 'saints' bore authoritarian attitudes associated with extreme Pentacostalism, 'Swingers' were adult drifters, 'Teenyboppers' were under-achieving teens, and 'black power' were politicized.[67] Wood's categories have undoubtedly been superseded—if they were ever adequate—but the significance of his argument, directed at social work, remains: social workers need to acknowledge that not all blacks are the same and

---

[63] *Ibid.* at 63.   [64] Smith and Gray (1983); Norris, Kemp and Fielding (1992).
[65] Brewer (1991) at 185.   [66] Wood (1974).   [67] *Ibid.* at 251–3.

that each category is associated with particular needs and problems. It remains a perspective seldom heard in the police. Community police are an exception here, as we will see. Implicit in the differentiating effort is the idea that the more you understand someone's background the better you can take account of their perspective, and the more purchase you will have in negotiations with them.

A sense of locally-relevant distinctions does not automatically imply that the police can access groups waiting with clear priorities and demands. Policing has been liable to the 'take me to your community leader' ideology which has dogged the race relations industry.[68] Research in one police division found that, while the demand for service by blacks was three times that of a similar white community, their views about police were confused. Self-appointed leaders often represented only their own interests, so trying to access those in need through leaders was fruitless. Those needing police service had expectations which were 'confusing and conflicting. They want a high level of law enforcement activity, provided it is not directed against them, and at the same time a high level of service provision. Lack of actual contact with police other than in crisis leads to a lack of knowledge and understanding of police problems, activities and operations.'[69] Nor are these problems confined to blacks. A study of Gujerati Asians' low use of voluntary sector services and limited participation in community groups found that this was not attributable to limited needs, ignorance of services or language problems.[70]

The idea of differentiating the community implies not only a grading of sub-groups in terms of esteem for, and need of, police. It also implies that some groups want no contact with police because they are involved in crime and deviance, and that some groups seek only conflictual contact. While ethnic minority relations provide community policing with difficult, sustained problems one cannot ignore white youths who seek confrontation with the police as an end in itself or a diversion from activities they want to conceal. Prior to the summer 1991 disturbances on Oxford's Blackbird Leys estate, local youths played a 'cat and mouse' game with police. The estate had reasonable amenities and many of the youths involved were students or in work. Large-scale vandalism began in 1988 by youths who eventually became involved in autocrime. Cars were stolen for dri-

[68] Keith (1988).   [69] Irving et al. (1986) at 120.
[70] Jackson and Field (1989).

ving 'displays' within the estate. When police arrived the car would be driven off ' "with the purpose of either causing a dangerous pursuit or luring the police down side roads so that other youths could throw missiles at the police" ' (*Guardian*, 21 September, 1991). Youths planned counter-attacks against police measures to reduce autocrime, making petrol bombs and gathering objects to throw. The driving 'displays' continued, with rising fatalities, and in some places allied with 'ram-raiding', where stolen cars were used to demolish shopfronts to enable looting.

The element of contest with the police which was increasingly explicit in these disturbances revived the idea of the police as a symbolic target for those wishing to express resentment at their lot, or simply to liven up a dull existence. Little had been heard of this since the rise of the new Right. The radicals of the sixties and seventies were engaged in defensive campaigns against Thatcher's regime, or were quietly prospering under it. Here, too, was a test of police abilities to detect the nuances of social change. Many of the libertarians and radicals had remained in the inner city, but age, affluence, and the effort required to maintain the dual career family had seen off any serious involvement in political agitation. What remained was a fondness for recreational drug use.

Unlike relief officers, community police would be well aware of this, and of where such people would draw the line. It was for community constables, not the reliefs nor senior officers, to decide what to do when, for example, one's neighbourhood watch contacts were also keen on cannabis. Their response was to differentiate within the drug-user category. Wishing to conduct observations from a local house, they might say to a resident worried about neighbourhood crime that they would happily stare out his lounge window to observe dealing in hard drugs while the resident kept his cannabis elsewhere in the house. It is important to recognize that, in doing so, the community constable's decision would be consistent with the tradition of ignoring an informant's petty crime in favour of information about serious crime. In other words, differentiating the community is something the police have always done but to keep one's categories up to date one has to be close to the people.

Relief Policing

To get a sense of the distinctiveness of community policing we need to know how patrol policing is conventionally organized. The term 'relief' refers to the groups of constables taking responsibility for a given eight hour shift of general purpose patrol. There is a rota system but, subject to abstractions from duty and illness, one generally works with the same colleagues, moving together from the 2 p.m. to 10 p.m. late turn to the 10 p.m. to 6 a.m. night duty and on to the 6 a.m. to 2 p.m. early turn, with periodic time off to allow for the ceaseless disruption of the officers' metabolism.[71]

Urban stations can receive in the region of 100 messages a day calling for police action.[72] It is normal, after abstractions, for a relief to deploy about half its nominal strength on any shift. Further, around half of an officer's time is spent in the station,[73] relieving specialists such as VDU operators, writing reports, making inquiries by telephone, dealing with prisoners and the courts and taking refreshments. Based on constables on the late turn at an inner city station, Irving et al. obtained figures of 13 per cent of time spent on law enforcement or providing service, 24.5 per cent on uncommitted patrol, 1 per cent on directed patrol, 9.5 per cent on assigned journeys, 9.5 per cent relieving station officers, 4 per cent writing reports, 2 per cent making enquiries, 9.5 per cent dealing with prisoners, 18 per cent taking refreshments, and 13 per cent on other station duties.

Time for organized contact with the public is thus very limited, leaving the principal burden on the Community Liaison Officer and community constables. The officers in Irving's study were aware of pressure for them to police in a different way to that which they would themselves choose. They were mildly unwilling to comply with the perceived wishes of friends outside the police, right wing political groups and senior police, and strongly unwilling to comply with the perceived wishes of ethnic minorities, local youths and left wing political groups. While 90 per cent of supervisors felt it was undesirable to always be looking out for and making large numbers of arrests, only 18 per cent of constables agreed. They saw the route to specialization and promotion as being arresting and summonsing people and conducting large numbers of on-street stops. Effective communication with other agencies was restricted because liaison was at managerial rather than operational level. This resulted in inadequate problem identification, a predominance of short-term tactics, differentials between police and public perceptions of crime,

---

[71] A factor neglected by researchers accounting for police action, but one of which officers are abundantly aware, see Fielding (1990).

[72] Irving et al. (1986).   [73] Ibid.

rumours concerning police action, isolation from the public, restrictions on the scope of policy and a poor public image.[74]

A good deal of rhetorical importance is accorded the relief role by senior officers, but suspicion remains that it is no more than lip service. Ostensibly this is the role on which all else depends, and no new entrant, no matter how qualified, can escape a period on the reliefs. Few would want to, because it is the basis of claims to membership of the occupational culture. But constables who remain too long on relief eventually find it an obstacle to horizontal and vertical mobility. Police officers widely perceive that the key to occupational advancement is to acquire specialist skills, such as being a computer operator or advanced driver. Further, for all the protestations about the centrality of the role, it remains a convenient pool of labour with which to satisfy short-term contingencies.

Several negative characterizations of the relief role have been articulated. One is its association with youth and inexperience, the first destination of probationers being a relief posting. Jones and Winkler found that 28 per cent of their research force's constables were aged 18–23 but the age group comprised 41 per cent of those on patrol duties; 'it is the relatively raw who walk the beat'.[75] Another reason to be less than enthusiastic about remaining on the reliefs is the feeling that while you are responding at full pelt to the despatcher and message pad your more specialized colleagues are busily reaping the benefits of your routine police work. Relief officers may feel they are forever hearing the first stage of an intervention while being denied any follow through. They often must 'clear up the mess' after an incident such as a fight, processing the details and the parties into terms which are organizationally 'neat', without credit, liaison, or the satisfaction of knowing the outcome. Because the demands of despatcher and message pad are perceived as intense, continuous and unpredictable (whether they are is another matter), relief officers find it hard to plan or to achieve proactive team-based intervention.

The reactive mode robs managers of power and authority, which lodges with citizens who activate police service and the ranks who deliver it. A superintendent commented, 'everything was done on the basis of what had happened in the past so the policing system was totally reactive and we had no ability to be proactive. Unless you can be proactive you can't problem-solve. I had no information base and no junior management that had any problem-solving skills. What I had was a very good reactive machine . . . so that individuals were dealt with effectively but problems were not dealt with effectively.'[76] This Surrey officer gave the example of a pub whose young clientele caused problems passing through alleys and urinating, throwing glasses and being noisy. The customary response was to position several PCs at letting-out time, which 'represses it for a little bit but as soon as you take away the policemen the problem is back again'.[77] Under the superintendent's new proactive approach, an inspector received long-term responsibility for the neighbourhood. He contacted residents, the local councillor and licensee, and set up an action committee. 'They are now improving the lighting, changing the parking, the licensee has upped his age to 21—his staff are policing people as they go out to make sure they're not taking glasses and we're closing two alleyways so that the only exit . . . is to go very quickly into a non-residential section.'[78]

Further, relief constables 'don't see any result for what they do apart from the odd charge sheet when they've got a successful prosecution. His measurement of his own efficiency will be how quickly he can do the call.'[79] The inspector gave the example of domestic disputes.

There have been many domestic situations where there was something the police could have done constructive . . . by talking to people and perhaps making a referral . . . Where that hasn't been done . . . domestic violence has arisen. The relief officer's attitude is, 'Oh Christ, another domestic, there's nothing I can do.' No follow-up, nothing. Common assaults between neighbours, nothing's ever done. So the next time its not common assault, its GBH. The number of times you turn up crime figures [and] find a history of common assaults and domestic disputes and yet we're never trying to resolve it there . . . Its because of the pressure . . . You've got a death message to deliver here and a disturbance there and you think, 'I'm not going to do that disturbance because I'm this end of the ground, I'm going to get this little message out of the way.' Who can blame them when they become efficient but sell the public short so they can get on with the next call.[80]

Community constables contrasted the knowledge of social geography held by relief officers and community constables. '[T]he problem on the relief is that . . . [if] you are posted to a beat on one day

[76] Supt. Tate.   [77] Ibid.   [78] Ibid.   [79] Insp. Adams.   [80] Ibid.

you might not be posted there again for another four weeks, if ever.'[81] On relief 'there were bits that I didn't appreciate were actually our ground and I'd never been before. You were put places [with] no system of learning the ground. You do one beat one night and another beat the other and you were supposed to learn all the streets.'[82] Another threat to 'beat awareness' on the relief officer's part was the despatcher. 'Take the P estate, where it would take ages to walk. You'd get there and . . . they'd say "could you deal with a call the other side" (of the divisional "ground"). So you've got to walk all the way back. They give you a beat and you take one look and ignore it.'[83]

The community constables professed that relief officers were insulated from public contact of a normal social kind. 'The reliefs feel it's too much trouble to say "hello" to somebody. They walk around [people], or turn their eyes away, or worse. Its as if they're afraid of the people out there.' 'I think seriously some are.'[84] The investment of time by relief and community officers was a key difference. 'People don't realise how much of a big jump it is to have that luxury of talking to people. I went on the home beat when I had 30 years service, and how much of a change it was to talk to people and just be interested in whatever they told me. If someone says "this has happened to me" you've got to say, "oh my gosh!" you know. You've got to be in there with them.'[85] All the discussants agreed with the contrast. 'As a relief officer you go from one call to the next, one extreme to another.' Another likened it to being a production worker. 'It's very much "thank you very much, somebody will be in touch" and away you go.'[86] Whereas, 'with a home beat you've got time for a bedside manner'.[87]

The station's chief inspector (operations) also saw differences of commitment. 'The relief officer comes on at 2 o'clock and goes home at 10 o'clock and doesn't think of [division], is not interested in [division], and couldn't care less if this whole place burnt down in the remaining 16 hours. The Permanent Beat Officer leaves here at 10 o'clock and is still thinking about things that are going on on his beat and be quite concerned if his beat burnt down . . . I'd like the whole station to have an interest with this area.'[88] However, home beat postings meant isolation from the occupational culture and sources

---

[81] Group Discussion 1 (hereinafter, all Group Discussions shall be referred to GD).
[82] *Ibid.*   [83] *Ibid.*   [84] *Ibid.*   [85] GD 2.   [86] *Ibid.*   [87] *Ibid.*
[88] C.I. Wills.

of 'easing behaviour' which helped officers through the job. 'They don't like losing their identity with the relief. With the relief there's a lot of *esprit d'corps*; after work they go out drinking and all the rest of it. You don't quite have that with the permanent beats.'[89] Differences in after-hours socializing could relate to the shift system. There can be few alternatives to socializing with one's workmates for those working a 24 hour rota, whereas community constables work a shift akin to a normal working day.

Police forces have reacted to criticism of relief policing, experimenting with 'geographic', 'neighbourhood' and 'team' policing. A stable group of officers take total, 24 hour responsibility for a given area. This system was introduced throughout Surrey during 1990–1 and the Metropolitan Police adopted the idea as 'sector' policing in 1991. An area, or 'sector', would have a team led by an inspector and staffed by the former reliefs and community constables. 'This is a radical change in police organization but not of policing objectives; rather it is a natural development of current practice that seeks to make the best possible use of available resources.'[90] In 1992 the Metropolitan Police confirmed its intention to establish community-based sector policing as the cornerstone for the next five years.[91] Described as 'a community-based policing style', sector policing was 'the most significant strategic initiative being undertaken' and could be closely tailored by divisions to meet local needs. 'As the smaller local teams develop, they will pay further attention to the specific needs of their own designated parts of the community and develop relationships with local residents.'[92]

The rationale highlights the issues taken up in this book.

Through continuity of policing by the same officers a thorough knowledge of local matters is obtained, enabling officers to identify local concerns more quickly and gain crime intelligence. In turn the public get to know and identify with 'their' officers and, gradually, better trust and understanding develops. Problems can be identified at an early stage before they escalate and require major police resources. Rather than just responding to recurring symptoms police are able to get ahead of the problems by identifying the underlying causes.[93]

[89] C.I. Wills
[90] Metropolitan Police (1990), 'Sector Policing: Guide for Divisional Management Teams'.
[91] Metropolitan Police (1992), 'Corporate Strategy'.   [92] *Ibid.*
[93] Metropolitan Police (1991), 'Sector Policing: Guide for Divisional Management Teams'.

Whether these objectives will be achieved remains to be seen, but the statement is plainly imbued with the reasoning behind the law enforcement version of community policing. Despite official statements that the model will be extended to all forces, there are concerns that the programme has foundered in the Metropolitan Police Force due to non-cooperation by mid-ranking officers. The early evidence is that sector policing has fallen foul of the problems of manning, internal relations, community definition and occupational culture we have noted.[94]

Moves to extend community policing confront relief officers' preference for established practices and, as Black noted, patrol is 'invisible, non-reviewed (and reviewable) and highly discretionary'.[95] Even if they had the time, one survey found that 66 per cent of relief officers wanted to continue working on relief rather than taking responsibility for a beat and only 14 per cent thought contact with local residents and agencies was important.[96] Recruits who express enthusiasm for patrol soon learn that it differs markedly from expectation. 'Boredom, easing, discretion and the search for action all play a significant part in determining the nature of the patrol.'[97] In much patrol the low level of work elicits easing behaviour, police-initiated encounters or over-reaction to the few calls that do occur (such as a five car response to a man wandering along suburban lawns who, it emerged, was negotiating parked cars in the dark on his way home, an explanation police originally on the scene could have gained by asking him what he was doing[98]).

Thus, far from the reactive mode being forced on relief officers by the fearsome level of demand, it is often willingly and wilfully adopted because it suits officers' interests, not least because it conforms to their preferred, crime-busting image.[99] Yet a Home Office study found that, of 981 police/public encounters, arresting someone was the central activity in only eleven, and was involved at some stage in another 25, under 4 per cent of total encounters.[100] The fifteen most common types of encounter were burglary investigation (9 per cent), vehicle stops (8 per cent), police-initiated social/casual conversations (8 per cent), enquiries at domestic premises (7 per cent), giving time or directions (5 per cent), foot stops (4 per cent), missing person reports (3 per cent), public-initiated social/casual

[94] Dixon and Stanko (1993).   [95] Black (1980) at 9.   [96] Irving *et al.* (1986).
[97] Norris (1983) at 25.   [98] Surrey fieldnotes.   [99] Holdaway (1983).
[100] Southgate (1986) at 24.

conversations (3 per cent), domestic disputes (3 per cent), damage to private property/vehicles (3 per cent), enquiries at business premises (2 per cent), moving vehicles along (2 per cent), complaints of rowdy youths/children (2 per cent), enquiries from the public about matters already in police hands (2 per cent), assaults/fights (2 per cent). Like other studies,[101] 60 per cent of contacts were initiated by the public. Some 73 per cent of encounters were initiated while the officer was patrolling, consistent with the fact that in only one in 50 encounters was any warning given to the officer as to the likely ease or danger of the encounter,[102] which suggests one reason why relief officers seldom feel able to plan interventions, instead reacting as best they can to exigencies. Not only does this deny any inclination to plan, it indicates that limited information is available to relief officers about the situations and people with whom they must deal.

It is known that victims put as much store by the officer's display of interest and sympathy as they do by the officer pursuing offenders and solving the crime.[103] About one in six of Southgate's encounters involved a person who was clearly distressed, but officers frequently ignored this. It avoided investing time in discussing feelings and offering consolation, some officers primarily seeing distress as 'being difficult', and it offered a coping mechanism against emotional involvement.[104] Another aspect of demeanour which reveals whether one starts from co-operative or conflictual assumptions is apologizing for mistakes; Southgate noted that relief officers often failed to apologize when it would have been reasonable to do so.

Southgate's emphasis on interactional skills is partly founded on the ephemeral nature of police/public encounters. Only one in 100 took more than an hour, 10 per cent between 30–60 minutes, 14 per cent between 15–30 minutes, 28 per cent took 5–15 minutes, fully 30 per cent between 1–5 minutes, and 17 per cent took under a minute.[105] In these circumstances officers need to work fast to maximize the information which is the basis of an informed decision, and to draw on as many sources as are available. Formal legal action, such as an arrest or making a report, terminated one in six encounters while one in five ended with 'informal' enforcement, such as a promise or threat of future police action. One in fourteen encounters were closed with the officer giving advice, arbitration or

101 Southgate and Ekblom (1984).   102 Southgate (1986) at 18.
103 Burns-Howell and Jones (1982).   104 Southgate (1986) at 29.
105 *Ibid.* at 47.

referral.[106] In 3 per cent of the encounters people were persuaded they could cope with the matter themselves. The character of the interaction affected its outcome, with police enforcing the law 'by the book' where people were difficult and using discretion with similar offenders who were more amenable. Formal law enforcement action was taken in 22 per cent of encounters where citizens were civil in the closing stage but in 45 per cent of those where they were hostile or rude.[107] Among Southgate's conclusions was that relief officers seldom got to grips with issues underlying disputes, seldom made referrals to other agencies, and concentrated on whether an offence had been committed.[108] The preoccupation with arrests is symbolized by the display in many police canteens of 'informal' league tables showing arrests relief-by-relief.

When managerial policy tackles this rather predictable orientation, resistance is stubborn, so that implementation requires direct monitoring and pressure by managers who want to make innovations last. Derbyshire's community policing experiment in Derby East exposed the depth of the challenge posed by such innovations.[109] Whereas police anticipated strong opposition, it emerged there was high support for police among residents. However, the view of relief constables was 'that's been done at the expense of policing, that's negative policing'. They claimed patrol cars were not allowed into the area; 'We're coming down to Toxteth, that's diabolical. If someone from West division wants to go into East division you have to get the permission of the inspector.'[110] A chief inspector insisted that 'all they're saying is you have to be sensitive about the policing you exert'. Constables commented that getting close to the community was failing; if you went into a café in Peartree you could not get to know the community because they asked if you had a warrant as soon as you entered. The chief inspector linked the idea of discretion to the routine practice of policing, justifying the idea of selective enforcement. He asked a constable 'Do you police S differently to how you do C?' 'Yes, because at C you're talking to the middle class, but at S . . . they have different attitudes.' The chief inspector asked if this was fair; fair or not, the constables thought, it was practical. 'So the idea that we treat all the same has never been true. So Scarman isn't coming up with something totally new, we accommodate special groups and special people?' The PCs still insisted 'they'll take the

[106] *Ibid.*   [107] *Ibid.*   [108] *Ibid.* at 50–1.   [109] Fielding (1988b).
[110] Fieldnotes.

foot and the yard and the mile' and this was a policy of weakness which had not worked.

The exchange revealed the depth of relief officers' resistance to constraints on their action. If community policing is characterized by 'partnership' with the community and a more liberal exercise of discretion, a clearer idea of the challenge it poses to established practice should be becoming apparent. The meaning of community policing is the focus of the next chapter.

2
Community Policing

Community policing, as Weatheritt[1] noted, is not a single concept. It may mean a *contrast* to rapid response and enforcement-oriented policing, so that constables are closer to the community and can represent its norms; a *process* by which crime control is shared with the public, as in neighbourhood watch; or a *means* of developing communication with the public and interest groups. This book largely concerns the first of these, the long-term assignment of constables to geographical areas ('permanent' or 'home' beats) under specialized supervisors. This approach employs similar personnel as relief policing and focuses on the work which also forms their predominant concern. In other words, the focus is on the hardest case, the area requiring change on the part of officers and organization which goes most against the grain.

During the 1970s, particularly in the United States, 'community policing' effectively described short-term tactics to repair police-minority relations, a largely cosmetic exercise masking reluctance to make major changes when entrenched patrol and investigation methods failed.[2] Latterly it has embraced problem-definition with (sections of) the community, attempts to reduce the fear of crime, and extended foot patrol. The term 'community policing' evokes images of police-community relations in stable, consensus-based and homogenous neighbourhoods where crime is a mere irritant and disorder largely consists in minor vandalism. Social control here is based on public-police agreement and tacit consent.[3] This idealized view is one in which police define, and strive to enact, a posited 'common good'.

The effectiveness of community policing depends on assumptions which are dubious in the case of some communities, and innovations in policing can produce unanticipated consequences. Those setting

---

[1] Weatheritt (1983) at 4–5. [2] Bucqueroux (1988) at 2.
[3] Manning (1985).

goals must be clear about whether it is intended to increase arrests, prevent opportunities for crime or manage reported crime rates. Each produces different 'foci' for evaluation. Further, a 'crackdown' in one area may prompt displacement so that foot patrol areas show a reduction but motor patrol areas an increase. The point is not to run down community policing but to be realistic in assessing its effects. Research comparing beat and motor patrol has criticized community policing because beat officers proved neither more nor less likely to prevent crime than their colleagues in cars.[4] While that may be so, it can also be interpreted as showing that beat patrol is no less effective than car patrol, and may enjoy advantages of image and accessibility.

The Claims Made for Community Policing

Despite latent negative effects that may be associated with community policing, confusion surrounding the term, and problems in measuring its effectiveness, large claims are made for what it can do. In the United States a key emphasis is on preventing civil disturbances, and this is also so in inner city areas like those in our fieldwork. It should be remembered that the prompt to community policing has been the need to develop policing sensitive to youths and blacks, and to address the fear felt by those in confrontation with such groups.[5] While Trojanowicz was director of the 'National Center for Community Policing', he plainly recognized the problems for community-policing-as-outreach in black and Hispanic inner cities. Age is a key factor. Over half those arrested in the 1967 Detroit riot were aged 15–24, and 80 per cent between 15 and 35.[6] The contemporary situation is dominated by drug dealing, also a young man's business. This group is singularly unpromising for police efforts.

When we look at an urban hot spot plagued by open dealing, will the community support more aggressive police action? How far will dealers go in protecting their turf? Will they exploit racial frustrations and manipulate the community into battling the system for them? Will young people help the police, stand and watch or . . . pull a gun? Should trouble start, are there enough adult authority figures with sufficient clout—and motivation—to help bring the situation under control?[7]

---

[4] Clarke and Hough (1980).   [5] Trojanowicz (1989).   [6] *Ibid.* at 14.
[7] *Ibid.*

Another complicating factor is the growing friction between minorities. Trojanowicz cites the 1988 Super Bowl riot, whose roots were in black/Hispanic tensions, and the increasing involvement of Asian immigrants in the drug trade.

Against this realistic appraisal of the problems, Trojanowicz poses the alternative to a community policing response. Once rioting starts, the question is whether to deploy the National Guard, to 'borrow from the Koreans and use tear gas and clubs? . . . [to] follow the example of Northern Ireland and issue rubber bullets? . . . [to] imitate the Israelis and ask troops to break bones instead of shoot?'[8] Put this way there is little alternative to 'prevention'. But there are two unanswered questions here. One is whether, when the inner city is not in riot, tough policing within the bounds of due process may not be more effective against key groups (of course, this is to respond only in terms of policing rather than the wider causes of urban malaise). The other is whether community policing is itself an adequate preventive measure. Trojanowicz believes that community policing achieves prevention by 'gathering superior intelligence that allows us to identify areas at risk, the level of threat in those areas, and weaknesses and strengths within the community', and by enlisting the help of the law-abiding.[9]

Trojanowicz cites evidence that community policing has prevented disturbances, including an event in Flint, Michigan during the 'Neighborhood Foot Patrol' experiments. Car officers responded to a call about a double homicide in a black area. Residents challenged what they saw as an unwarranted influx of heavily armed police.

Tensions continued to mount until several foot patrol officers arrived. They recognized people in the crowd and started moving through the area, explaining that they knew about the homicides and encouraging them to 'cool it'. The people trusted the foot officers, not only because they knew them but because daily contact had made them uniquely accountable. They knew the foot officers would not dare mislead them, because those officers would be back in their neighbourhoods the next day and every day, where people could confront them if they hadn't told the truth.[10]

It is notable that, rather than any programme with which the officers were associated, their effectiveness derived from their simple identifiability. Interestingly, the Flint research found that the foot officers felt safer than their car counterparts. Trojanowicz suggests

---

[8] *Ibid.* at 16.   [9] *Ibid.*   [10] *Ibid.* at 19.

this is because most people obey the law most of the time 'and people who live in underclass neighbourhoods have good reason to want to help police protect them from victimization'.[11] It is an important observation. Above I suggested there is a logical alternative to community policing and that is harsh conventional patrol exercising minimal discretion in applying the law. Since inner city Britons also differentiate community officers from other police this evidence does suggest an advantage for community policing in the preventive role. As Trojanowicz implies, identifiability also brings police to account. Elsewhere he writes 'having the same officer in the same area every day facilitates a two-way information flow, where the officer receives input on community priorities in exchange for which the residents provide vital information'.[12] Whether this ultimately happens depends on whether the police act on local priorities.

As well as controlling civil disturbances, it is claimed that community policing has advantages in controlling drug dealing. Enforcement at the street dealing level is emphasized.

The problem has been that we have focused so much of the police effort at Mr Big, ignoring that he's never the one actually selling drugs to kids at school or to the addicts who steal to support their habits. The retail-level dealer at school may well be another teenager who sells [drugs] . . . to indulge himself for free. The crack dealer on city streets is often someone like the 14 year old interviewed by CBS in the District of Columbia . . . who had only been dealing part-time for two months [but] averaged $800 a night.[13]

The removal of 'Mr Big', as these authors go on to argue, will have little effect because such high stakes mean he will instantly be replaced. What they do not appear to perceive is that precisely the same point applies to Master and Miss Small. Nevertheless there is merit in a policing style involving long-term presence rather than bursts of intervention, if only in providing a visible deterrent. Trojanowicz and Bucqueroux report that community policing addresses retail-level dealing by such measures as deploying officers to stand at the door of known dealing premises. Each time the officer appears the stash is flushed, and it also puts off customers.[14] Relief and community officers can even play on the 'visibility' issue together. Dealers gauged one community officer's

[11] Trojanowicz (1989) at 22.   [12] Trojanowicz and Moore (1988) at 15.
[13] Trojanowicz and Bucqueroux (1989) at 1.   [14] Ibid. at 2.

schedule and waited for him to leave before resuming business. So the officer arranged for another officer to drive through. As soon as the car was out of sight the community officer entered on foot and made arrests. The same officer pruned foliage so that dealers could not hide what they were doing.[15] Another approach is to combine coercion with assistance; Trojanowicz and Bucqueroux cite a Florida officer who offered dealers a threat of arrest or the opportunity of being found work through his good offices.

A further claim is that 'community policing can gather better information about retail and even high-level drug dealing with less danger and expense than traditional undercover operations'.[16] Drug squads target dealers, at great risk, while community policing garners the trust that leads to disclosure from informants. Trojanowicz and Bucqueroux cite evidence that more detailed, actionable information was received from such sources than the conventional tip-off, which seldom includes more than an address. It may involve listening to the 'neighbourhood busybody', but time is one of the community officer's best resources. Revenge is less likely, too, because informants are harder to target when officers are routinely seen to chat with local people. A further argument is that community policing attacks street dealing without overwhelming the system, as do mass crackdowns, which overcrowd courts and prisons and lead to a 'revolving door' situation, with dealers on bail hustling to pay legal fees. Community policing also uses lower-level charges, such as misdemeanour disorderly conduct charges which discourage retailers and customers, in preference to felony drug busts where stringent standards of proof apply and bail may be granted. Units dominated by an arrest mentality are susceptible to abuses of the law, entrapment and fraud, whereas, because community police are more visible, people are more likely to complain if they seem to have strayed. Another mooted benefit of community policing is that community officers' detailed knowledge offers a basis for the targeting and identification of crime patterns upon which problem-oriented policing relies. They can collate lists of youths whose relatives worry that they are involved in drugs and, as with one officer in Flint, work from contacting parents to arrange counselling through to rewarding youths for making curfew by conducting visits to amusement parks

---

[15] McLanus (1992) at 5–9.   [16] Ibid. at 3.

(the officer actually took them to an art gallery; most had never been further than a city block from home, and responded well).

Trojanowicz has advanced an imaginative range of possible benefits. But the relatively innocuous measures noted above hardly challenge civil liberties in the way that some American developments do. In Aurora, Colorado, the police interrupt traffic in problem areas by having officers do routine paperwork in front of crack houses, and issue housing code violations on the properties. They instruct apartment managers on screening prospective tenants for drugs.[17] In Lansing, Michigan, officers were stationed 16 hours a day in 'drug-infected areas' and barricades were erected against drug and prostitution customers. Long Beach, California, police have a squad of 'Drug Recognition Experts' who can, apparently, visually detect if a person is under the influence of drugs and, if so, what kind, with a 97 per cent success rate.[18] In Newport News, Virginia, community police issue trespass tickets to drug customers and 'act as agents for landlords and owners of drug-ridden apartments to eliminate problem tenants'.[19] These potent officers also demolish buildings that have become 'shooting galleries'. In Baltimore, Maryland, drug crackdowns are followed by community police conducting citizen surveys into whether the enforcement has been effective. They encourage landlords to add instant eviction clauses to leases for tenants suspected of substance abuse. In Alexandria, Virginia, public housing was a particular target. Tenants enjoyed complicated eviction procedures, 'so Alexandria worked with the agency to develop a quick eviction process for drug dealers'.[20] The tendency of other tenants to applaud whenever a dealer was led away need not blind us to the potential for mis-identification, false tip-offs motivated by grudges, and the difficulty, at retailer-level, of distinguishing 'dealers' from 'users'.

It hardly seems necessary to indulge in such measures when many mooted benefits of community policing arise from the simple long-term presence of officers on foot. The Flint experiment is again relevant. It began in 1979 with 22 foot patrol officers assigned to experimental areas comprising 20 per cent of the city's population. The crime rate fell by 8.7 per cent, but more dramatic was the reduction in calls for service, by 42 per cent between 1979 and 1982,[21] reflecting the increased tendency for citizens themselves to handle

---

[17] McLanus (1990) at 6–7.   [18] *Ibid*. at 7.   [19] *Ibid*.
[20] *Ibid*. at 8.   [21] Trojanowicz (1982).

problems, with officers acting as informal mediators.[22] Citizens reported feeling safer, and two thirds of residents could either name or describe their foot patrol officer. They felt that such officers were more effective than mobile patrols in encouraging crime reporting, promoting neighbourhood crime prevention, working with juveniles and following up complaints. — P Culture

The experiment was funded by a charity but in 1982 Flint's citizens showed their enthusiasm by voting to pay for a city-wide programme. The renewal three years later passed by an even higher margin,[23] despite Flint's falling tax base as the car industry collapsed. While motor officers made six times the number of felony arrests, no doubt related to being assigned three times the number of investigations by despatchers, the foot officers initiated twice as many investigations themselves and provided 7.5 times the number of services to the public.[24] Self-initiated work by motor officers was traffic-related, while the self-initiated work by foot officers involved direct, proactive community contact, like home security checks. While 91 per cent of foot officers' community contacts were non-adversarial it was exactly the opposite with motor officers, 91 per cent of whose contacts were adversarial.[25] Despite these differences, the two groups spent the same time on patrol. Foot officers averaged an activity (such as a suspicious person check) once every 41 minutes of patrol, while motor officers managed a self-initiated task (such as issuing a hazardous vehicle tag) only every 81 minutes. The drift of these data is not to prefer one approach over another, although community policing is so much the poor relation that advocates can be forgiven for trumpeting its advantages. Rather, the point is to compare so as to understand better each, and to be aware of ways they can work together. Quick car response to burglary alarms can secure arrests. Equally, foot patrols can prevent burglary by teaching owners how to harden targets. But together they could prove effective 'because the foot officer advised the owner to install the alarm that brought the motor patrol'.[26]

Community policing consistently seeks a more 'proactive' and preventive mode of operation. Yet communities are increasingly marked by division. Jefferson and Grimshaw analysed the approach to mediating 'sectarian' demands in their account of a controversy over a

[22] Trojanowicz (1986) at 11.   [23] Ibid.   [24] Ibid. at 16.
[25] Ibid. at 16–17.   [26] Ibid. at 19.

National Front meeting in 1979.[27] Southall council decided election law obliged them to permit the meeting. Some protestors advocated a peaceful, symbolic protest and some wanted to stop the meeting by force. As well as protestors, police construed the community as including shopkeepers, white residents and the Tory council, all of whose interests had to be protected. The balancing of interests offered something for everyone. 'Thus the strong police presence was designed to ensure that the meeting took place, yet the provisions for "limited" demonstrations attempted to ensure the community protest was catered for . . . The cordoning attempted to ensure a controlled, if limited, mobility, yet arrangements existed to seal off the area completely.'[28] The National Front had its meeting, with some public attendance, older Asians had their sit-down protest, though not exactly where they wanted, younger Asians were allowed to picket, again in a different place, and the roads were kept open for a time.

These efforts to strike a 'balance' seem consistent with the normal relation of police and state, but the community policing doctrine does include an element of reforming society by arbitrating conflict and supporting interests that promote what police perceive as order and stability. In evaluating such claims it is granted that the autonomy police enjoy as a state institution is debatable. The police, 'irrespective of occasional truces with labour, the disavowals of [officers], and occasional actions against the immediate interest of members of the capitalist class is . . . concerned with the implementation of legislation which will maximize the social reproduction of appropriate labour, repress the "social dynamite" of threatening . . . marginal groups and combat the power of organized labour'.[29] Police may wish to maintain neutrality as servants of law rather than the state but their actions are useful to the state and preserve an inegalitarian social order. Against this, the ameliorative efforts of community policing are likely to remain a minority voice within the police institution.

We have examined claims made for community policing, and indicated the scope of social change which could realistically be expected from it. Such change is more likely as a result of order maintenance than from police efforts at community development. One reason is that policing varies because it adapts to the diversity of different areas; for example, there is considerable variation between forces in

[27] Jefferson and Grimshaw (1984) at 113–15.   [28] Ibid. at 115.
[29] Brogden (1982) at 9.

times spent on particular tasks.[30] There is no prospect of a uniform blueprint for community policing. Its chief form is foot patrol on long-term beat assignments plus 'outreach' efforts, but there are approaches to maintaining order which do not involve police, or only peripherally. The concept of 'community policing' has provided an opportunity to spread policing functions to other agencies.

Police in Milton Keynes, New Town, were worried about civil order in the central, privately-owned shopping centre. It is policed by security staff and police, with the former in the 'front line'; troublesome youths 'were firmly warned by security staff and thereafter asked to leave the building'.[31] However, and unusually, for most shopping centres are owned by insurance companies or pension funds with limited interest in the quality of the environment,[32] this action was followed by inviting youths to become involved in the shopping centre. 'Groups of youths are not "moved on" if they are not causing trouble, and security staff are encouraged to talk to them. If they have a grievance, attempts are made to resolve it.'[33] Schools and local organizations are encouraged to use display areas, and there are consultations to see that 'as wide a variety of the local population as possible is catered for'. The Youth Information Service has offices in the shopping centre. Unemployed youths are given jobs there, and run a café for unemployed youths. Cleaners are called 'orderlies'.

Here we see some elements of an approach to maintaining public order which involves police only peripherally and indicates some conditions under which a 'community' can 'police itself'. As Roger Birch, then chief constable of Warwickshire, observed, 'without the force of law, this privately run organization has sought the same ends as the police—the preservation of public tranquillity and the absence of crime. Without statutory authority they have been obliged to search for a system that is acceptable both to the organization and the public.'[34] He goes on to say that the attractiveness of the shopping area helped because people were proud of it. The real problem would be to induce such feeling in 'decaying urban areas'. But here he takes a revealing line. 'Milton Keynes suffers from the same political imperfections as other parts of the country. It identified many of the social and economic factors present in other new towns, yet suffers little of the social disorder that has become synonymous with

[30] Bennett and Lupton (1992a).   [31] Birch (1982) at 6.   [32] Landry (1991).
[33] Birch (1982).   [34] *Ibid.* at 6.

them. The management of Central Milton Keynes has achieved what the police seek—a non-political solution to a grossly political problem.'[35]

Thus, in their preoccupation with the maintenance of order, the police do not act simply and only to preserve the *status quo*, to stabilize monopoly capital, but sustain a political analysis. By their own lights these senior advocates of community policing are campaigning for social change, and it is both characteristic and disingenuous for them to depict it as apolitical. In a commentary on Toxteth, Birch suggests that, thus placed, any reasonable person would resist authority. Referring to a housing scheme dubbed 'the Fortress' he notes that 'the stairways and corridors are impossible to police and consequently crime is very high. The residents have little to be proud of, feel neglected by authority and attack authority in any form whenever the opportunity arises.'[36] Later I will show that at constable level, too, officers' sympathies are engaged by the problems inner city people face. The point is not that police have feelings—though sometimes this does need to be acknowledged—but that their awareness of the consequences of government policy and the workings of the market economy can motivate actions which place crime control behind order maintenance.

At individual officer level, the use of discretion takes this into account. The police aspire to political neutrality. As the example of the National Front meeting suggests, they often adopt a literal and pragmatic notion of 'balance'. For their continued acceptance it is vital they are perceived as neutral. Consider this observation on target selection in the Toxteth riots. 'Prior to the riot a gentlemen's club was located in Upper Parliament Street. It was used extensively by a rich upper class clientele. This building was so severely damaged by the rioters that it has consequently been demolished, and it is interesting to note that next door the local community centre remained untouched.'[37] The very selection of this, against all the events in Liverpool, suggests a particular awareness, a class analysis.

In a column headed 'The solution through police eyes' we see how the threat to neutrality, and with it popular acceptance, is resolved; the police perceive the 'sides' in conflict and, just as at a demonstration, place themselves carefully between, by virtue of their 'objectivity'.

---

[35] Birch (1982).   [36] *Ibid.* at 7.   [37] *Ibid.*

The police see themselves in several respects at advantage in looking at the problem . . . They can be objective. Their perspective is not political but at the same time they have close daily contact with those who form a community. Their view is not from the remote comfort of an air-conditioned planning office but from the reality of the street. They are in a position to understand the feelings and reactions of those whose surroundings bring them close to despair: they are accustomed to gathering and piecing together evidence.[38]

Birch later comments on the 'cruelty of pouring money into inner cities for expensive housing re-development which is then beyond the reach of those formerly living in the area'; the grousing about 'yuppies' and gentrification I heard from the community constables reciprocates Birch's concerns. While remedies for urban malaise can be identified—'pride in neighbourhood; a sense of purpose; the possibility of neighbourliness; freedom from fear of attack on the person or property; proximity to work and the chance of finding it; confidence in public servants; facilities reasonably accessible as well as affordable for welfare, education, sport and relaxation'[39]—police are neutral arbiters and cannot force the pace: 'they are anxious to share their knowledge, to invest in building contented communities, for by so doing they will be making their own task less burdensome but, as with high rise flats, they cannot step in uninvited'.[40]

In practice chief constables enjoy considerable power to implement change by administrative policy. As chief constable of Northumbria, Sir Stanley Bailey formed a Community Services department combining the Crime Prevention, Race Relations, Accident Prevention, Community Involvement and Schools Liaison sections.[41] The Special Constabulary, 'the uniformed arm of the community', was placed in the new department plus a 'volunteer cadet' programme with 300 members, some of whom later joined the Specials or regular force. They meet weekly 'for instruction and project work, or expeditions of historical or educational interest, to increase their knowledge of the area'.[42] Activities include charitable collections, learning map reading and life-saving, and traffic censuses. This lay involvement in policing is obviously aimed at giving youths a prideful sense of identity. 'Every Volunteer Cadet wears a white tee shirt with the words "Northumbria Police-Volunteer Cadets" emblazoned across the front and back.'[43] It was also

[38] *Ibid.*   [39] *Ibid.*   [40] *Ibid.*   [41] *Ibid.* at 10.   [42] *Ibid.*
[43] *Ibid.* at 11.

recognized that the hours worked and places to attend for duty put some adults off joining the Specials. The force devised the 'Home Beat Special' who was only expected to work when requested by the Permanent Beat Officer on whose beat they live. Duties included 'patrolling shopping centres in the late evening, keeping a watch on troublesome car parks or public houses, or observations on other areas'.[44]

Sir Stanley was aware the new department would encounter problems within the force; here he also gives a revealing view of where community constables stand in relation to the community. 'A primary task is to establish the credibility of the department with the rest of the force. No one pretends this will be easy but it is essential if the community is to recognise that Police Officers are not divided into two sorts: those who work with them and those who work against them. At the halfway point between these two extremes are the Permanent Beat Officers.'[45] Here is 'neutrality' and 'objectivity' again. The 'between extremes' position means they will combine crime prevention with crime control, where crime prevention is construed broadly. Thus, 'not only will they be expected to work closely with leaders of local community organizations and youth clubs; and get involved in communal social and sporting activities, but [to] . . . detect crime, arrest offenders and otherwise perform what the community expects of a police officer'.[46]

These innovations fall well short of those made to meet a harsher situation in the United States but still exceed the standard ingredients of community policing in Britain. The stock approach is represented well by what was, in 1982, sufficient of a 'new policing formula' to be subject of a television documentary about its application in Brixton. There were three elements. First, local officers were assigned in pairs to beats and instructed to get to know the people there. On minor offences they were to 'advise, guide and warn—talk to the people first' (London Programme LWT 17 December, 1982). Secondly, Immediate Response Units were deployed, specially trained and equipped to 'crush street disorders'. A senior officer said the Immediate Response Units were specifically there 'to protect my officers' and 'nip public order problems in the bud'. Thirdly, a consultative group was created to bring police and community leaders together, convened by the divisional commandant, but chaired by a

---

[44] Birch (1982).   [45] Ibid.   [46] Ibid.

local clergyman. Police claimed that reduced crime figures, including violent street crime, were due to the scheme.

This scheme remains the model for others in the inner city. Also enduring are the anxieties expressed by local people. Community members on the programme criticized use of stop and search powers. They spoke of the danger of resentment, but the police asserted they only did stops in response to violent or drug-related crime. The commandant insisted it would be improper to inhibit 'these dedicated teams'. The council leader and some community leaders suggested that stops and searches were being imposed as a penalty for securing public order, and that resentment would lead to more civil disturbance (as has occurred several times since). They cited the police designation of the Brixton 'Front Line' as a 'symbolic location' with its own contingency plan with which police would suppress disorder. Police were engaging in saturation patrol there in what was seen as a tactic to stop it being used by youths to 'hang out'. They reported a mood of 'sullen despair' among young blacks.

It is obvious that a scheme with the mixed 'hard' and 'soft' elements cited above must inevitably excite such concerns. Later I will examine what senior officers think of the mixed strategy. But such approaches seem inevitable in that the Association of Chief Police Officers' guidance to senior officers on handling disorder preserves considerable latitude for the commander on the ground. Nor will it have escaped readers that Sir Stanley Bailey's Northumbria, for all its innovative schemes, was the site of new disorder in the 1990s. No one is sufficiently convinced of the preventive effectiveness of community policing to forgo the option of main force *in extremis*.

Contemporary Community Policing Practice

Experienced officers recognize the resonance of past policing practices in the claims made for long-term patrol assignment. For them it is the rediscovery of the beat. With it come the skills and virtues of self-reliance. Such qualities were forced on constables by the general practice of solo patrol, punctuated only by brief contact with supervisors at 'fixed points'. The negotiating skills required to resolve trivial incidents and minor conflicts were necessary survival techniques. Technical means of assistance were seldom available, so situations which would today provoke a heavy response, posing dangers of confrontation, were resolved without help. Young notes that his first beat included a pub where trouble was frequent, but that he 'quickly learned to "see the pub out" and the patrons off home by methods which avoided conflict'.[47] The beat box containing a phone was 400 yards away from the pub, so assistance meant considerable delay and his leaving the scene.

Young, a former superintendent neither uncritical of police nor nostalgic for past practices, nevertheless maintains that

this technological gap helped generate self-reliance and produced a style of policing which required the foot patrol to calm and dispel disorder, and created . . . a certain reluctance to call for assistance. Calls for help suggested you were incapable of resolving local problems, so although the arrests of 'prigs' were justified, the gratuitous arrest of those who could have been 'talked into going home' was not always looked on favourably. Calls for 'the van' could seriously interfere with the activities of the inspector, the station sergeant and the shift driver, who might well have a game of dominoes interrupted.[48]

This was a small force (Durham) whose style reflected the 'social, economic and structural etiquette' of the time, being one of 'visible calm and containment'. The inclination of constables to cope with contingencies on their own was the manifestation at individual level of the force's projected image and posture toward other social institutions. 'Everything was geared to suggest all was well within society, that known disorder and calamity was contained within acceptable statistical terms, and the police were in command of the small amount of "real crime".'[49] A further overtone to the cope-alone preference lent pragmatic humility to the constables' policing style. '[T]here was little opportunity in such a system for the isolated, patrolling police officer to present a tough, crime busting image.'[50]

Autonomy is a theme carrying over into contemporary policing.[51] While relief officers spend some 57 per cent of their time outside the station, Bennett's national activity survey[52] found community constables spend 64 per cent, a statistically significant difference. As Grimshaw and Jefferson note, variation in approach among 'resident beat officers' was 'a corollary of the "freedom" of RBO working' which related to 'relative freedom from colleague influence or socialization'.[53] Thus, 'the result of choosing hours of work and how to fill them on . . . patches with their own particular clientele and

[47] Young (1986) at 278.   [48] Ibid.   [49] Ibid.   [50] Ibid. at 279.
[51] Kelling and Moore (1988).   [52] Bennett and Lupton (1992a).
[53] Grimshaw and Jefferson (1987) at 153.

correspondingly peculiar policing problems is a set of "unique" work conditions for each RBO . . . Relative freedom from a group "working norm" is the result'.[54] Bennett suggests the time difference relates both to the brief of community constables and their lower involvement in legal process, with its accompanying paperwork.[55]

Enhanced ability to decide how to spend patrol time, relative to relief officers, promotes distinctive policing 'styles'. A 'public relations' style maximized regular contacts, seeking new ones and using excuses for chance encounters, marketing 'the self as representative of a cordial and benign police *service*'.[56] The 'educator' style maximized contact with 'at risk' populations such as schools and youth clubs, emphasizing crime prevention (rather than public relations), a concern with the causes of crime, and a constituent emphasis on mediation. The 'spy' style maximized opportunities for 'gaining criminal intelligence or information'. Befriending was a manipulative tactic to cultivate informants rather than for public relations. Such officers were more concerned with crime than the preceding types and hoped for eventual assignment to the Criminal Investigation Department (hereinafter CID). The 'patrol' style maximized foot patrol interspersed with public contact, akin to the traditional 'bobby', emphasizing deterrent value and reassurance. An example was a constable who saw himself as 'the dutiful community servant, careful to respect its wishes and tolerant of its foibles rather than an interventionist in the PR or educator style',[57] suggesting a liberal use of discretion was also characteristic.

These styles emerged in prevailing circumstances of little guidance on how to go about community policing patrol. For instance, while Hampshire shifted officers from reliefs to 'area beats' in the early 1980s, they received no clear job description, statement of objectives or training.[58] The officers emphasized conventional enough aims: to be a front-line police resource; build a knowledge of local residents; take a long-term approach to law enforcement, and investigate and prevent crime. The researchers found that the officers were indeed functioning as a 'front line' resource, handling a fair proportion of most kinds of incident. They had significantly more contacts with citizens than relief officers and handled a high proportion of crime complaints.

[54] Ibid.
[56] Grimshaw and Jefferson (1987) at 154.
[58] Horton and Smith (1987).

[55] Bennett and Lupton (1992a).
[57] Ibid. at 155.

Police service can be a major resource, and the reciprocity intrinsic in long-term, negotiated relationships will be motivated on the citizen's part by instrumental needs such as the application or inhibition of police 'resources'. Reciprocity is a form of exchange having three characteristic features.[59] First, it develops as part of a social relation. Secondly, reciprocity extends beyond single transactions. Thirdly, it is not governed by laws of supply and demand. Reciprocity is achieved and maintained through sharing burdens by 'taking turns' in contributing to joint projects. In reciprocal networks the exchange moves beyond burden-sharing. Members behave toward each other with familiarity. Reciprocity strengthens social solidarity. We can see the relevance of reciprocity if we consider Grimshaw and Jefferson's list of community constables' reasons for initiating public contacts. These were '(1) to acquire information about particular crimes or . . . relevan[t] to the processes of criminal detection [intelligence]; (2) to prevent crime amongst especially the potentially delinquent or "at-risk" populations [education]; (3) to build up a credit balance with the public [public relations]; (4) to succour the weak and helpless [welfare]; (5) to pass the time [social]'.[60] All this requires regular contact. Because regular contact 'both requires and produces consensual relations' it may lead community constables into ineffective agreements and alliances. In Grimshaw and Jefferson's study the regular contacts were 'respectables'. As well as pensioner police officers and schools (officers were told to visit these), regular contacts included youth clubs, social service departments and other statutory agencies, 'groups variously "representing" the community, local "worthies", publicans, shopkeepers, people in the street or the elderly at home'.[61] Even contacts maintained for criminal intelligence were respectables; for instance, one community constable's informant on the drug scene was a vicar's wife.

This genteel approach has an obvious problem, not only for the quality of information which is being laboriously collected but also for the public relations or 'outreach' mission. 'The absence of systematic contacts with "toe rags" . . . means the RBOs have built up systematic consensual relations with all sections of the community except the regularly "policed" . . . [T]his . . . can account for "explosive" relations building up between sections of the community and the police, even . . . where community relations are said to be

---

[59] Polanyi (1957); Dalton (1968).   [60] Grimshaw and Jefferson (1987) at 150.
[61] Ibid. at 172.

"good".[62] The contacts of the not-'respectable' remain with CID, reliefs and Special Patrol Group-type officers. Grimshaw and Jefferson found their community constables little involved in offence-related activity (only 16 per cent of contacts concerned criminal intelligence, 60 per cent public relations, welfare or sociality). This ensured consensual relations were everywhere apparent but excluded the very group most likely to challenge police. This is parallel with other agencies treading the community outreach path. Research concluding that detached youth work in Islington was 'misdirected and largely useless' found workers were retreating from the street into the 'safer and controllable environment' of youth clubs,[63] whose clients were already socialized into youth-work culture, whereas those at risk of criminal involvement remained outside the system.

The relatively unrestrained public relations/outreach approach by Grimshaw and Jefferson's community police and their low involvement in law enforcement meant they were less subject to the legal constraints on other officers. 'Their infrequent court appearances, together with their infrequent involvement in law enforcement work, makes them less routinely susceptible to the constraints of either judicial advice and admonition or [public] complaints.'[64] The absence of legal work made their work unquantifiable and beyond the reach of conventional supervision. Sergeants were forced into an 'egalitarian' mode of supervision by the lack of conventional performance measures.

This also explained the absence of a 'cohesive peer group culture', because of the lack of a means like comparative arrest rates through which to socialize 'deviants' into expected working practices.[65] Community constables could exert considerable leverage, provided senior officers adopted 'community reputation' as a performance measure instead of crime figures. Indeed the community constables' ability to marshal apparent public support through their contacts was indicated by inattention to stationary traffic offences, taken as a sign of reciprocity. Thus, 'given the nature of much RBO work, consisting to a large degree of . . . personal interactions the *quality* of which is known only to the participants, and the effectiveness of which defies easy measurement, the most important general form of assessment becomes "community reputation" which lies largely in the hands of community contacts'.[66] But this depended on senior

[62] *Ibid.*   [63] Pollak (1990).   [64] Grimshaw and Jefferson (1987) at 179.
[65] *Ibid.* at 180.   [66] *Ibid.* at 181.

officers prioritising community relations over law enforcement. This was not the case in the divisions on which the present study is based.

Researching community policing in five forces, Brown and Iles also found crime work a negligible part of community constables' duty. However, under 14 per cent of duty time by their sample of 300 officers was spent on community involvement,[67] suggesting the emphasis of Grimshaw and Jefferson's officers was distinctive in its skew towards public image and acceptance. The greatest share of time (over 22 per cent) went on preventive policing which involved little or no verbal contact with the public. Most of the remainder went on activities off the beat or was not directed at community policing objectives. Time withdrawn from the beat, and general duties, accounted for over half the working day.[68] Crime work fell a poor fifth in priority and public order work was negligible. Community involvement averaged five hours per working week, including informal contacts, school liaison, clubs and statutory agency contacts. Contacts were casual and brief. Brown and Iles depict community policing as a place to put old officers 'out to grass'.

Liaison with statutory agencies took a ridiculous five minutes per constable/week. Being off the beat for 'general duties', which accounted for nearly a third of time, was dominated by paperwork. Some 60 per cent of officers felt these withdrawals hindered their work. The 20 per cent of working time spent on preventive policing was dominated by foot patrol, but only a fraction went on crime prevention advice or checking the security of premises. 'Preventive foot patrol' denoted walking the beat as a visible deterrent without speaking to anyone. Crime work averaged 10 per cent of duty time, mostly 'trivial' crime, follow-up investigations and enquiries for other forces. Brown and Iles use the word 'contempt' to describe relations between community constables and other police. In two forces some 30 per cent of constables reported poor to non-existent contact with mobile patrols and overall nearly a third reported poor contact with CID. It was up to community constables to initiate contact, and the information they held was scorned by detectives.

Bennett's more recent survey[69] found patrol was the most frequent outside duty for reliefs and community constables, but, at 22 per cent of time and 28 per cent, respectively, there was a statistically

---

[67] Brown and Iles (1985) at 19.   [68] *Ibid.* at 17.
[69] Bennett and Lupton (1992a and 1992b).

significant difference between them. 'Patrol' included contacts with individuals, in which community constables invested three times as much time as reliefs.[70] Community constables spent longer on community contacts (i.e., with groups and schools), patrol and preventive police work.[71] Bennett remarks that, while these differences are in the expected direction, they are not as great as one might expect. He particularly criticizes the small time spent in community contact. However, individual contacts, most likely to yield crime-relevant information, appear in the 'patrol' category, where, on his own data, there is a real difference between relief and community police.

Despite Brown and Iles', and Bennett's, pessimistic assessment, community policing continues to be practised, even in distinctly unpromising circumstances. Brewer found that, paradoxically, the 'troubles' in Belfast had produced benefits for community policing, including managerial support.[72] As an antidote to the RUC's partisan image the delivery of routine policing is no doubt helpful. An obvious question is whether police preoccupied with terrorism can exercise community policing. Brewer found little contamination of community policing by the paramilitary role because officers did not perform both roles simultaneously. But community policing was not tried where the 'troubles' were endemic. Outreach has its limits.

Brewer's study shows that, even in divided societies, there are areas where 'routine' policing still occurs, although where 'hard' and 'soft' policing co-exist they affect each other. Thus, community policing has both conventional crime prevention and outreach meanings and a specific meaning of overcoming Catholic hostility. Brewer found only one neighbourhood constable who saw his role as crime detection rather than prevention. The emphasis was on informal contacts, visible deterrence and local knowledge. Officers patrolled in pairs, with guns and flak jackets. One constable provides cover, so each spends only half the shift on their particular area. To enhance identification as local constables, and allow fire to be returned, officers are meant to patrol separated by some distance; in practice they often walk together. Following a fatal attack on an officer they began patrolling in threes, which was resented as it became virtually impossible to establish rapport, and took three days for a circuit of the beat.

[70] Bennett and Lupton (1992a) at 209.   [71] Ibid. at 208.
[72] Brewer (1991a).

An unintended consequence was an improvement in police views of Catholics, categorizing most residents as decent, honest and essentially friendly. This is gratifying when one notes an officer's remark that, in West Belfast, his constables 'risked their lives for community policing'; every pair of neighbourhood constables was accompanied by 16 soldiers, and sometimes another squad protecting the soldiers protecting the officers (and landrovers and an army helicopter). Here, where a neighbourhood patrol amounts to an armed convoy, no more can be done than demonstrate police presence. Sensitive to the dangers for those seen in contact with them, the officers use interactional skills to give the appearance of issuing route directions as they conduct their contacts.

Inner cities can themselves be depicted as divided societies. A study of police-citizen interactions in Philadelphia[73] involved a longitudinal design at whose mid-point the MOVE incident occurred (where police bombed a house containing black activists, killing eleven and rendering 240 homeless). Greene and Decker found citizen support for police declined dramatically but antagonism also declined. '[T]he environmental effects of the MOVE and other police incidents were perceptible to the community . . . but day-to-day interactions of police and community residents remained less conflictual.'[74] But police attitudes to the community declined. Citizens' 'business-as-usual interpretation suggests that the community participants were less sensitive to the generalist criticism of the police, then were the police themselves'.[75] Both Brewer's study, and Greene and Decker's, hint that community policing may be on a better footing in unpromising areas than we may first imagine.

Community constables need to make direct contact with favourable people because in the inner city it is unlikely to be initiated by residents. But one must wonder how adventurous their interpretation of 'favourable' will be, especially with the evidence that community contact is a limited claim on their time and that they are drawn to 'respectables' rather than the community's 'undecideds'. In 1986 there were half as many schemes for neighbourhood watch on inner than outer London boroughs (Metropolitan Police Crime Prevention Service, letter 10 April, 1987). Half the chief superintendents Donnison et al. interviewed in 1984 identified high crime areas in their division where it would be virtually impossible to establish

---

[73] Greene and Decker (1989).   [74] Ibid. at 115.   [75] Ibid. at 116.

a scheme because of general public apathy or endemic hostility to police.[76]

Community constables amount to little more than 5 per cent of the establishment of the average force. Even in those such as Hampshire, which emphasizes permanent beats, they still account for only 15 per cent of officers up to inspector rank.[77] Career incentives are needed to secure commitment and real continuity. At present, too few officers are allocated to beats, and the beats are too large. They are called too often to other duties. Community patrol too often lacks effectiveness and purpose. Limiting the size of beats is necessary if constables are to have close enough contact with residents and local organizations to take account of them.[78] But one of community policing's key advantages is that beat patrol is still seen by police as the generic basis of law enforcement. The Police Federation's Manchester representative declared at its 1991 conference that 'we have lost our way. Current emphasis on specialised squads and units has been to the detriment of the uniformed patrol officer. "Fire brigade" policing means we are losing control of the streets' (*Guardian* 22 May, 1991). The chair of the Federation commented 'keep the police in police stations and vehicles and they'll remain remote, authoritarian, separate from and uneasy with the people they're meant to be helping'. Because the resolution of conflict is central to the community police mission, and conflict is unpredictable, police-initiated activity is hard to plan. It is therefore difficult to define a set of concrete tasks for community police. Nor is there consensus on the best ways of resolving conflict. This implies the need to document exactly how community constables go about their 'impossible' mission.

[76] Donnison *et al.* (1986) at 22.   [77] Smith (1987).   [78] NACRO (1988) at 19.

3
Settings and Sources

The Fieldwork

Community policing was very much a live issue at the time of the fieldwork, which was conducted in two divisions in the Metropolitan Police and one in Surrey Constabulary. The Metropolitan Police was implementing 'neighbourhood policing', which had three compulsory elements. While the first, participative management, was indeed functioning throughout the force's eight areas 'in some cases manning problems have put strains on the participation process'.[1] District Information and Intelligence Units, vital to information transfer, ran in six areas but there was 'still a long way to go before DIIUs are working as planned'. Graded response 'failed to get off the ground'; in only one area were even half the divisions implementing it. Availability of officers was uncertain, they were reluctant to hand over messages, progress was difficult without geographical responsibility.

Of the three optional elements, geographical responsibility was so labour intensive that most divisions had not implemented it. Where it had been tried it was being restricted or abandoned due to under-staffing. (The same appears to have happened in recent moves to 'sector policing', or geographical responsibility. Police sources suggest it was being supported in appearance only, with prevailing, relief-based methods continuing, and a reduction by half in sectors originally designated in one area. This meant officers operating on much larger areas, effectively reverting to relief mode.) 'Alignment of administration' [between different units in a given area] was restricted by lack of accommodation. Most Areas considered that introducing crime desks fulfilled this element.[2] But, under 'Police and public contract', all areas were seeking closer liaison with the community, through neighbourhood watch, neighbourhood policing and

---

[1] Metropolitan Police (1986) 'Force Appraisal' at 38.   [2] *Ibid.* at 39.

consultative groups.[3] This latter, optional, element was the only one on which real progress had been achieved.

The image of policing founded on relief work suggests a policing effort with little teamwork, a limited collective memory and restricted planning. All is subordinated to the message pad, clearing calls as they are received, delivering on-the-spot resolutions in haste and hurrying to the next call. Researchers know that the actual volume of activity does not in fact support the image of constant pressure. But the myth still has power. One effect is to obscure how relief policing contrasts to traditional beat patrol in documenting information about the community. From the earliest days patrols passed records of their activity to supervisors, who compiled reports for senior officers, ensuring continuity and transmission of information. These records, or 'beatbooks', are no longer universally compiled; one has to go back to the 1970s to read a lament for their failure to be as full, and fully-used, as in the past.[4] They described occasional visitors, the location of facilities like telephone kiosks, details of hawkers and gypsies, special constables, people who would volunteer to help in times of need, crimes that had been committed.

This patrol tradition was preserved by the Permanent Beat Officers of our inner city research sites. The source documents are the 'Homebeats monthly returns' compiled for each beat. Each includes 'Permanent beat action sheets' which summarize highlighted issues, and an Action Plan. The documents are largely compiled by community police sergeants, and their usefulness is attested by an inspector's comment: 'Chief Superintendent: an excellent profile, much of which will be of use in my action plan. I have congratulated PS Jones.' These books offer an insight into the range of community policing concerns and into what the officers feel it important to record, serving as an element of the organization's 'collective memory'. To the researcher they offer a methodological resource because an established way of confirming the validity and reliability of data is from records of similar events from different sources.[5] Beatbooks offer a means of 'within-method triangulation'.

Surrey, a force near the main fieldwork sites, was in the process of committing itself to 'total geographic policing', a system based on a community policing approach where the former reliefs take responsibility for particular local areas. Because of this policy shift,

---

[3] *Ibid.*   [4] Evans (1974) at 95–6.   [5] Fielding and Fielding (1986).

community policing ideas were much in currency, and some of the data presented here arise from interviews in Surrey. Opportunities to observe community policing in the force were limited. Until the change to total geographic policing, most policing in Surrey was still organized on the relief model, and all but two of the observational incidents discussed here derive from inner London. This calls for comment on criteria for the inclusion of fieldwork data in this book.

The methodology of this book is qualitative. Beatbook accounts are used along with observational fieldnotes, plus interviews and group discussions conducted with officers by the research team— Charles Kemp, Clive Norris and me—as a comparative base for analysing community policing practice. We observed over 1,200 police/public incidents in hundreds of hours of fieldwork, and interviewed officers of all ranks and functions in the three research sites. The group discussions were jointly conducted by all three of us, while we worked in pairs in conducting the intensive interviews. We agreed that project data would be available to us all to write up singly or jointly. The present analysis is the author's.

The interview data were transcribed *verbatim* and analysed by compiling sets of themes and sub-themes (or 'categories') and assigning the categories as appropriate to the text. Text relevant to a particular category was then retrieved and extracts chosen either because they represented essential qualities of the theme or added nuances and refinements to it. This procedure is conventional in qualitative research and, indeed, many of the new software packages to assist qualitative analysis are based on it.[6]

With a large set of data of observed police/public interactions it is not possible to present them all, and only a fraction appear here. In many instances the interaction was routine, or superficial, or community police played a peripheral role. While these incidents entered our statistical database (and were primarily used for quantitative analyses of the effects of police and citizen demeanour, status and dispositional variables[7]), extensive fieldnotes were not written on them. Incidents where community police engaged in more extensive interactions were recorded in full fieldnotes, and these are the source of the observational data included in this book. Although all three team members compiled fieldnotes, our observations were conducted individually and all of the observational data presented here were

6 Fielding and Lee (1993).   7 For example, see Norris, Kemp *et al.* (1992).

collected by the author. Because we were observing officers based in the same stations there were many occasions where we could 'compare notes' on the same incident at different stages or as it was discussed by different officers, and reference is made to this where relevant.

The incidents appearing here were selected because they represent key elements of community police practice. The key elements themselves were identified by drawing on several criteria, as is usual in ethnography. Study of the literature (much of it discussed in chapters 1 and 2), group discussions and interviews (informal and formal), repeated reading of the fieldnotes, and introspection about experiences while accompanying the officers, all contributed to the set of key practices which form the basis of the substantive chapters. Once these elements were identified the fieldnotes were reviewed in order to select cases illuminating the element in question. Qualitative research must guard against prematurely claiming generalizability, but it can be said that the incidents are 'representative' in that similar incidents were collected which do not appear here. Where an incident is exceptional this is indicated. While reference is made to statistical findings from quantitative studies, notably the roughly contemporary research by Southgate,[8] I am less concerned here with how often particular practices occur than with detailed exposition of key practices. I regard the present analysis as part of an incremental effort, motivated by the absence of a literature conveying just how community police go about their work. Data from Southgate[9] are largely consistent with our own in respect of quantifiable aspects of interpersonal tactics and proportions of time spent in particular activities. Both statistical comparisons of relief and community policing, and our observations on relief shifts, inform the statements about the character of relief policing which are used as a contrast and comparison with community policing.

Qualitative data are, in an important sense, themselves interpretations. Observations are mediated by the researcher's perspective and behaviour. Interviews add a further layer, being affected not only by the researcher's characteristics but the traits of respondents. All are capable of adding 'colouration' to the data (quantitative instruments bear different but no less tangible mediating qualities). This is inescapable and, following Wright Mills,[10] it is incumbent on

---

[8] Southgate (1986).   [9] *Ibid.*   [10] Wright Mills (1959).

researchers to offer procedural details to help readers see where the data are 'coming from'. Access was gained to conduct research on competent community policing practice. All were aware that 'competence' could also be identified by its opposite, and that community policing could be understood partly by the relief policing with which it contrasted. Briefings to this effect were given to all participating officers. Different community constables were accompanied on different occasions, but these sections are not large and nearly all were accompanied at least once for a full eight hour shift, with a number being accompanied up to five times. Relief officers were also accompanied, on a similar basis, but their larger numbers meant that some were not accompanied.

When we accompanied individuals from either group we repeated the statement of the research focus above and explained that we would be writing fieldnotes. We minimized note taking in the presence of officers and/or citizens, using the stock ploy of a weak bladder to get time to write detailed notes where necessary. We wore 'smart' civilian clothes and if citizens asked who we were our first response was a noncommittal 'I am with the officer today', followed by the plain description that we were conducting research if there was a further query (which happened surprisingly infrequently). We infer from the few occasions where even the first account was called for that, because we always arrived with police officers, most citizens assumed we were police. We did carry a police access letter but seldom had occasion to show it. The events the police deal with generally have their own dynamic and this is helpful to observers.

We avoided reacting evaluatively to police actions although there were occasions where we consciously displayed similar perspectives on citizens' actions to those expressed by officers, either to maintain a sympathetic fieldwork posture or because we agreed with them. Sometimes we joined in with a chase or some other action, as will become obvious. When we did not agree with what the officers were doing, we sought to control overt displays of our views and reactions. We all had considerable prior experience of participant observation and were used to presenting a neutral guise in the field; the principal case in which I departed significantly from this is discussed in Fielding (1990).[11] We had also agreed the circumstances under which we would report an action to a superior officer. Maintaining

---

[11] Fielding (1990).

this posture is trying and we sought to manage the stress by frequent, lengthy debriefings—or a session at the pub. All person and place names have been given pseudonyms. Further details of our fieldwork may be found in Fielding, Kemp and Norris (1989)[12] and ethical matters are considered in Fielding (1990).[13]

About two thirds of our observational fieldwork was concentrated in one of the London divisions. This primary research area was a part of inner city London undergoing significant change in its socio-economic composition. Traditionally mainly working class with large council housing estates, there were major concentrations of people of Irish origin and, latterly, Afro-Caribbeans. More recently there had been an influx of young, prosperous people who valued the area's convenient location. The community policing inspector, Inspector Adams, said, 'four years ago it was very much . . . a working class area with a large amount of council tenants, which, because of the yuppies that are moving in . . . there is more wealth coming in, which is also generating the possibility for more crime, particularly burglaries and autocrime.' Among the monthly beatbook entries was this in the 'Environmental changes' section: 'there is a constant refurbishing of property on the beat by housing associations and private developers and with Council property on the fringes this is giving quite a "mix" of social classes which will inevitably lead to friction'.[14]

The community police

Primary responsibility for the community constables resided with an inspector, who had four sergeants working under him. One was the '10 to 6 man' responsible for duties rostering and neighbourhood watch 'because it is important to have an office manager who can be contacted, he is also the link with the outside world'.[15] The other three sergeants each supervised seven constables. The 'ground' was divided into six beats, and each sergeant took two, which equated to two wards. The rota system provided community policing seven days a week from 7 a.m. to 11 p.m. Each sergeant was responsible for the whole division when on duty but had particular responsibility for his two wards.

The inspector saw case papers and allocated work to the sergeants. All correspondence was routed through him. He was

---

[12] Fielding Kemp and Norris (1989).   [13] Fielding (1990).
[14] Beatbook 4 (hereinafter all Beatbooks are referred to as BB).
[15] Insp. Adams.

briefed by his sergeants and responsible for seeing that monthly reports on each beat were compiled. They included crime figures on particular beats, the number of abstractions from duty, where the constable had been and an account of the constable's time. Constables had to include details of community involvement work, so supervisors knew whether schools and neighbourhood watch coordinators were being visited. 'Changes in the environment' updated information held by the divisional intelligence unit. If crime figures on a beat changed the inspector sought 'any feature, like the abstractions which are recorded, that would indicate that "because he hasn't trodden the beat, crime has gone up" '.[16] A community constable had broken an ankle and burglaries and autocrime rose 25 per cent, 'now she's resumed service its gone back to the preceding level'.

The inspector had no quota of arrests because he accepted that not all beats were 'busy'. 'I would never demand a quota for arrests, but I do expect them to take an interest in crime, to investigate crime and show arrests wherever possible.'[17] One constable had a dozen 'good quality' arrests in a month 'but he had a particularly good period when he was getting good information from his informants on the beat. Anybody could have solved them . . . because suspects were turning each other in . . . You can't apply what happened to him to everybody because there are beats where its middle class where there is very little community spirit, people just like to see the policeman walking the streets, they don't want to contact him, take part in anything.'[18]

The reports were not the inspector's main way of checking up. 'I speak to my officers whenever I get the opportunity. I get a good idea of what they are doing.'[19] He also held quarterly and impromptu meetings. On occasion he patrolled with his constables, and attended public meetings, such as neighbourhood watch, in which they were involved. He thus saw how they reacted to the public and gauged the public's relations with the constable. He devoted little time to the exercise of formal discipline because 'my officers are the better quality of bloke'; the tear-aways were on the reliefs. He had not had to report anyone for indiscipline.

Above the inspector the most significant ranks to the community constables were the two top officers in the station. The superintendent was responsible for community involvement. The management

---

[16] Insp. Adams.   [17] Ibid.   [18] Ibid.   [19] Ibid.

team had changed prior to the interview with the community policing inspector at the principal site, but 'certainly in the past the superintendent has played an active role, there's been a two-way flow of
information with me which has permeated down to the permanent
beats. He has attended meetings with the PCs. We have had really
good support.'[20] An example was a problem with a shebeen in a
black community. The superintendent and chief superintendent co-
ordinated and led the operation. 'Its not an easy thing because you've
got observations, which they both took an active role in, which cul-
minated in a well-coordinated raid which utilized homebeats, crime
squads, CID, relief officers. It was a divisional effort and it was very
successful. The local community were very pleased.'[21]

The inspector felt that the outgoing superintendent and chief were
not typical of management. 'We've seen genuine participative management where anybody could make his point of view and it would
be considered. It had a cohesive effect on the station. There was a
sense of common purpose.'[22] With their departure this was unlikely
to be sustained, threatening community policing. 'There is a
significant change in atmosphere. My role, I think, will disappear.
There is no communication. Nobody at my rank . . . knows what is
going on or what is planned.'[23] This was widely confirmed by other
officers and relief constables.

The community policing system at this principal site was distinctive. Community policing was a route into the prestigious Crime
Squad. As the chief superintendent confirmed shortly after retirement, 'we made it known that, if a bloke wanted to specialize,
whether Crime Squad or even Special Branch, let him prove himself
as a competent, all round officer, as a home beat officer'. It was
important to set community policing on a career path.

We laid down that the way to progress was through permanent beat and a
lot of officers took it on that basis, not wanting it, and then realized that
they thoroughly enjoyed it and do a very good job. We set a period of six
months trial [and] the number that opted to go back [to the reliefs] was very
small . . . ones and twos out of 23 at any one time. A lot of those original
permanent Beat Officers were press-ganged. You try and get them off now.
They'd come off if it was for their advantage in specialization or progress
or inter-district transfer. People like [X] were press-ganged, they were happy
on the relief running and tearing around. But having got into depth and

[20] Ibid.   [21] Ibid.   [22] Ibid.   [23] Ibid.

knowledge on their beat and the problems of that beat, I don't think you'd wedge them away from it.[24]

The community policing effort had profited from managerial support of the most manifest kind.

They will be supported in any application later on if they wish to specialize. If an officer wanted to join the Divisional Crime Squad he would be expected to gain some experience on the home beats because there he would get some idea of how to investigate crimes. He would get practical experience, more so than on the relief, and if he did a good job he is more likely to come to notice so that senior officers are going to be able to report on him properly and extol his virtues when he's going up for a board.[25]

The community policing inspector said 'the proof of that is the number of officers that I have lost elsewhere, at least ten to the Crime Squad over the last two years'. The carrot was very attractive: the chance at a career in detection. 'If an officer wants a CID career he has got to be able to convince somebody before he goes onto the Crime Squad, which is a stepping stone into the CID, that he is worthy of that post. It is a sought-after post by PCs and obviously they're going to do what they can to get on, its quite competitive. We've been very successful, I've only had two rejected.'[26]

Chief superintendents set the policy of the station, as much by manner and style as by formal pronouncements. Subordinates avidly interpret the chief's asides, reading much into the apparently trivial, preoccupied with whether the chief is a 'street' or 'management' officer,[27] ambitious or committed, supportive or officious. Of course, these are overdrawn bipolar distinctions but they give some idea of the pervasive influence that subordinates believe the person at the top exercises. Believing this they partly make it so; their actions are informed by their grasp of the chief's predilections.

The chief superintendent was a powerful, street-oriented manager. He was also approaching retirement, so that his officers knew his commitment to the station would not be diluted by having an eye towards his next career move. He had made his mark and established his style. He was well liked. Like Muir's 'paradox of face',[28] this esteem actually meant he could proceed with policies that were, at first blush, unconducive to the average constable. Such a policy was community policing, traditionally regarded with disdain by street

---

[24] Ch. Supt. Heath.   [25] Insp. Adams.   [26] *Ibid.*
[27] Reuss-Ianni (1982).   [28] Muir (1977).

officers. However, his interpretation of community policing ensured that it would be taken seriously. He emphasized its role in crime control through information gathering. He put less weight on school liaison, neighbourhood watch and 'gladhanding' the local people. He did not condemn these things but his most significant and distinctive interpretation was making a community beat a route into detection.

Here he is discussing his interpretation of the chief superintendent role.

It has been laid down that the chief superintendent is now very much the strategist, the planner, whereas the superintendent is the operational head. That goes hard against people like myself who have had 30 years operational experience of being involved and its something I could never release the reins of. If there were operational matters of sufficient importance I saw it not only as my responsibility to be there, but by being there you could win the total support of your men. I recall when I went to [station] carrying out a couple of raids, which was almost unheard of for chief superintendents, but I had always done that.[29]

He led the raids, in uniform. 'That was very much me but I was not restricted from above. Superiors might have said "Should you not be allowing your superintendent, chief inspectors, indeed inspectors to do that?" I don't agree. To maintain morale and get support you've got to show you're able to do it.'[30] This was not the way things were going, and trouble lay ahead. 'The current policies are encouraging the planning, the strategy at the expense of that ability and leadership. Officers moving up are likely to get to the command positions without having done an awful lot of commanding.'[31] The chief felt he was not typical, that 'I am one of the old school who came up under a different regime.' An orthodoxy had become established at the top, a cabal of insiders insulated the commissioner. 'The commissioner is closeted by a breed of officers that have been very much brought up with him . . . If you look at Area, Area DACs have been closeted by a staff, most of whom are that type. Very few real, hard, practical policemen.'[32]

The emphasis on being close to the troops as a 'practical policeman' carries with it a regimental, paternal concern—'my blokes knew my door was always open and if they had a real problem they could come and see me. And they did.'[33] It was a hands-on

---

[29] Ch. Supt. Heath.   [30] *Ibid.*   [31] *Ibid.*   [32] *Ibid.*   [33] *Ibid.*

management style which also emphasized the unalloyed value of information and personal contact.

[I]f you got this ear to the ground there's an awful lot more that you know that is not on paper, whether it be domestic problems or a very good piece of work an officer has done. I always thought you should call officers up if they've done good work and pat them on the back . . . I would go and see the individual in his own environment, in the canteen maybe, and say 'bloody good bit of work the other day, well done'. That meant more to the bloke then all the formality, in front of his colleagues particularly. He went out 'head and shoulders'.[34]

Looking outside the organization a similar traditional perspective was expressed. For instance, public meetings were desirable because they offered a venue in which to put the police view. In what follows there is little sign of an intention to be responsive.

Two years ago we made presentation of the [local] strategic plan to the public at the request of the [divisional] Policing Consultative Committee. I found that was a very, very useful way of meeting the public and putting over the police message and listening to what they had to say about policing . . . At a meeting such as that I would say that we identify our priorities and we explain why some things are not priorities, one of which was racial incidents. Now you can imagine that from some of the minority groups we got quite a bit of questioning on that. Then you can turn to the statistics and say there are so few, in reality, why should we? We are still going to deal with the problem. If it arises we will deal with it seriously, but we don't see it as our priority. Now if Area disagreed with that then I would still expect them to support me because it is the view of my officers and myself and of the public we come in contact with, in the main. You always get minority groups who scream and shout about various things.[35]

There was no sign of awareness in the statement about statistics on racial incidents that prioritization would increase reporting and therefore the numbers recorded. The chief's line is consistent with a crime control angle on community policing: crime figures, not community pressure, set priorities.

The meetings, then, were to inform the public of the choices the police had made, even though their best justification was when there was conflict over goals and priorities. In an adjoining division 'with a very, very supportive public . . . there wasn't a great value' whereas in his own division 'I felt the value was in going to the public as a

---

[34] Ch. Supt. Heath.   [35] Ibid.

whole and where there was opposition, saying "here we are, we're standing up and we're being counted. Here's your chance, let us know what you think about policing at [this division]".'[36] It became apparent that the meeting *was* the consultation, there would be no follow-up, no ongoing process of priority-setting and performance monitoring, at least not one involving outsiders. The chief also adamantly defended the meeting's representativeness, on the grounds that those who did not come showed they did not care.

You have got your leftie, you've got your support from neighbourhood watch, you've got your councillors from the Establishment, shall we say, you've got everybody there who had the slightest interest. Everybody had the opportunity to attend, which is more important, because we had public notices displayed . . . Police need to be taking the initiative more and saying 'this is what we've done, we've given you your chance. Now its no use your shouting and saying "we never had a chance to say anything about this, that and the other". If you didn't turn up, if you didn't take advantage of that, that's your fault, you had the chance.' They had one through that system.[37]

While consultation through public meetings had become accepted practice there were differences in approach among senior officers. The chief inspector (Operations) thought the outgoing chief's view was unsatisfactory.

Unless you consult the people out there its a complete waste of time. Even if the people say 'we're not interested in robbery, what we're interested in is parking' then we have to take that on board. I know you can never get the whole spectrum and, as you go round these neighbourhood watch meetings, you find that, certain areas, all they want to talk about are the rat runs . . . Other people are more concerned with robberies and burglaries. Inevitably when you go on this consultation line, people fight for their own corner . . . But we must make a concerted effort to actually speak to these people. [Chief superintendent] did a presentation of the divisional plan. That I can see no point [in]. It's no good doing a presentation. It should be beforehand. We should be going to them and saying 'this is what we did last year, tell us what you want us to do this year'. I know it becomes a bit of a bear garden if you're not careful and we'll probably still end up with the same result but that's what we should be doing.[38]

As well as the point about genuine consultation being before priorities are set, the chief inspector's (Operations) comment reveals an

---

[36] *Ibid.*   [37] *Ibid.*   [38] Ch. Insp. Wills.

awareness that consultation is inevitably selective and that police have to take account of views that are not directly put to them. As Jefferson and Grimshaw argued,[39] arbitrating competing demands is a role with which the police are comfortable. The interviewer asked the chief inspector (Operations) if he saw the police trying to 'educate' people on the need to reconcile competing priorities through consultation. 'That's half the process. Then it becomes apparent to people that when all these people are coming up with their own specific problems, somebody has got to make a decision and say "we understand your problems but there's got to be a priority, because we just can't do the whole spectrum".'[40]

The role of the chief inspector (Operations) was to maintain the overall mission of the station and provide the staff to do it. He gave the community constables a central part in the station's mission. 'I must ensure the reliefs are working well in combating crime and the permanent beats are able to fight crime in the most practical way . . . I define [community policing] as an operational role because that's the kernel of why we're here . . . We can do it by other means, neighbourhood watches and getting people on our side, but the most important thing, at the end of the day, are the crime figures.'[41] The chief inspector's emphasis on crime figures is entirely conventional, but note that he places permanent beat policing as part of the core mission, unlike neighbourhood watches and community 'outreach'. It is significant because the chief inspector (Operations) is the officer who must 'rob' less central functions to maintain relief strengths. As we will see, the community policing inspector specifically refers to conflict with the chief inspector (Operations) over just this issue. But the chief inspector (Operations) places permanent beat policing—as crime-related patrol work—alongside the reliefs, and against other community policing activities.

Consistent with this, the community police inspector, Inspector Adams, had a deserved reputation for getting involved on the street. Not all community constables shared the crime control version of community policing, but the inspector's energy and commitment were appreciated, and his involvement in operations created good morale. The point had registered with him early in his service.

People like to be able to measure their effectiveness. When I first joined I was at West End Central [where] there were something like 300 officers. It

---

[39] Jefferson and Grimshaw (1984).   [40] Ch. Insp. Wills.   [41] *Ibid.*

was quite common to have 25 officers on parade. You would go out and work quite hard, patrol the streets in Soho, arrest the doorman at clubs that were causing problems, get the beggars off the streets, even find something connected with crime . . . But you never saw how it affected the overall picture. There were often times when I thought 'what am I really doing? Am I giving the public a service? How do I know? How do I measure how successful I am?'[42]

The inspector offered a dramatic example of the ability community constables and their supervisors have to gauge their efforts.

When Trevor Todd was posted to his homebeat, which encompasses the W Estate, reported burglaries were running at 30 a month. He worked very hard and had some early successes which cleared up a number of burglaries. Within a short space of time people knew there was an officer who was about most days who obviously had informers on the estate who were giving him good information. The burglaries dried up and for six consecutive months after he was posted to that area we went down to four or five reported burglaries a month. He was able to see what effect he had, because nobody else was doing any work on that estate at all.[43]

The inspector's figures were subsequently checked against records; he was right. With such crime control successes, the community constables and their inspector had secured considerable autonomy. 'If there was anything specific that we wanted to do we would get the authority. I can't ever remember authority not being given because we would always pick a problem which was something that was permanent to the community . . . I have been given an awful lot of leeway, and the only thing that was required is that I told senior management what I was doing.'[44] Among the means he used to determine 'permanent' problems were the consultative committee meetings, occasional surveys (often through Neighbourhood Watch schemes), Neighbourhood Watch meetings, and findings from the British Crime Survey.

Despite successes, the status of community constable was not avidly sought after. The chief inspector (Operations) confirmed that several permanent beat vacancies were unfilled and that this hiatus was associated with the new superintendent and chief superintendent. 'The homebeats feel they're under threat. There isn't the commitment that there was with Mr Heath (former chief) but the management feel that, because there was so much commitment by

---

[42] *Ibid.*   [43] *Ibid.*   [44] Insp. Adams.

Mr Heath, they really can't back pedal at this stage. But they would like to reduce the number of Permanent Beat Officers and take the inspector away as well.' He would 'defend the entire department of beat officers' and if anything 'they should be increased', at least by restoring officers to unfilled beats. 'And there should be an inspector in charge of them, a line command structure to give them identity and somebody to fight for their cause.'[45]

At the second London site, staffing prevented the superintendent doing all he wanted in response to information about crime but he still met weekly with the District Information and Intelligence Units along with his chief inspector, Crime Squad sergeants and home beat inspector. He told them, 'I want you to put me on the spot, tell me, "Governor, that's what's happening, because of our Intelligence, and we can actually attack that problem successfully if you will put the manpower into it." So then I will discuss with the Crime Squad sergeant and the Home Beat inspector.'[46] Thus, the community policing section was closely involved in the intelligence exercise. There were 24 Permanent Beat Officers at this station, on eight beats; 'the problem is the consultative group would have 124'. Of one of the home beat sergeants he remarked, 'his danger of course is he is doing the job I put him there to do, to take that personal interest and make his sector the only sector that matters . . . but he is forgetting the needs of the rest of the division . . . His whole philosophy of policing is towards homebeats and I believe its absolutely 100 per cent right, but it ain't practical because there ain't the manpower.'[47]

It was a matter of balance. 'I worry that in community policing you do need the other sort of policing as well'. The superintendent was reviewing the system and had just attended one of their weekly meetings. Familiar complaints were aired of their being taken off for public order and relief cover. He suggested ' "we could make eight of you untouchables. You select them amongst yourselves with the inspector . . . We would still have the others supporting".'[48] The suggestion was left with them. The new chief superintendent was also looking at re-structuring the homebeats. The uncertainty marking community policing at the principal site was also being visited on the second site.

This was not the only way in which organizational problems confronted community policing. Like other organizations, police forces

[45] Insp. Adams.   [46] Supt. Vine.   [47] Ibid.   [48] Ibid.

are also domestic institutions providing succour, accommodation and sustenance for their members. Early in their careers, constables are likely to be housed in police houses or 'section houses', dormitories providing all domestic services. While some may find it nurtures camaraderie and a sense of affiliation never lost in their career, others find the experience overpowering, as the following fieldnote suggests.

Andrew was in the divisional section house with 105 other constables, mainly the younger ones. This was the atmosphere which bred the macho approach to policing. Andrew doesn't mind a crime-oriented approach, for in his mind, while there is a balance with service work, crime is still your *raison d'etre*, but its the attitude that all [those with whom police deal] are scum which he condemns. He thought the facilities reflected the macho attitude of management. For example, the cooking facilities: for 105 officers there was one cooker and one fridge, both next to the gym, and a microwave oven upstairs. A working party complained these facilities were excessive and they were in danger of losing the microwave. The facilities being next to the gym, they were under-used. It was assumed that PCs ate in the canteens. 'What you have is a total institution, as much as any prison.' Though rent was nominal, if he had his own place he would get mortgage/rent allowance and a completely different level of facilities, so there was a gulf between the predominantly young, male probationers [in their first two years of service] and the older constables, which accentuated the 'hard' image. Further, attitudes acquired early tended to become set.[49]

Andrew was a graduate with a desire to join Special Branch. He regarded police management as out-dated and insensitive. In our discussion, what is more important than his complaint of the impact of section house life on him is that he saw it as symbolizing a macho lifestyle implicitly antithetical to the philosophy of community policing. His plausible supposition was that the domestic arrangements conveyed and supported an occupational culture which affected the style of policing; the organization was reinforcing the wrong message by keeping its novices in barracks.

Even in a perfectly supportive organization, problems are not only set by the organization itself—its hierarchy, lines of accountability and authority, resources, mandate and duties, public image, and so on—but by its members' adjustments to the organization. In the main, the officers encountered in the fieldwork were ambitious, ceaselessly discussing promotions, transfers, appraisal, courses and

[49] Fieldnotes.

the like. Despite unusually strong senior support in the main field-work site, the community constables seemed particularly touched by careerist concerns. This was inevitable because beat assignment usu-ally encountered resistance and the incentive used to 'persuade' officers to accept was the route to investigative specialisms and/or promotion.

One obvious trouble this presented for community policing was disruption to continuity on the beat. 'Sergeant Mint mentions that over the next two months five PBOs will be transferring out. Lack of continuity is not just a result of organizational policy but of indi-vidual option in pursuing careers—all the transfers arise from officers applying for courses, promotion or specialist functions, e.g., DSU or Special Branch.'[50] Transfers are not only a problem among the ranks but disrupt managed change. A superintendent referred to implementing area policing. 'When we were setting up the scheme the inspector in charge was selected for a job at headquarters. Although he set it up he had no ownership because he was going. He was replaced by an inspector who was only there for six months because he's going to university. So I now have the third inspector in six months. The strongest sergeant was continually taken out for training and most of the other sergeants were inexperienced.'[51] For the promotion-minded the transfer is a crucial way of gaining broad experience and a record of expertise on which to capitalize. For the manager the transfer is not only disruptive but removes skilled staff.

These matters lead to some very mixed motives.

If you promote them the chances are you'd lose them in the police service, so there's stronger reasons for you dissuading them. In industry you'd get somebody a promoted post in the hope that you were going to give them extra money but use them in the same skills. You can't do that in the police service . . . Rewarding the individual for particular skills they have devel-oped is very difficult . . . In industry you can pay them bonuses . . . You can't do that here so you have got to find other ways of rewarding people . . . Other than patting them on the back publicly there's not a great deal you can do.[52]

Of course, instrumental ends can be served by accepting the post-ing. In the case of one constable, it offered the only way to maintain the essential quality which attracted him to policing. On the reliefs, Bill did a computer course and a police national computer course.[53]

---

[50] Fieldnotes.   [51] Supt. Tate.   [52] *Ibid.*   [53] Fieldnotes.

He could see that the consequence would be his being 'cooped up inside a lot'. He described himself as crime-oriented, preferring to be outdoors and 'active'. He disliked paperwork intensely, talking openly about his limited vocabulary and having to labour over reports and statements on forms, which still came out in a stilted way compared to others.

As Bill saw it, a bargain was struck that the price of his staying outside was his accepting a permanent beat. It was not his choice. He had applied for Special Patrol Group training when he was offered the Police National Computer course instead. He still wanted to return to the reliefs, but had a long-term interest in CID. It must be added that Bill appeared to be a skilful community constable, with a detailed knowledge of his beat and a contacts network that was both numerous and extended to many ordinary residents rather than resting with commercial premises, schools and neighbourhood watch co-ordinators. His reservations about his articulateness did not impede his efforts to persuade such people as Neighbourhood Watch contacts to do things they did not want, despite the gap between his own working class background and the titled people involved in Neighbourhood Watch at the opulent end of his beat. (His negotiation with a reluctant Neighbourhood Watch co-ordinator is examined later.)

Another reason community constables came to appreciate the function and put its case to other officers was to ensure that their work was seen as valuable and not marginal, both with a view to future appraisals for their next career move and to sustaining a sense of personal satisfaction. But we should not underestimate the instrumental sophistication of the canny constable looking to get ahead. In the following there is no doubt that the officer is playing the system, but in exchange the system has its own ends met. 'There was discussion of inter-departmental transfers. Dick was at the five year point at Christmas but bought more time by agreeing to leave his former beat and accept a posting to the D Estate beat, knowing vacancies there were hard to fill.'[54] To a superior examining Dick's pattern of postings, this would look like a highly-committed beat officer wishing to maintain himself in the specialism. Not so. 'It presently suited his career plans to be on permanent beat and on [this] ground. He is preparing for his sergeants' exam and values the

[54] Fieldnotes.

autonomy he has on permanent beat.'[55] Having duty times similar to conventional working hours was also an incentive. With such career planning in currency, we may identify dysfunctions of the organization's personnel policies.

Dick pointed out that, since one was transferred on promotion to sergeant in any case, the prospect of an IDT transfer, followed by promotion transfer eighteen months later, would be too disruptive both in his ties to people on his beat and relations with colleagues. No sooner would he get accepted and learn the ropes than he would move again to start as sergeant. Consequently he played the permanent beat system to see that he stayed where he was until promotion.[56]

Dick's commentary combined both instrumental and beat-oriented thinking. He strongly saw his tie to local people as the key to good policework; through this came the crime-related information he needed to maintain a good activity level and see to his advancement.

It would be wrong to conclude this look at the troubles of community constables without noting that trouble could also be caused by personal incompetence. In a study based on participant observation fieldworkers will always be drawn to construe events from the perspective of those observed; appreciation of their world view is one of the things we pursue. But this should not mean that fieldworkers sanitize the data to conform to some idealized notion a group has of itself.[57] In fact, community and relief constables proved to be preoccupied with estimations of the competence of their colleagues, within and across specialisms. The following fieldnote reviews one obvious problem, with details making clear its effect on the service given by the officer.

Discussion of the previous officer assigned to this beat, also a WPC. The transition was less effective than Sophie wished because the previous PBO had been ineffective and uninvolved. The problem arose because her boyfriend was the PBO on the adjacent beat. As a result, she tended to walk his beat with him, to the neglect of her beat. This was to the extent that, when she was taking Sophie round to introduce her to 'contacts' on her beat, in several cases when they entered premises such as schools it was the first time they had seen the outgoing WPC. Also in the case of the schools, the WPC told Sophie that, due to the attitude of the headmaster/headmistress, most schools on her beat did not welcome police and had a policy of discouraging their entry onto school premises. Sophie found this to be false—

---

[55] Fieldnotes.   [56] *Ibid*.   [57] Fielding (1990).

all welcomed her and wondered why they had not previously been visited.[58]

Relief officers have no monopoly on inefficiency but each function has its characteristic forms. Each makes different options available and privileges some accounts as plausible while making other accounts of action less so.

The community constables were increasingly being seconded to reliefs to cover absences. In the following case a community constable temporarily serving on relief proceeded to minimize involvement and terminate contact as hastily as possible. The relief-type demand the officer experienced, the limited degree of supervisory oversight and the limited account expected to be offered of such incidents, encouraged him to take this approach. Two Home Beat Officers were asked to staff the station's 'front desk'. One of them, Richard, parleys to get a car for half a shift to deliver Neighbourhood Watch newsletters he would normally take on foot, in exchange for sitting at the enquiries counter for the other half. Once in the car he is subject to despatchers, who start sending him messages as if he were on the reliefs. One is a burglary report.

Richard has a bad feeling about the 'burglary' the moment he arrives. The front door is open and a Cypriot woman in her late forties with curly red dyed hair and heavy make-up emerges onto the road, whispering for him to get inside. She ushers him into the lounge, decorated in bold, jarring colours and featuring numerous posters of herself with various family members. She is Mrs Baglar. There is no mention of a burglary, instead she seeks to present her life story.

'I am of the best family. Related to [top politician's] brother. Been in this country the 17 years, had many children. Too many. Now, I have to take pills.' She points to several phials on a table. 'Pills because I hear the voices. Inside my ear. Inside my head. I hear them. Tom Jones and his wife.' 'Yes, madam, but what about the burglary. When did you notice your loss?', Alex said loudly and slowly. 'I coming to that but first I have to tell you the backgroun'.' Apparently, Tom Jones, his wife, and Simon Templar had all obtained keys to the front door. They would spirit in at night, and 'they are inside my ear, they come through the keyhole and then they touch me. They are inside my clothes, they paw, they put the penis in. Here, I show.' She reached through a screen dividing the lounge from an equally ornate bedroom. Richard rolls his eyes in disbelief. 'I bought sweater yesterday and its gone. Eight pouns'. There's my loss. And it was just like this [a blue striped sweater] only black. Before it went they burn a hole in it. I stitch up and its gone.'

---

[58] Fieldnotes.

Richard has got her name and is putting details in his notepad. By humouring her he is taking a burglary report, he seeks information about her next of kin. 'Is your husband with you?' At first he is said to work at a pub but it emerges that he actually works next door to a pub and after much discussion it is said he washes up in a restaurant. He is at work. 'But don't tell him I report this. He must not know you are investigate. They come and they touch me. I don't want to be touched.'

Richard is edging from lounge to hallway. 'It is too hot in the summer to be wearing the track suit. Look, I show you.' She returns to the lounge and Richard reluctantly follows. She produces the bottom half of a pink track-suit. It is wet around the crotch. 'Now you will investigate. They try to touch me but I don't want to be touched. Tom Jones and the Simon Templar. And that wife of his, bloody woman.' 'Yes, Mrs Baglar. They shouldn't do it. But we have another burglary to report.' Richard is speaking loudly in a gloss of the normal procedure. His note is simply name, address, husband's place of work. His responses are the absolute minimum. She thanks him as he leaves. As he starts the car she runs out. 'Please you remember, don't tell my husband about this. He will get mad. He and Tom Jones.' 'No, madam, we certainly will not contact your husband about it.' Driving off, he remarks that the woman was patently in need of psychiatric treatment. The incident is reported in the hackneyed phrase, 'woman suffering from harmless delusions. No burglary to report.'[59]

The time Richard had been given to cover the front desk was fast approaching. By coincidence the 'burglary' address had been on his beat but he had not attempted to establish whether there was anything to the woman's allegations; she was 'deluded' and that closed the matter. Any prospect of trouble with her medication or her husband was not to be followed up, yet Richard volunteered that he would have checked both matters if he had been in his normal beat role. (He later wrote himself a brief *aide memoire*.)

While relief officers dealt similarly with such cases their role provided an excuse to legitimate minimal involvement, a legitimation temporarily available to Richard. Both in the literature and in police thinking much of the distinctiveness of community policing is established by contrast to relief policing. It is important to recognize that this is not a matter of the personal disposition of officers but of the function to which they are assigned, and, in particular, the means by which they may account for their action.

[59] Fieldnotes.

4
First Contacts

After a period on relief or perhaps in a specialist function, an officer is assigned to the community constable role. The officers regarded their first task as being to make contact with local people. Scissons cites several tactics associated with developing and maintaining good public contacts, including 'a friendly and outgoing manner for the initial approach; use of humour to sidestep potentially "touchy" situations, demonstration of active listening skills when interviewing citizens who report criminal activity, [and] ability to vary type of response in dealing with the public, depending on reactions'.[1] To the chief superintendent at the main site, the necessary qualities equated to those of police constables with fifteen years' service: 'the knowledge of the law, experience in how to deal with situations, handle people, get on with and understand people. A policeman's job really is talking and getting on with the public, whether criminals or the local populace . . . And not to interpret it black and white.'[2] A friendly manner and being seen to listen, with interest, to what people say, are tactically desirable. The emphasis is on displaying this; 'there are many things officers do—particularly not looking at [people] or seeming to respond to what they say—which can make it appear they are not listening'.[3] An outgoing disposition, age and experience were advantages in dealing with the public.

Controlling encounters is a subtle business. Gross physical control is rare, with under 4 per cent of encounters resolved by arrest and under 1 per cent by threats of arrest or the use of force. Officers raise their voices in only 5 per cent of encounters. Physical restraint, issuing orders or threats are rare in relation to verbal reasoning and persuasion. Southgate found officers more likely to look directly into the face of people they spoke to rather than vice versa, and that officers stand close to those they address. In 70 per cent of encounters the officer stood between 18 inches and four feet from the citizen, rated

---

[1] Scissons (1990) at 43. [2] Ch. Supt. Heath. [3] Southgate (1986) at 26.

as within 'personal distance' rather than 'social distance'. Interactions were characterized by displays of deference, where citizen and officer displays were highly asymmetrical; 'pronounced deference was accorded to the officer in nine of ten encounters, whereas officers showed such deference on only one occasion in 100'.[4] Gauging local expectations and norms in this interactional respect is very much an individual matter on which little guidance is given.

Nor is there a sense of taking on a brief with a clearly-defined mission, which might assist initial contacts. Asked if priorities were set when he was assigned, one replied, 'none at all. I've started in the last couple months and nobody said a word about how it was to be done and what was to be looked at, what guidelines for an operation . . . It was left entirely to me. Nobody said "come and have a chat, this is what we want you to do". I was just asked to join and, when I joined, left alone.'[5] Asked if this was others' experience another commented 'Basically yes. No one says to you when you take it over that you've got to do this, that and the other. I was luckier, I went around with previous homebeat for two days before I took it over and got a couple of guidelines. But she was doing the job completely differently to me and you decide your own priorities.'[6]

One respondent was told he would have a week patrolling with the old homebeat 'but I didn't because of manpower problems'. One other respondent had no hand-over, another had a two day hand-over, two others had one day. They plainly saw value in handing-over. Otherwise 'you are starting from cold. You know [the division] as a whole but your particular area you know vaguely and its up to you to get involved.'[7] To be effective the hand-over needed to introduce new community constables to established contacts; new constables would only know notorious offenders on the patch. 'You only know the bad guys when you first move into an area. A constable who's been there five years might talk to you about what's going on. You have to rediscover these people and that takes time, regular contact.'[8]

In making initial contacts, the constable begins to differentiate the community. What may have been labelled by a single trait—a 'yuppified' district, a 'rough' estate—must become a variegated network of individual contacts. The constable learns that a 'community'

---

[4] Southgate (1986) at 35.   [5] GD 1.   [6] *Ibid.*   [7] *Ibid.*   [8] *Ibid.*

is not a solid social reality but a setting for many individual realities. Several tactics relate to making contact: establishing an interpersonal knowledge base (identifying the friends and enemies of the police among local people), establishing agency relationships (cultivating relationships with 'opposite numbers'), and establishing one's own persona (by refining and broadcasting a locally-appropriate demeanour and role).

Making your way 'into' the community was a matter of inheriting some contacts, being seen 'out and about', and discussing events with the more experienced.

If his is the same face that's seen every day, just by being there he will be approached by some of the public. But because we investigate crimes, and there are neighbourhood watches, most officers taking over a beat know they can plug into certain contacts because they are briefed about them [and] told 'go and make yourself known'. They get each contact's perspective on the problems of the beat and get filled with information. Most officers would think "I've got some problems here and I need [to] see the Governor and sergeant and see what I can do."[9]

Apart from advice on tackling initially-identified problems, the extract indicates that, no matter what the officer's patrol procedure, some contacts will 'make themselves'. A community constable explained the role of the police surgery. 'Its not very successful, but its getting involved, getting myself known, my face, name, telephone number. If you're known you're their policeman. As their policeman you're going to solve their crime. They are going to tell you if they hear anything, what they've heard or what their suspicions are. The deeper you get involved the more they tell you.'[10] The last remark suggests a reciprocal relationship, where the provision of deeper information is contingent on 'results', be it an arrest or simply information about police handling of a case.

In establishing a knowledge base, community constables are inclined to rely on relatively fleeting signs in order to infer the citizen's attitude to police. Constables learn this habit doing relief work, working on minimal information to achieve quick, temporary resolutions of incidents. Bipolar (pro-police, anti-police) distinctions predominate; subtlety comes later. Many officers begin where they guess a tangible stake in established order exists, with local shopkeepers. I asked one who was new to his beat how be began.

[9] Insp. Adams.   [10] GD 1.

He sought out local shopkeepers, let them know of his presence and asked them to let him have information about people involved or suspected in shoplifting, street crime or causing disturbances in the premises. It gave him a chance to judge whether the shopkeeper was sympathetic to police and those that were not he did not thereafter visit. Although there was at least one 'bent' shopkeeper on the beat it was not always such people who were unsympathetic; Barclays Bank recently had a major robbery and when he called to see if they wanted any help he was coldly dealt with and it was made clear they did not want police help so 'I won't be going there again.' He added that he only meant there was nothing wanted of him as a PBO.[11]

Clearly this officer appreciated that simply being in a local business did not make the contact pro-police. His mental map was already becoming more detailed. But constables are still drawn to alliances they predict they can count on. Thus, a beatbook records,

during March all schools were visited. St David's received a lecture from the youth and community section. All shopkeepers were visited by myself and PC Brent. I visited my friend 'Chakra' in the Asian grocer's shop in . . . and urged him to pursue a criminal injuries claim in respect of the injury he received when the shop was held up with shotguns. I supplied details of Victim Support. Sister Brown from St David's has been away tending her sick father, who has now sadly died. We have kept an eye on her house and I reported to the Church Wardens that her fence had been broken down, rendering the downstairs rooms vulnerable. I have been telephoned by a contact who informed me that her friend in . . . Street had been the victim of rape . . . She wanted some money for her husband's fare from the USA. I referred her through my contact to Victim Support.[12]

In like vein a community police sergeant writes that, 'referring to the section of the Action Plan concerned with Vandalism, an initiative has been set up aimed at local Churches. I have been in touch with various Ministers and encouraged the inclusion of propaganda in Church Magazines and Newsletters.'[13] An article by the officer was to appear in several newsletters, and he would speak on vandalism and neighbourhood watch in services at two churches. Drawing on predictably pro-police contacts is also encouraged by sheer numbers; single officers cannot expect ever to know more than a fraction of those on their beats.

Participants in community activities, and those in the locale for long periods of time, are key initial contacts; the elderly are important in both categories.

[11] Fieldnotes.   [12] BB 4.   [13] Ibid.

I'm visiting as many clubs as I can regularly. Old people's homes and clubs, whether its cooking, karate or whatever. Pop in during the evening, once they have seen you, once they say hello to you when you walk in and you get more and more involved. Not just walking in and saying 'hello' and coming out but something like a bingo session, where you've got lots of tables to go round and chat with each, if only for a couple minutes, about something completely weird and wonderful, just to get them used to you and know your name. A lot of the information isn't important but its surprising what old people notice . . . The old people's clubs are more than happy to see you because it boosts their confidence. There's so much problems round here for old people. Especially if its an evening club, if there's someone around in uniform it boosts their confidence.[14]

This stock port of call was confirmed by all the homebeats. They spoke of the need to be open to any contact, to appreciate that dramatically useful information was rare, and that information often came as part of some *quid pro quo*. 'I wouldn't say as yet I've had any information—road fund licenses, that sort of thing. But beyond that, nothing yet, but one's only been doing it a few months.' 'The other way is just by investigating burglaries, because you're helping them. Its a bargain situation, they do something for you because you're literally doing something for them, and that way I've built up a rapport.'[15]

School liaison has been a political issue, with boroughs barring police from their schools. For their part, some community constables dislike the role, which involves both children and public speaking, taking them far from their notion of 'what policing is about'. However, in this example, the 'stand-offish' attitude of school and parents is overcome by community police intent on dealing with robberies from pupils by local youths. The preventive, deterrent emphasis is also notable.

An example which did lead to one arrest but was more a preventative thing is a public school where we have youngsters from all over London who walk from school to catch their transport and kids from a local school are mugging these pupils. Nick Baker, the homebeat, working with his sergeant, has spoken to the headmaster and set up a formal reporting system. Because these kids won't dial 999 when they are robbed, they go home and tell mummy and daddy, and they ring up the school and the school won't pass on any information to us. We've gone into the school, impressed on the

[14] GD 1.   [15] *Ibid.*

headmaster how essential it is that we get immediate information: 'can your little lads give us a phone call as soon as it happens'. As a result we cleared up a robbery where we got a description and were able to catch the guy, and through Nick and his skipper, who has put additional resources out there, managed to stamp out the robberies completely. We were getting five a day, schoolboy stuff, dinner money, but its still robbery. Knives have been used, but for some reason the parents haven't [acted]. We hadn't really had co-operation from people who you'd think would be responsible and would realize the need to let the police know immediately.[16]

The example suggests that community police, having more time and autonomy than reliefs, can combine 'outreach' and crime control. A normally 'respectable' agency spurns police help but police actually press to solve the problem for the school. The prospects of relief officers doing the same are remote.

Contact with 'respectables' sometimes has especially clear benefits for both sides. Here a beatbook shows the officer's awareness of the commercial advantage enjoyed by an insurance company supplying 'educational' leaflets to schools. 'I have ordered a further supply of the "Stranger danger" and "Woman Alone" leaflets from [company] . . . and asked that they pay the carriage. This was agreed as obviously it is a publicity venture for them.'[17] Reciprocal relations do not mean losing a realistic sense of the conditions under which co-operation obtains. Nor do they mean that those involved abandon an agency perspective on events, although it may mean 'pulling your punches' in the knowledge that opposite numbers will now possess a better grasp of your agency's perspective, and an awareness that it will need to be taken account of at the next stage of any negotiation. Here is a community sergeant's *aide memoire* on borough housing policy.

A retrograde step (in my opinion) by the Council is withdrawing caretakers at blocks of Council flats. Local knowledge of flats is so essential, i.e., where stopcocks, water tanks etc. are situated, we can expect increased vandalism and burden on police to act as caretakers for old people etc. The idea is to cover the flats by mobile patrols, apparently on the grounds of economy. As most caretakers I have spoken to will be going on the dole and getting assistance for their (at present) rent-free accommodation I fail to see where the benefits will accrue. As Police officers we will lose a valuable source of assistance and information.[18]

---

[16] Insp. Adams.   [17] BB 4.   [18] *Ibid.*

Parts of the entry were highlighted by the chief superintendent, who pursued them with the council. The case also speaks to the 'political' perspective police can adopt.

Contacts with agencies like local government (especially environmental officers and highways officers), social services (especially those involved with juvenile bureaux) and housing estate managers, are among the most regular, and functional, contacts. A friend in the council's evictions unit could be a most useful contact for address and name checks. The kinds of contacts involved are shown by a sergeant's beatbook entry. 'I attended the Housing Office to discuss the T Estate. All aspects of social work and police-related matters were discussed. No specific conclusions were reached. The meeting was mainly an opportunity for the various agencies responsible for the estate to meet each other.'[19] The list of participants was attached, including representatives of social services, a local urban renewal project, a ward councillor, the local hospital, a housing management assistant, the community constable, the borough's senior technical assistant and the district housing officer.

I asked the 'contact' question of a constable who had said he was fortunate as his estate had two experienced community constables already who were able to introduce him to their contacts. I noted that,

he construed 'contacts' as the official and semi-official agency workers, mentioning the housing manager particularly, with whom he was impressed and had a co-operative relationship—'he's hard-working, knows everybody and is very, very savvy, doesn't let anything pass him by'—the youth and community centre workers, volunteers at a craft workshop project for unemployed youths, the social workers. Notable among the semi-official contacts is an American sportsman whose anti-drug, black pride programme was being imported. 'He's a fantastic guy, I really like him. He's great with the kids and nothing fazes him.'[20]

The officer was a keen athlete, and, as with contact with shopkeepers, put priority to those with a presumed identity of view. Community constables play on aspects of biography that give them an angle from which to approach negotiation with the public, another example being parenthood. Asked about differences in how community constables approach the job, one said 'I've got two children . . . I see myself as a father image, if you like, to some of the

[19] Ibid.   [20] Fieldnotes.

kids on my beat. The way I speak to them, the fact that I'm a father comes out.'[21] This beatbook entry by a community policing inspector suggests that officers recognize personality factors play a part.

New links are being forged by WPC Reed, who has taken over from PC Till. I have urged her to establish good rapport with Reverend Breed, following his complaints about lack of police interest. I feel I have done much to heal old wounds and I want Jane to carry this on. There wasn't the 'chemistry' between PC Till and the 'Rev' for a good relationship and although I have personal misgivings about that gent, personal dislikes are a luxury we cannot afford.[22]

By the same token, there are social groups with whom the police have such a poor 'chemistry' that any deviation from abuse or sullen denial of contact is notable to officers. An indication of the distant relationships that prevail between police and some groups is the fact that it was thought worth recording, under the heading 'Movement of Industry or Population' in a beatbook, that 'At no. 9 . . . Road, I gave and received a friendly wave from a Muslim family.'[23] Much store is set by this elementary activity. Thus, another entry records 'it is significant that when one tries a friendly greeting towards the [black] youths outside the shops [at the edge of a "problem" estate] one is either met with insolent stares or just ignored'.[24] Greetings give an important, initial toe-hold on social contact. Community policing, the constables assert, is very much policing 'with one's personality'.

While this makes for variety in the way the role is construed, some community constables are clear on the interactional tactics they use to establish their own persona as an image of local police.

Bob (a PBO sergeant) and Andrew agreed it was necessary to reveal things about oneself, to project one's personality to give people something to latch onto. It was as simple as offering them something they could know about you that would enable them to chat until they could get an impression of you and raise the matters they wanted to put over to police. Bob felt one had to have confidence about oneself to do this. Working on the reliefs helped to shield the shy or diffident from confronting their lack of confidence, and the 'macho attitude' was often a smoke-screen enabling them to indulge in superficial dealings with people which were, ultimately, counter-productive. To get an 'in' initially, you had to do 'cold canvassing', going from door to door introducing yourself and seeing who was responsive.[25]

---

[21] GD 2.   [22] BB 4.   [23] BB 4.   [24] *Ibid.*   [25] Fieldnotes.

The 'campaign' imagery was widely chosen, for the assignment of a community constable is a luxury mostly 'enjoyed' by precisely those areas where 'community' is problematic. It is intrinsic in the idea that beat officers must be responsive to local interests, that there will be variation between beats, to which they must become oriented. 'My beat is different from D's in that a lot of crime isn't committed by people on my beat, it's from surrounding areas. So I'm on the defensive in that respect, setting up NW to counter-attack the people coming into my beat from D's or L's . . . They're the type of estates that are attracted to the type of area that I'm responsible for.'[26] This is different from individuals having their own set of priorities; to an extent, the beat's nature sets priorities. 'The more people who report burglaries then that is a priority over something you might like to have done . . . I can't go into council estates and say "I know him, him and him." I have to ask D or L, "look, who are they over there who are committing offences on my beat?" So the priorities are to an extent dictated by your beat.'[27]

Recognizing diversity was essential in establishing oneself as responsive to the local standards from which civil order seen as appropriate by residents was built.

Andrew said his beat was not like a middle class area, where police and public shared values and saw law enforcement from the same perspective. Apart from a few lower-density blocks '95 per cent of the tenancies are council', people he described as traditional white working class, with high proportions of blacks on one estate. Most residents on his beat had a different perspective to police, with different priorities and concerns. While local manufacturing industry had been considerable, it was now virtually gone, places like [DIY store] replacing the Factory. Unemployment was high and opportunities for young people negligible.[28]

Andrew felt that one problem was the numerous recruits from outside London who were ignorant of urban life, and had never experienced the disjunction of values between themselves and a heterogenous community. This was not just true of ethnic or class groups. Andrew pointed out the ignorance about homosexuals that fed the scathing attitude of relief officers to a group which, he noted, numbered in the millions. It was important to him as a beat officer to put over to blacks, gay people, squatters and lower class youths

[26] GD 1.   [27] Ibid.   [28] Fieldnotes.

that there was at least one officer who could co-operate with them without interfering with their way of life.

Yet here community constables encounter a profound contradiction in the role, for the more they succeed in securing the good local relationships from which reliable information is gained, the more likely they are to be placed in the position of excusing the everyday delicts which, to relief officers, provide the bread-and-butter offences of patrol. It may be why community constables are so keen to cultivate informants, placing selected (and hopefully reliable) citizens in a relationship which it would be dangerous to encourage more widely. Thus, Andrew suggests that his ideal of 'non-interference' with others' values stops short of compromising his own.

This was largely a matter of 'using my personality'. Yet it also involved getting them to accept that, as a constable, he had his own values and they could not expect him to give up his law enforcement function. 'Its *me* that's policing that beat down there.' It was not just the uniform but his own presence through which he tries to achieve his ends. He comes on to kids, youths and others involved in crime by trying to make himself a known quantity. He sought to emphasize that he was reliable, that if he said he would do something he did it, and sought to be perceived as 'just and fair', weighing up the pros and cons of enforcement. 'I also want to present myself as firm. I weigh things up and when I have decided, I adhere to it.'[29]

The tactic by which community constables seek recourse from the role contradiction is to promote themselves as mediators, arbitrating, rather than imposing, the relationship of police and community.

To do so they inevitably refer to the concept of discretion. Discretion must be attuned to local standards in order to reflect community norms and thus gain maximum support for police actions. A superintendent was discussing why ranks above inspector seldom become involved in operational policing. He rarely led operations now because he could not draw on knowledge of prevailing local standards as a base-line for his discretion. 'If you are not on the street then you lose a sense of what is proportionate for that time. Take youths coming back from the pub making a lot of noise. If that's happening every Saturday night it is disproportionate to go out there and tell them to shut up or else they're going to get lifted. You haven't got a mean to apply that particular experience to. Your leadership could be misleading.'[30]

---

[29] Fieldnotes.   [30] Supt. Tate.

Often, as suggested above, community police are trying to bring about a community where one no longer exists. The problem of leading without appearing to lead has to be confronted. However content the constables may be with securing co-operative contacts, they know their success in getting their organization to accept them as interlocutors is by giving it a focus through which its own demands can be channelled into 'the community'.

Andrew considered how he went about establishing an 'in' with people on his beat and developing points of community contact, particularly where there was no prior focus from NW or residents' associations. His role was to assist in developing tenants' associations as a step towards NW schemes. His role was that of facilitator, not leading developments, but he also felt the process of developing community spirit was worthwhile in itself. He would identify an individual willing to take the lead in getting an association going, and liaise with and support that person.[31]

The community constable is led towards an intangible goal ('community spirit'), one which is unfamiliar to the police organization and whose quantification as a means of performance assessment is impossible.

Community constables learn what type of information to expect from people on their patch, as well as the proportion of their contacts likely to offer information useful to police. They sought to guide some, such as neighbourhood watch participants, to appreciate what information was useful. 'Things like NW. You are really educating them . . . [O]n my beat 60 or 70 actually know my name but they will never be able to give me information because they are not that group of people. But if they see anything they will go to the police. I have had robbers, muggers and burglars arrested on a regular basis . . . They would never be able to act themselves because they wouldn't know, but when they see something suspicious they do respond.'[32]

While community constables find that simply being an available, known face brings information, they must also play an 'educational' role, both in information management and 'moral education'.

Particularly the older people will save things up until they see you again. They will hang onto things for weeks until they see you rather than phone up . . . Bits and pieces, even if its only lost property, they will carry round with them. You try and instil some personal integrity in them, certainly

[31] Fieldnotes.   [32] GD 1.

where I work, largely council estate. You have got some traditional antipathy towards the police. There are a lot of nuisances being done by young kids. The people who live there, although they find it an annoyance, don't want to be responsible for young children being arrested. It's difficult to persuade them that your aim is not just to arrest people but to put an end to the problem. There are plenty of other options open to you to solve these problems. So you try to build up credibility.[33]

This implies that, as one confirmed, 'it takes a lot of time', another remarking 'I've been there twelve months and it will be a lot longer before I really have the trust of the community. It's coming. A lot of people talk to me now whereas before they wouldn't. It takes a long, long time.'[34]

Beatbook entries regularly report the failure of local people to call at the 'surgeries' and mobile 'offices' that police use to encourage residents to maintain contact. Most monthly entries record no visitors, making these facilities unpopular with the officers who have to staff them. Since they are likely to be sited where community 'spirit' is lacking and there are public order problems, their failure seems a foregone conclusion. Some officers claim few call in because it would be in sight of their neighbours, establishing their 'unreliability' or status as possible informers, a perspective that says much about police/public relationships in these areas. A beatbook notes 'it should be remembered that persons entering the Surgery Building are observed and may be regarded as "Coppers' Narks" by the villains and it takes some courage for the law-abiding citizens (who fear reprisals) to attend'.[35] A beatbook entry identifies another demerit. 'At the time of writing I manned the S Surgery with PC Mount from 5 p.m. to 6.30 p.m. and the Neighbourhood Watch Co-ordinator, there were NO callers. I have submitted a report through Chief Superintendent suggesting the Surgery should be discontinued. One point was that local villains knew exactly where their local "Bobby" was for those two hours and were free to indulge in criminal activities without let or hindrance.'[36]

Unsurprisingly, some prefer a more limited construction of the role. It is easy, given the recurrent emphasis on crime control by the community constables, to lose track of the problems which exercise community members on a daily basis. The emphasis on crime control may be a symbol of an effort at self-persuasion, a litany whose

[33] GD 1.   [34] Ibid.   [35] BB 4.   [36] BB 3.

repetition helps to make the symbol real. The constables are well aware that they invest time in what other officers regard as rubbish. While they have several reasons for doing so, sympathy plays its part. 'A "major incident" to these people is stopping the lads playing football. Then they get their night's peace. To stop them mucking about in their lifts. That's their major incident. Half of them aren't affected by crime; that's what they are affected by.'[37] Faced with disjunctions between their own priorities and those of the community they patrol with limited co-operation, and the intangibility of community 'spirit', community police pursue the accessible. Rather than chase the distant ideal of community spirit, they offer to interests they consider legitimate a service role by taking to the limit the routine services police can offer.

Sophie found keyholder enquiries a useful device to develop community contacts. Most officers take keyholder details only where premises have a burglar alarm. She used them more liberally. She would record keyholder information on any non-residential address . . . including schools, churches, youth and community centres, shops, restaurants, industrial premises, pubs and clubs. It gave her a reason to gain admission, something to discuss and information to exchange, keeping her on the premises long enough to get a conversation going. 'Otherwise its "hello, I'm your homebeat" and the person would say "Oh thanks very much" and there'd be nothing more to say.' While completing keyholder details she could convey something of herself to the person naming the keyholder so they had some purchase on her personality when they next saw her. Likewise, the process of identifying a keyholder and their details led the person to discuss their own social network. This gives Sophie background knowledge about the person. In addition to the filecard, Sophie records in her own notepad the information gained, such as opening hours of premises.[38]

As we will see, the ability to 'spin out' a conversation proved a useful occupational skill. It is to be noted that, by developing it, community constables are doing precisely the opposite of the characteristic stance of the relief officer. Rather than welcoming urban reserve and the civil but closed demeanour of the everyday public contact, these officers are exploring devices to stay on the scene and, however instrumentally, get to know their public.

---

[37] GD 1.   [38] Fieldnotes.

5

Keeping Community Contacts

Assuming that the initial contacts we have been examining succeed in securing acquaintance, the constable must now maintain it. The 'costs' of maintaining contacts, even with those deemed respectable, should not be underestimated. Officers must attune to the expectations of a variety of people, from individuals on their beat to representatives of local agencies and groups. Maintaining working relationships with representatives of organizations ostensibly sharing core concerns with the police requires its own kind of forbearance, as with youth and community workers involved in multi-agency programmes on 'problem' estates. The multi-agency approach is established policy in respect of a range of social problems and it is worth examining an instance to get an idea of the limits and potential of such ongoing co-operation in respect of order maintenance policing. Divided loyalties make the experience frustrating, as this beatbook entry shows: 'I get the impression that these "workers" either: a) Have no influence on the problem youths b) Have influence, but don't use it to assist us. I appreciate that we must do anything to improve living conditions on the estate and that in line with the Commissioner's policy about meeting community groups, we must attend these meetings, but when are *they* going to show a constructive contribution?'[1] As well as differentiating the public according to their attitude to police, 'partner' agencies must also be measured up.

Such complaints were regularly documented. A month earlier the beatbook stated:

there was the usual meeting between Police and 'Community Workers' on the estate, which was attended by Supt. Webb, Ch. Insp. Heal, Insp. Richard, Insp. Adams [community policing inspector] and Permanent Beat Officers. I can see no benefit from these meetings. I have been attending them since they began over 14 months ago and they have had no benefit of notice in establishing better relationships between us and those who disrupt the

[1] BB 2.

lives of the many law abiding and decent members of the public who reside on the D Estate.[2]

Apart from the jaded tone it is noteworthy that so many senior officers attended the meeting. It also bears comment that, while the 'tiny minority versus decent majority' idea is an established theme of police rhetoric, the estate spoken of is nearly 100 per cent black. The sergeant compiling this note not only is in a position to perceive divisions between the agencies involved on the estate but divisions within a 'hostile' community. These divisions were manifest in contacts with older blacks, who often expressed disapproval of the behaviour of the estate's youths.

Apart from the tenor of the meetings, the sceptical police attitude toward the youth and community workers can be traced to a crown court case. Five members of the 'Tough Posse' had been charged with serious assault on three police officers. The involvement of two estate workers attracted as much resentment as the outcome. (A finding of guilt would be, an earlier note states, 'a major break-through in bringing an increased quality of life' to estate residents.) 'The only person convicted . . . was sentenced to two years conditional discharge. Two "workers" on the estate, Mary Knoll and Stephen Cooper, gave character references for the group. Detective Chief Inspector Grant said that there was little to fault in our evidence. I do not understand how such a group of youths are believed against the word of Police Officers.'[3]

Later in the monthly report it appears that one of the community workers had helped police with information about gangs on the estate. 'Mr Mike Gott, the Borough Council special estates officer, has recently been suffering from verbal abuse from a group of black youths. These youths are older than the "Tough Posse" and are known collectively as "MG". This information came from a community worker, Mr Cooper.'[4] As we read on, however, we discover that the information was hardly volunteered.

The incident took place when two men from this group applied for a flat. They had been drinking brandy and crème de menthe, and were very abusive towards Mr Gott when he explained the council rules about tenants having to be over 25. This was repeated some days later and abuse was directed towards Mr Gott and his staff. I would have liked to have been told about this incident earlier, because we have good contact with Mr Gott and

[2] *Ibid.*   [3] *Ibid.*   [4] *Ibid.*

am sure we could have assisted (arrests for 'Threatening behaviour' at least)
. . . This affair was brought to my attention when Ch. Insp. Geeves and
myself were touring the estate with Mr Cooper and casually met Mr Gott.
As a result of a conversation between Mr Gott and Mr Cooper I asked questions and was told what had occurred. I know that my officers visit the council offices on the estate both before and after this incident. At no time has
any such incident been mentioned. I have explained to Mr Gott that in
future, all such occurrences must be brought to our attention whether action
is required or not.[5]

Apart from the identity of the gang the community worker had
not volunteered anything about it, perhaps wanting to 'protect' this
group of older black youths from police harassment. (By the time of
our fieldwork the group had a reputation for serious drug-dealing
and autocrime and, officers said, scrupulously shunned confrontations with police.) The denial of information by those with whom
police thought they had good relations may well account for the note
of betrayal in the beatbook entry. From such episodes police derive
a keen grasp of the multiple divisions, not only in the 'target' community but in the agencies alongside which they are supposedly
working.

This incident itself had a similar predecessor, showing that police
had continued to expect the community worker's co-operation after
more than one occasion when he had not sided with them.

[In July] two members of the 'Tough Posse' were arrested for an offence of
'Threatening behaviour' and 'Highway Obstruction'. They were arrested by
PC Ayre [District Dog Handler] and immediately ran into the 'Family
Centre' in an attempt to avoid arrest. . . . Officers assisted PC Ayre to
remove the arrested persons from the Family Centre. As the event was witnessed by a large number of people, several claiming to be interested parties
attended the station. One was a community worker in the community workshops who police have a close liaison with, a Mr Cooper. It became apparent, that despite almost a year of dialogue with local police officers, there is
still a fundamental mistrust of Police activity and actions by persons claiming to represent persons living on the D Estate.[6]

The community worker's failure to support police action is
resented, and he becomes one who merely 'claims' to represent local
people. It should be noted that the original incident involved relief
officers. It is plausible that Cooper repudiated their action. It is also
plausible that the community police sergeant compiling the beatbook

⁵ BB 2.   ⁶ Ibid.

entry expected the community worker's support regardless of which officers conducted the intervention. The entry goes on to note that the Family Centre provided a lawyer, the local Member of Parliament became involved, and that 'it is a pity such resources are not provided for the victims of crime'. The 'nonrepresentativeness' of the community workers became a recurrent theme. 'The community workers seem absolutely powerless in assisting us with establishing a "Police Office" on the estate . . . Community workers were quick to point out that such an office would attract stigma to residents. They can only gauge response on the estate from the residents who use their agencies, e.g., The Family Centre, The Tenants Action Committee etc. They cannot speak for the majority.'[7] Community policing and public consultation is often criticized on the grounds that community organizations and 'leaders' may not be representative of the community. Here we see police capitalizing on just such divisions to query support for a policy they oppose.

Accounting to outsiders is a jarring experience for police. The form of relief policing and, ultimately, that of police accountability, makes them particularly resistant to attempts to make themselves more responsive to public opinion. Consequently, it is an unfamiliar experience for most officers to find themselves having to respond to public criticism of police efforts or account for local policy. A relief inspector was asked about his involvement in Neighbourhood Watch.

I've been to a few meetings; I've probably went to [sic] more meetings than anybody else did. Inspectors rarely go and I took a bruising one evening from a gang of hooligans at a NW meeting and they complained of my attitude, basically because I wouldn't give in to them. My attitude was perfectly correct but they became very abusive. The Governor took the wrong attitude without talking to me about it and got complaints from councillors and things like that and I never went again. He wouldn't let me go again but he wouldn't tell me why.[8]

The incident clearly rankled, but there is more to it than unfamiliarity with accounting to the public. It emerges that what was at issue was the nub of community policing, a willingness not only to discuss options and requests but to concede (some) demands as part of a long-term negotiating relationship. The interviewer was surprised to hear of the conflict as the area was a calm one.

[7] BB 1.   [8] Insp. Sharp.

No, they wanted me to give them concessions. (Mimicking:) 'It's just our particular little interest, surely you can let us have it?' And I said, 'No, I can't. If I give it to you I've got to give it to everybody.' They said 'Oh, only this for us, you can do it for us.' If I'd made that commitment to them it was a huge commitment for the whole station . . . I wasn't going to give in. And 'why weren't they informed on two crimes'. They were rapes. One of them was a local resident. What I couldn't say to them was, 'I'll come round and start talking to you about rape. You mentioned your wife had been raped', which is basically what it was. Then I'd be talking to somebody else in the scheme, telling them 'Gor you should have seen him, gor bobbing up, gor, bloody hell, great drawers she had on, you know.' You can't talk about things like that to a scheme, can you. Burglary yes, but you can't talk about crimes such as that . . . Then they criticize us! They just had me down there as a knocking exercise. I sat there and took it for an evening and came away very disillusioned and very concerned about some Neighbourhood Watches that, if we're not careful they will be used to manipulate us. They only need to be criminally motivated once . . . The left wing councillors at the moment haven't taken them on board but when they realize what they can do with them the tail will certainly wag the dog. It's a lever.[9]

Liaison meetings can undoubtedly be conflictual. Here the unfamiliar experience led the inspector directly to the doctrine of political impartiality, a vital buttress of police accountability: 'they [left wing councillors] could take them over, they've got control over a little group of people, direct access to the police, and they're telling them what to do and when to do it.'[10] This relief inspector's immediate translation of public consultation into the spectre of political control suggests how challenging the community policing function, with its emphasis on discretion, is to the customary practices of the organization. The idea that consultation could afford sectional interests scope to exert influence, rather than simply offering police a chance to manipulate public opinion, challenged the inspector's fundamental understanding of police accountability.

In contrast, the extensive contacts community constables are enjoined to make can increase the realism of the police grasp on the nature of local demands. The experience of discretion operating over a long period of time can educate officers that first demands are negotiating positions, establishing the scope but not the detail or final form of public demand and police response. 'As you get older there's not exactly black and white, is there? There's grey, isn't there? That's what I found. When I was young it was either black or white, all or nothing. A lot of times people are happy just to get a hearing.'[11] When we asked another constable whether he felt he was too young for the role he commented, 'I was literally told that I was going on a beat to square the odds up, as a young, crime-oriented officer. I do find it hard to get involved in the community, I must admit.'[12] The older police constable argued that experienced community constables did control crime but in a more sensitive way. 'You've watched the children grow up. As they grow up you can say "I'll have to watch him" . . . I'd been told before about what he'd been doing. There was a robbery in . . . Park and just by the description and what I was told I knew who it was.'[13] Such perceptions resulted from long-term knowledge. Good public relations helped carry people with you in formal interventions. 'You are ideally suited because you know the children . . . I like to be known up there. I've known people for years up there . . . I arrested some young boy and his mam says "Oh, you are Tam that I've been hearing so much about" . . . People know you on the beat, "That's Tam, that's our local policeman." That's the essence of the home beat.'[14]

Differences in the style of community policing emerged. An important difference, which cannot simply be mapped onto a crime control versus social service bipolarity, is between high and low visibility approaches. The high profile police constable emphasizes 'putting yourself about', so that making his way is 'basically by saying "Hello, I'm the home beat officer for this particular ward. This is what I can do for you. What can you do for me?" Its important that you come across genuinely. If you go in there with a couldn't-careless attitude they will think you are a fly-by-night, they're not going to trust you. You've got to come across as caring . . . try and sell yourself.'[15] Some contacts were cultivated over the years and by successive officers, others came from agency staff in regular police contact, e.g., housing officers: 'they have problems with their tenants . . . Their problems usually merge with out problems and we can help. Some contacts are handed on and others are cultivated by individual officers.' In sharp contrast was the approach of another, who emphasized low profile information gathering: 'I don't like being seen too much. The information you gather has to be out of the view of other people.'[16]

---

[11] GD 2.   [12] *Ibid.*   [13] *Ibid.*   [14] *Ibid.*   [15] *Ibid.*   [16] GD 2.

This gives some idea of 'costs' and techniques in maintaining community contacts, and we will continue in this vein before examining the benefits. The account continues with the need to maintain civil contact with discreditable, low status people, develops by examining the need to act as legal adviser and moral counsellor, and culminates with the most profound problem, ignoring or excusing offences in order to maintain relations and/or gain other advantages. It is a demanding trial ground for the officers' use of the discretion they are given in law.

Most community constables interpret their role as being open to contact with one and all, and this obliges them to seek civil relations with people with whom relief officers are often offhand or worse. The beatbook records that 'complaints have been received from [garage] that youths are glue sniffing at the rear of premises. PC Davis is looking into the allegation. It will be remembered that there were cases of this adjacent to the Red Dog.'[17] Having picked through the deserted garage forecourt looking for syringes and cans of glue, a Permanent Beat Officer walked to a low door set in corrugated sheet masking the entrance to a derelict building. Inside was a courtyard, rubble and trash everywhere.

A fairly well-groomed young man stood there with a bike. Bill asked if he'd been to the party. A sign with the word 'party' pointed to another building. It was at the weekend and bands had played to punks, hippies and squatters, Bill said. The youth had been but left early. Bill asked if he was visiting the occupant—'He's an Australian, isn't he? It's a squat, yeah?' The youth had been visiting, said it was a squat but the occupant wasn't Australian. After a few more words he said 'I don't know why I'm telling you this. I'm probably getting somebody in trouble.' Bill told him not to worry, he was only keeping in touch. It was down to the council if they wanted to move people. His manner of address to the youth was the same as if he were speaking to a conventional householder.[18]

The ability to negotiate a fruitful course through this kind of edgy community contact is not built into the role of police officer. It is important that officers are able to see things from the citizen's perspective, and to have a good knowledge of the different interpretive frames attaching to different roles. The 'normative scripts' embodied in role expectations are seldom complete. 'Role reciprocity may be the product of extensive and subtle negotiations with others

---

[17] BB 4.   [18] Fieldnotes.

whose purposes are not complementary to ours.'[19] Rather than a purely goal-oriented approach to negotiation, the officer needs to take into account processes by which parties guide and draw inferences, and the rules which structure their interaction. Such negotiations are marked by a working consensus; for the purpose of the negotiation actors take up context-bound or 'situational' identities. An element in this process is 'identity bargaining', action seeking to establish certain situational identities for participants as terms of the working consensus.[20] Skill in establishing and maintaining desired identities is central to interpersonal competence. It hinges on accurately taking the role of the other, possession of a large repertoire of lines of action, and employing tactics appropriate to the situation. Accurate role-taking hinges on exposure to a broad range and variety of social relationships.[21] People presume they can freely claim the assistance of police, but the community role obliges Permanent Beat Officers to extend greater tolerance and invest more time than relief officers. That they are dealing with people whose performance is inadequate and/or whose manner suggests volatility implies that an element of 'humouring' the citizen often imbues these contacts.

A West Indian woman in her forties simply began talking at Rodney as he crossed an intersection . . . Initially she spoke to him in the middle of the road but he got her to move to a traffic island, around which the traffic swirled as they conversed. There was no preliminary 'excuse me' or 'hello' and her manner was vague; she seemed somewhat under the influence but not excessively. Her manner was of someone Rodney already knew [but he did not]. She was returning from a local pawnbroker. She had gone to collect a ring but he had sold it. Rodney established that six months had elapsed and said that the pawnbroker was in his rights to do so. She claimed not to realize he could do this. He said he had written advising her what he intended, but she had not received the letter. Rodney thought there wouldn't be any mileage in claiming not to have received the letter . . .
    . . . He advised her she couldn't expect to get anywhere on the sale but that, although he was rusty on it, he thought that she had a right to the lion's share of the proceeds. She elaborated; the ring had been given for an engagement that was broken. Although she would therefore never want to wear it, she did like having it around; it had sentimental value and had been valuable, £179. The pawnbroker had not offered a share of the proceeds. She had intended to get it out of hock. He advised her to call in at [police

[19] Weinstein (1969) at 762.   [20] Weinstein and Deutschberger (1964).
[21] Weinstein (1969) at 763.

station], asking 'are you driving at the moment?' She didn't have a car and it was a long walk. He explained how to get to a closer police office. The pawnbroker problem was not something that came up very often so if they looked at her in puzzlement she should explain that an officer told her there was a procedure to follow and for them to advise her on the law. He also advised her to return to the pawnbroker once she had established the legal position and invite them to pay her what she was owed. If there was any further problem she could proceed legally. At this point she began to repeat the entire story . . .

The second time through the story he added a rather pompous remark that was nevertheless received as appropriate in light of the seriousness the woman, though vague, was attaching to it. 'I can see the sorrow that you feel about the loss of this ring, and you have my sympathy for your loss. I do sympathize with your position.' He then quickly reiterated what she should do and left before she could recycle the story again. As he walked away he remarked that 'I had to cut her off then cause I think she would have talked for another half an hour.'[22]

As well as being generous of his time the officer had judged the rectitude of the woman's complaint, and it appeared that his sympathies had been engaged. The delicacy of his broaching whether the woman had a car, and the regret expressed at electing not to hear the story a third time, appear to be related to this. Conversation analysis suggests the importance of 'affiliative agreements' in building rapport, where an accord manifests itself in talk, leading to (often extended) sequences of mutual agreement and affiliation by interactants.[23] The methods used by salespeople, counsellors and interviewers to elicit expressions of affiliation from prospective customers, clients and respondents, and the 'episodes of rapport' triggered by these communication skills, display regular properties and sequential patterns. They are not dependent on the topics under discussion or the identities of the interactants.

The parallel to the community constable's communicative practice is clear. In order to secure their goals (which may simply be to exit gracefully, leaving the contact receptive to future interactions) it is a useful tactic to demonstrate a degree of common perspective by affirming agreement with something the contact has said. In the case we have just examined, Rodney's responses show several signs of this. Importantly, the sales research found that affiliative agreement was not just a self-contained form but had consequences for the

---

[22] Fieldnotes.   [23] Clark *et al.* (1989).

overall course of the interaction. Further, the type of affiliative response by the customer related directly to the salesperson's first reaction to the evaluative statement by the customer, the initial exchange. Where the salesperson produced only minimal agreement with the customer's evaluative statement there was little for the customer to 'latch onto' and the exchange often stalled there. The salespeople often had to expand on their own previous evaluation, or change the topic, or ask questions in the hope of eliciting further evaluative statements to build on. This gave prospects more with which to agree, and, importantly in terms of officers seeking compliance with their own objectives, made it harder to break the affiliative form by an outright refusal. 'These junctures of agreement and rapport allow salespeople and prospects safely to express and infer ideas, opinions and assessments about one another, and the likelihood of a sale occurring, in a way which enables both parties to maintain [one another's] face . . . [T]hese activities obviate salespeople and prospects having to officially address the issue of whether they are "getting on" with each other.'[24]

By analogy, police and public can gauge through the interaction the likelihood of their achieving particular objectives, and in a way which appears to defuse the irritation of finding that on this occasion they cannot. As well as the mode of interaction, the content of each expression of affiliation 'comprises an "on the record" and thus accountable expression having some indirect relevance for the underlying purpose of the interaction'.[25] So as well as managing face, the form renders more likely the provision of details germane to the outcome. One last point is that this was an interactional tactic consciously engaged in, rather than a coincidental similarity of views. '[T]he salesmen were attempting indirectly to "get on" with and accomplish sales . . . by selling (a particular version of) themselves. The "personality" of the salesman (and the prospect) emerged within these sequences, and the "similarity" attraction that developed between them, was essentially a social artefact.'[26] It need hardly be pointed out that community constables emphasize that they make and maintain their contacts by 'policing with their personality'.

The relationships promoted as important to this work come to exact demands on the officer. A major cost to community constables

[24] Ibid.   [25] Ibid. at 40.   [26] Ibid. at 40–1.

is maintaining a relationship when given occasions of contact can be predicted as unlikely to bear any police-relevant information.

Arthur had given Dick a lot of unwelcome attention. A boy of 19 from a traditional working class family, he had cottoned on to the beat bobby idea in a big way. He befriended Dick and initially this was fine but his calls became increasingly persistent and were invariably for help and bore no crime-related information. Dick had become 'something of a laughing stock, the others were forever leaving me messages from Arthur and they were embarrassing, made me look an idiot, silly little things'. Dick eventually told him he was pestering him and 'he was as good as gold, no hard feelings' and had not got in touch for three months. He had now gotten back in touch and Dick felt obliged to call. When Dick arrived, Arthur and members of his family were working on Arthur's car at the roadside. Arthur initiated by asking Dick's advice on fixing the bonnet shut; Dick is a keen mechanic. He and Arthur puzzled over the catch . . . The women were pouring petrol but got most of it on the car and the road . . . Dick had taken his helmet off to work on the car and they were captivated by it . . . Dick established that Arthur had just bought the Jag, his first car, for £495 from a backstreet garage.

He noticed a tax disk lying on the dashboard and found it had the index number of another car on it. It was six months out of date. 'I'm not saying for a minute that you've done anything wrong but we'd better get this sorted out, Arthur. If we don't you're going to get pulled over by one of my col-leagues.' Dick ran a check on the car's index number. He wanted to see if it was stolen. The car was clean. Dick then turned to the procedure for tax-ing the car . . . He told Arthur not to say, when he taxed it, that he had only just started driving it, because he was liable for tax from the day of purchase if he was keeping it on the road . . . Arthur takes what Dick says very seri-ously and goes over points to ensure he has understood, with which Dick patiently co-operates. Dick emphasizes that he must get taxed as soon as possible because the police are hot on this. (He remarks after leaving that, looking the way he does, Arthur is bound to be pulled everytime he goes out in the car.)

Attention turned to the inoperative car horn. Dick got himself oily but couldn't determine the fault. After ten minutes it became clear Arthur's father had a point to make to Dick. While Dick worked on the catch Arthur's father explained it was to do with reopening the community cen-tre. Dick had no good news to report but counselled patience as he fiddled with the catch. Meanwhile the women periodically mobbed the men but mainly revelled in the helmet. Dick reiterated his point about the tax, joked a while longer and took his leave. 'His mum is especially bad. She's killing herself through drink. You heard how she spoke? It used to be a lot more clear when I started here. The alcohol has begun to soften her brain.' Dick spoke of them as solid, old-time types and rather admired what an unre-constructed old devil Arthur's mother was. 'She's still well into shoplifting and she's done assaults on police. She throws wobblies, and when she does she's incredibly strong.'[27]

Dick may have reflected on what policing-related objects were secured by this contact. Had he done so, he could have identified the advice he gave Arthur on taxing the car (which might preclude police time being spent on an untaxed car) and the discussion over the community centre with Arthur's father. The community centre was a hotly-debated local matter and having support from Arthur's father would be useful if the police line on the admission of young blacks was questioned by the working class whites who mono-polized it prior to its temporary closure following disturbances. A measure of 'glad-handing' is regularly required to maintain relationships, as a community policing sergeant noted in a beat-book: 'During PC Mount's driving course I hope to bridge the gap and get around to his contacts to reassure them of our continuing interest.'[28]

As officers get involved in the community they feel a greater oblig-ation to local people, and relevance to 'policing' concerns is con-strued increasingly broadly. In the following case the returns for police are reduced to the value of having one friendly contact in an all-black apartment house. The point is that, while the present benefit may all be to the citizen, if the disturbances that made the estate a police 'no go' area in the past recurred, such contact could be valuable.

Someone in one of the tower blocks wanted advice after a burglary. Dick called but they were out. However he was greeted by a forty-ish black woman a few doors down. She was gossiping with her neighbours. 'I didn't recognize you without your clothes on', he called, referring to her thin sum-mer dress. She made a jokey reply. 'What do you want me for?', he asked. 'Something you can't do by day', she giggled. After a little more banter he said he would call tomorrow. They had met by chance several years ago: she was getting married and wanted advice on renting a limousine. Later he met her on the street and she said she'd thrown her husband out. Then, when Dick came onto [the estate] she found the contact useful. She liked her neigh-bours to see that occasionally a policeman visited her. It was good insur-ance.[29]

[27] Fieldnotes.   [28] BB 4.   [29] Fieldnotes.

In order to maintain the *potential* benefit of contacts, officers must invest considerable time in a series of 'community contacts' which, singly, can hardly be construed as police-relevant at all. Indeed, officers find themselves obliged to extend a friendly hand to those they might personally prefer to shun. In the following case, the officer engages in a contact with individuals he sees as the lesser of two evils; while the business activities of the new management of the amusement arcade would not bear close scrutiny, their tough policy on customers had helped reduce shoplifting.

Rodney introduced me to the manager of the arcade, Luke. He was a southern European in his late 40s/early 50s, somewhat shabby. Rodney explained that the arcade had been particularly rough and a distinct problem on the beat until the new management had taken over. It then had a pool hall at the rear where youths hung out. They used to steal from an adjacent department store, run to the arcade and disappear into the pool hall. The pool hall was now closed. The youths had intimidated the previous management, openly looting the machines in front of them.

The new management had 'sorted them out'. Luke, who had run clubs before this distinctly downmarket arcade, introduced Rodney and me to Dave, a tough young skinhead whom he had taken on. Dave's handshake was like a vise, and he said he liked the work . . . Luke's conversation was both pro-police and imbued with authoritarian views on criminal justice. Rodney blandly reciprocated these. At one point a black youth came to ask if there was another stool and there was not; Rodney gave him his. Once he was out of earshot Luke told Rodney that the youth was involved in street-crime and shoplifting, and Rodney scrupulously got from him all that he knew about the youth. Apart from the 'mutual' admiration, this information was the chief gain from the visit. When it became clear there was no more to be gained, Rodney left.[30]

Even in such low-key contacts, then, officers may work the situation for something of value; it is simply that the criterion of value becomes extended and indirect. But such an indirect criterion is implicit in one of the main identified benefits of community policing, the giving of crime prevention advice. The benefit to police is seen as the reduction of demand for reactive policing as a result of advice leading to target hardening. The following episode, a visit to a delicatessen, illustrates how the officer may develop an opportunity to impart such advice from the most mundane contact.

[30] Fieldnotes.

During the chat [the owner and her female assistant] stated they'd had little recent trouble but there'd been some shoplifting they dealt with themselves. On entering the shop Bill had remarked the new lay-out. They said it let them see the whole shop from behind the counter. Bill chatted about renovations to his kitchen, food he'd had from them, the recipe for a cocktail and the price of champagne . . . A large wooden spoon hung from the ceiling inscribed 'Shoplifters will be bashed'. She [owner] told Bill about a shoplifter, as a result of Bill's remarks about the renovation. When the shop was busy shoplifters would block their view of the cabinets and take expensive wine as well as food. She described the particular shoplifter as 'a young hippie' . . . He'd filled his pockets with food when only three people were there and she stood behind, and when he turned round she said 'please put those things back' which he'd meekly done. She'd coped and didn't call the police. 'You really ought to have called me. If we don't find out it's happening we don't know that person's active or how they go about it.' The information could benefit other shopkeepers.[31]

A noteworthy feature of Bill's conversation was that he gave out information about himself to sustain the talk; befriending as a device for seeking information only works if one also gives out information about oneself. When there is no more direct service that officers can offer it can be the only resource to maintain a relationship they hope to capitalize on later. Maintaining the relationship exacts costs from community constables, as these examples all variously indicate. The costs take different forms. One illuminating form is the sparring that goes with attempts to get the officer to excuse or sanction some infraction. Such interactions have elements of the joking relationships which feature insults made in jest, direct reference to sexual behaviour, comments about anatomical features with sexual meanings and *double entendres*. Joking relationships contribute to social equilibrium, particularly by reducing tension and conflict at critical junctures.[32]

On the ramp at the station entrance is a fruit vendor, black. Trevor calls him 'Chalky'. He greeted Trevor warmly and offered fruit. During the chat Trevor made sassy comments about the vendor to his customers, who appreciated it; some responded in kind. Trevor asked him about his new van, a rusty Transit. He said he'd bought it just yesterday and it needed some work, £200 worth, and then he would have a good vehicle and get it taxed. The man was attempting, in a charming way, to get Trevor to warrant his not taxing it until he had fixed it up. (Trevor later remarked, "Did you see

[31] *Ibid.*   [32] Radcliffe-Brown (1965).

what he was trying to do there?") Trevor told him he needed the tax disk before he drove the van again but took no further action.

Talk turned to upcoming events, particularly the . . . Festival; the fruit vendor couldn't get a licence to trade at this, which he lamented. This led to a similar attempt to enlist Trevor's support in circumventing the law. The vendor raised an opportunity he had to put up a stall in the doorway of a solicitor's office that was closed on Saturdays. The shop adjoining was friendly and the office did not object. He wanted Trevor's advice whether he would be causing obstruction if he set up there. Trevor said, 'You're asking me there. I've got to admit I'm not an expert on this.' He asked if he'd traded on the street before and what the licensing arrangements were for that. The vendor said that in his only previous experience the council had prosecuted him under hygiene regulations. He then revealed that he already knew the objection would be that he did not have anywhere to wash his hands if he was trading from the doorway of a closed office. When Trevor realized this, he advised the vendor, 'Well, you can't do it then, can you? You mad bugger, you'll have the Council on you.' The obstruction issue did not come into it if he already knew there was a hygiene objection. 'You're not licensable to trade from there even if I tell you its not obstruction.' The vendor immediately caved in; he wouldn't pursue it further . . . After further chat about profitable lines in seasonal fruit, Trevor left.[33]

There was no visible sign of negotiation in this episode. It came over as a rambling chat about the complex obstructions put up by bureaucracy to honest business. After leaving, the officer remarked that the vendor had clearly been trying to get him to agree to two things, the car tax and the street trading, and he had to think hard to put the right point of view without offending a useful contact.

Skills of talk are crucial in negotiating the inevitable conflict of expectations in reciprocal relationships, as between Tevor and the fruit vendor. Reciprocal relationships inevitably call for forbearance, and the point applies at all stages of negotiating about suspected, or proven, infractions. Private institutions such as large shops and educational institutions claim the right to assign sanctions internally, arguing that formal legal avenues be avoided to protect their reputation or that of their members. It is often up to the officer to decide whether to assist an institution in maintaining an unblemished reputation. A beatbook records a clear instance. 'Information has been received from the Headmaster of . . . College to the effect that drugs are being sold in the School by pupils. As a result, four youths have been suspended and a small amount of cannabis seized. PC Davis is

---

[33] Fieldnotes.

awaiting the outcome of a meeting of the School Governors as to whether they wish Police to be involved. PC Davis is strongly advocating Police involvement.'[34] Importantly, the form of 'involvement' is not specified, leaving scope for the officer's discretion. We also need to see that there is already police 'involvement' because the officer knows about the offence, but is standing to one side to hear the decision of the Governors before negotiating his response.

Community police were quick to recognize that a key need of the public is for information about cases in which they are involved, another sign that a reciprocal relationship has been taken to heart. Reporting a neighbourhood watch meeting, a constable states that 'the meeting was not very well attended, however, the "Old Chestnut" came up that residents, having troubled to call the Police, were never told the outcome of the incident. We really must be more professional about this.'[35] Such negotiations as Trevor's with the fruit vendor, the interaction with the school, and awareness of the public's desire to keep informed, considerably complicate the officers' appreciation of discretion. They develop a sophisticated sense of the concept which renders the bald expressions of the law less and less satisfactory.

The favours the constable can give are considerable, from acting as a sympathetic listener to ignoring certain infractions. The long-term assignments of community policing promote the need for forbearance. Officers are obliged to work in such a way that they gain the trust of the community, particularly local youths. It takes a long-term view of policing strategy not to 'force the pace' by rushing into action on the first crime-related information received in what may be an opening move by youths. There are a series of such gambits, and officers' patience can be rewarded once they orient themselves to the 'rules of the game', appreciating that, because they are engaged in a relationship of negotiation, they must expect to give as well as take. Essentially this means ignoring petty infractions in order to get information on major ones, but canny officers build physical resources into their strategy, such as obtaining grants for sporting facilities for local youths, giving a short-term bargaining counter and the opportunity to develop routine long-term contact.

The features of a negotiated police-public relationship include the willingness to refrain from full enforcement. There would be little

---

[34] BB 4.   [35] Ibid.

point in entering into a relationship of negotiation if one's intention was always to drive for a prosecution. When constables move a group of noisy youths along or glare at a crowd noisily leaving a bar they put into operation their criteria of appropriate behaviour, providing a tangible meaning of local order. However, these criteria are seldom rigid. The contingent nature of discretion implies that the constable's action is shaped in the unfolding course of interaction. Indeed, the very uncertainty of what the next contact will bring militates against a rigid approach by even the strongest believer in stereotypes. The 'backchat' in many such encounters gives them the appearance of a duel between equally proficient parties. The course of such interactions is not pre-defined but emergent.

A more regulated exercise of discretion would remove one of the officers' key tactical devices, and one which prevents the courts becoming clogged with nuisance cases. The technique is threat, to which skills of talk attach which can meet the challenge of stroppy citizens. Threat is made believable by the general awareness that officers are powerfully backed up and *could* deploy such threats; the technique is used much with youths. As a step between avoidance and coercion, threat and counter-threat afford officers the chance to handle challenges without escalation or loss of credibility. A home beat officer decided that he was investing too much time pursuing heroin addicts, and that his enforcement efforts had yielded scant return. He prepared printed cards about local drug treatment projects and 'street agencies'. When he subsequently encountered users he put it to them that they needed help, not law enforcement. He would give them the information card and tell them that, if they contacted the agencies and participated in one of their programmes, he would stop pursuing them for drugs and related offences. After giving out the card he would ring the agencies to see which individuals were responding.

Another tactic in the officers' armoury of discretion is persuasion, sometimes involving the need to present a rationale for the fundamental assumptions of the law. A community constable who embarks on an educative rather than narrow law enforcement course of action may need to make a case for the law where none exists in the offender's outlook. Such a use of discretion speaks to the give-and-take which lies at the heart of discretion. 'You've also got problems when you are taking people back to parents, parents don't see there's anything wrong with them. They can't simply enforce standard behaviour on kids if they don't see wrong in what their child's done. You've got a bit of a paradox really. You're trying to make policing *for* them while policing *against* them.'[36] This last comment very nicely captures a reality of the role, that the community policing rhetoric emphasizes policing sensitive to the wishes of local people whereas in some cases the community constable has to directly contradict their wishes by enforcing law contrary to their perceived interest.

Brown reports that citizen satisfaction with police is greater in areas with small police establishments but was often associated with greater leniency.[37] Community constables are well aware of the pressure on them to use their discretion maximally, but tend to see it as part of negotiation or 'give and take', where leniency may be excused by greater gains from citizens who feel bound by their part in the negotiation. When this is not the case and law is to be enforced despite a negotiating relationship the constable has to 'educate' and persuade. Thus, the dilemma the community constables raised above was tackled by efforts at explaining the officer's (and the law's) view, 'being an education to our way of thinking': 'you have to bridge that gap from a member of the public. To do that you need that liaison to break it up in some way, to make them aware that you are human beings as well.'[38] When one recognizes that the application of the law is contingent upon the situation in all but the most trivial cases (e.g. parking regulations), one seeks one's own standard and one's own thresholds in the search for consistency. In a sense officers become the arbiters of equity in those incidents where they play a direct role.

Although John's [a 16 year old black male] family were involved in crime Dick [the PC], needed to make this kind of contact. Even if it meant dealing with someone who had assaulted a police officer he had to cultivate his contacts 'and I'll do it by fair means or foul'. Dick commented on his interpretation of discretion. He was keen on school visits and had decided what he wanted the kids to call him. 'It can't be just Dick and it can't be PC Dyer. So I get them to call me PC Dick. I want them to be friendly but there's got to be that edge, just that bit of formality. They have to know that I'm authority, like their teacher, but friendly authority. Then, when they get older, if its just "Hello Dick" that's OK.' As to dealing with discretion, he let it be known that petty things would be dealt with informally first but that if something was serious they had to accept that he was a police officer and would act. There were so few contacts available with the youths that it meant making his point about discretion to people he knew might well exploit it.[39]

The practice spoken of here can be illustrated. It refers to the balance officers must strike between cultivating informants and condoning infractions. In the case that follows the officer feels obliged to provide information his informant wants, knowing that by doing so he can control the version of the incident to be heard by those his informant will inform. After this exchange he stated why he was prepared to parley with the informant.

[At a sidestreet farrier] a girl is sweeping up at the stable, white, about 14, punk tomgirl. Bill grins at her, she calls out 'what are those scars on your face then' (there aren't any) . . . She knew Bill had been in a fight with a 19 year old black youth who lived locally. He had fought with punks and hippies she hung round with. The youth had also been in scraps with her brother, a 'Mohican', over some drug-dealing dispute. On one occasion the youth, with other blacks, had set upon her brother at the side of a main road and she went to help; in the ensuing mêlée they got the youth to the ground and she proudly said her friend, also a girl, had controlled him by sitting on his face. Bill found this amusing and so told her some details of his encounter with the youth. She was curious, and actually raised the subject herself – 'Did you find anything on him?' He explained that as he walked towards the youth he had stuffed something down his trousers. Bill asked to search him. The youth refused to be searched on the street so Bill called a van. The youth agreed to be searched in the back of the van. However when it arrived he refused and Bill said he had no option but to take him to the station to be searched. At this point the youth began to struggle and 'we ended up rolling round on the ground. It was so stupid cause he knows I know him, he lives on my beat. I'm going to be coming across him again and again.' 'So was he carrying?' 'I'm not able to tell you that, the matter's still under investigation.' 'Oh', she pouted, 'go on.' 'No love, but I can tell you it was pretty stupid, only a little thing. He needn't have fought over it.' 'Well, he's a shit isn't he. Me and my friends are going to keep him in order.' 'You do that, love. Anything going on?' 'No, I'm just here this morning.' 'Well, see you around.'[40]

It emerged that when the youth was got under control and arrested all he had concealed were two stolen foreign banknotes worth under £1. The youth badly lacerated the tip of one of Bill's fingers and was charged with Assault occasioning Actual Bodily

<hr>

[39] Fieldnotes.   [40] Ibid.

Harm (ABH) and criminal damage to the officer's uniform. Contact with this and other girls who worked casually at the stable yielded information about local drug-dealing, fights and vandalism. It was a useful source, despite the fact that the girls were all clearly truanting. 'If I come on too heavy-handed and report them for the truancy the information is going to dry up.'[41] A *quid quo pro* based on this bit of leverage had evolved. 'It's in my interest to keep it going.'[42] The nature of the girl's casual allusion to the fight with the youth and her curiosity about the charges against him suggested that this information contact was not simply an *ad hoc* favour by a pro-police citizen but part of a negotiated relationship in which the girl sought to manipulate the officer as a resource (in his full knowledge) in her effort to get at the youth who had crossed her brother.

Information rendered often involves a grudge in which the police exploit one person's desire to get even by 'snitching' while the informant exploits the need of the police to enforce the law beyond the superficial level of routine offences at the surface of the community. The informant has to ensure that the attempt does not rebound, because the possession of discreditable information (and the willingness to 'snitch') reflects stigma on its owner. The officer may file the informant as crime-involved, and has to ensure that it does not rebound by poisoning his relations with others in the community whose involvement may not be immediately apparent but whose being affected may be a bigger cost than the benefit of the bust. An example was the arrest of a councillor's son, the embarrassment having occurred when officers investigating ructions between Hells Angels and hippies were caught in a manipulation by a hippy with a grudge against an Angel.

One difficulty associated with getting close to community members, and their schemes and interests, is corruption and graft. Until recently the police discipline code discouraged close community contacts in case sections of the community gained extortionate advantage and officers were compromised. It was under this rubric that the common practice was discouraged of calling at 'tea spots' where officers knew they would receive a welcome, a short break and a chat which might include information of note. In the police world it is sometimes suggested that community constables are par-

[41] *Ibid.*   [42] *Ibid.*

ticularly prone to becoming ensnared in extortionate relationships with locals.

The fine line between cultivating contacts in a difficult area and the dangerously corruptive liaison is apparent when drugs are involved. In 1992 allegations were made against a group of London officers, involving the offering of immunity from prosecution to drug dealers in exchange for money, the giving of protection to drug dealers working on their behalf, and charging drug users with possessing smaller amounts of drugs than they were arrested with (*Guardian*, 31 January, 1992). A headline linked the allegations to the police station's role in community policing. A woman found guilty of drug dealing was sentenced 'on the basis that your dealing stemmed from the advances of a corrupt police officer', although the judge stated this did not mean he accepted the allegations (*Guardian*, 11 July, 1992). However, it is worth noting that whatever the efforts of the community police, press reports indicated that the relationship between police and the local community was extremely poor. Thus, while the alleged corruption arose in an area noted for drug-dealing, it did not appear to stem from community police getting 'too close' to the community.

A further complication arises from the charge on community constables to become aware of, and responsive to, local standards of normality and deviance (ostensibly incumbent on all constables). Rather like the 'going native' problem in ethnography, the problem can be where to stop. Officers may come to identify with local people, particularly if their own values and experience are similar to some established perspective in the community. This very identification is, of course, what critics complain about when they perceive the police identifying with mainstream values, but the problem is more apparent when, for some reason, the values the officer espouses diverge from the mainstream. In the upcoming example it is relevant that the officer, a graduate, identified with the despair local people felt at the decline of traditional working class employment and community, and was hostile to the gentrification of the borough.

The abandoned Cortina that's been here for weeks has now lost its wheels. It's right in front of the [DIY store] car park. Andrew was friendly to the uniformed security man. Having been asked to call by the manager, Mr Ing, he made his way to the office. Also there was the Area Manager, Mr Moses. Both suavely dressed. Andrew's attitude was cold during the discussion.

Initially Ing asked about the Cortina and Andrew explained it could be a long time before the formalities were concluded and it was moved. They asked what would happen if they moved it and he said he could see no objection though officially the police could not know. Ing asked who the children wearing smart blue blazers were that he saw but Andrew didn't know what school it was. Mr Moses said that Mr Ing was 'beating around the bush as usual: what he means is that we have a lot of vacancies here, especially part-time, and we can't find anyone suitable to fill them'. Andrew couldn't identify a steady source though he said he might suggest individuals. Ing said it wasn't easy to find anyone suitable 'in this kind of area', at which Andrew visibly bristled, remarking that the locals may not be like in [posh area] but they were probably working [in posh areas] anyway.

The talk turned to shoplifting. The chief methods were grabbing things and rushing out the fire doors or throwing things to confederates over the security fence. Moses wanted to know if there was an informal value below which police would not prosecute. Andrew was evasive, said there was no policy. Cases were assessed on their merits. He was not at all giving and when coffee in the staff canteen was offered Andrew refused and left with a civil but cool farewell.

Andrew walked to the garden department. It had a 15 foot mesh fence with two strips of razor wire, but pallets were stacked above its top. Andrew remarked that they were happy for the police to prosecute on any value of item because the police paid the costs. But he wasn't going to tell them a value below which the police weren't interested and they'd have to do it themselves. Shops like [department store] employed their own solicitors full-time on shoplifting and prosecuted everything. [DIY store] were a cheap-skate management and didn't want to pay if they could shift the burden to the police. [DIY store] were very bad payers. 'They're an exploitative management. To give you some idea, those managers would only be getting £8000. Nowadays for them to have unfilled vacancies there must be some-thing wrong. There are always people wanting a bit of part-time work. I worked at [grocery chain] for two years when I was doing my A Levels. They're [DIY store] just a bad company. I don't like them. The security manager is OK.' He was not prepared to play ball with [DIY store].[43]

The officer had developed a sense of loyalty to 'his' community, as his reaction to the characterization of the area indicated.

If officers are indeed to 'use their personality' in the community constable role, these cases suggest that police practice may be a lit-tle more likely to reflect individual traits and quirks as well as local norms. We have now reviewed and illustrated several respects in

[43] Fieldnotes.

which the maintenance of community contact imposes costs on the community constable. Some of the tactics they use to achieve their objects have also been identified. The working tactics of community constables can be further specified by examining cases where they take the initiative.

6
Tactics

The general view of community constables is that social service and the presentation of a friendly image are central to their role and that this is at the expense of their involvement in crime control. This impression is widespread among officers on reliefs[1] and common among academics.[2] Yet there are reasons to argue that this is an over-generalization. An analysis based simply on records of activities may miss the intention behind the activities. In describing tactics, goals are as important to identify as the means employed. Goals relate to the strategy, or grand design, which may be brought about by means of tactics. In Schutzian phenomenology, adequate accounts of human action require a grasp of actors' plausible goals, which bring different elements of their knowledge into play so as to activate means of achieving goals.[3] Analytic schema to account for action are formulated on this basis. When we examine police tactics we thus need to maintain an awareness of motives.

When officers' motives are brought to account, moral as well as pragmatic components are revealed. Indeed, an officer's wider sympathies can be engaged while a focus on crime control is maintained, as this beatbook entry shows.

We will be losing Miss Jill Barr as NW co-ordinator; she moves shortly. I dropped off newsletters and chatted with her and her friend, who lives above. They have an absentee landlord . . . There is a communal entrance door which is ridiculously easy to force. The entrance to each flat is a 'joke' (were this not such a serious matter) and the girls are so vulnerable to personal attack. This is the main reason for Miss Barr's move. She also has £700 worth of stereo/video equipment. Miss Barr has also been the subject of an attempted rape by a driving instructor, from whom she hadn't bargained for instruction in other matters. The whole house reeks of damp and backs onto the railway, the TV picture is interrupted by every train (three to four

---

[1] Grimshaw and Jefferson (1987).   [2] Horton (1989).
[3] Agar and Hobbs (1985).

minute intervals!!). Needless to say the landlord's interest is only in the rent and doesn't extend to repairs.[4]

Such discursive entries are encouraged in community officers as part of the craft of beat bobbying, but the construction of these narratives also helps officers keep in view the relation of their routine work to the strategy which validates it. In the police world the central debate over community policing is how it relates to crime control. The rhetoric remains directly rooted in conflict over the police mandate and is ceaselessly rehearsed as officers assess the worth of particular elements of their work. When senior officers are asked how they assess the effectiveness of constables at working their beats, they cite an awareness of those local problems which are susceptible to police effort, and good communication networks, including a system of contact with local organizations, particularly where these have a representative dimension. The beatbook entry above reveals both detailed knowledge and the maintenance of sympathetic contacts with the Neighbourhood Watch representative. But is it crime control?

Rather than de-prioritize crime control, community constables take a broader approach to it. As noted earlier, the community constables ran several 'surgeries' on estates where relatively few residents had a telephone. It is easy to be cynical about police hoping to offer 'help, advice and guidance' on an outreach basis in the inner city, but it would be wrong to think police are unaware of this, or have high expectations of it. However, it was a tactic they supported because there is no calculus by which a value can be assigned to the reassurance such facilities may offer to the lonely pensioner on a rough estate or the potential informant prompted to act on a whim as they are passing by. The activity was justified not on traditional, numerical grounds of arrests and 'process' but by public confidence and responsiveness to community representatives.

There are ironies in the crime control rhetoric. One is that, because community policing can be read as a return to the values of 'traditional' beat policing, it is apt to attract testimonials from the 'old school' senior officer, even though it is this same group that is most likely to champion a crime control interpretation of the mandate. Equally, the relief 'mentality' is often represented in aggressive, crime-busting terms when it is the reliefs who most often work along

[4] BB 4.

with others and the 'soft' community constable to whom the maverick style of the urban cowboy falls. Community constables are more isolated than reliefs, spend long times in solo patrol, are vulnerable as they patrol the often more demanding areas to which they are assigned. The relief officer, often mobile, has more cause to call for assistance, as they cannot be expected to know a particular locale sufficiently well to handle all contingencies. To the chief superintendent, the car and personal radio robbed constables of resourcefulness.

This business of leaping out of cars and calling for assistance . . . When I was a PC I didn't have anything to call assistance with. And you got on, flanneling, bullshitting through a situation. You used commonsense, tact, good humour. That's something missing because all they do now is call for assistance and the poor PC calls more often than the good PC, not standing on their own two feet and sorting out their own situations. It makes it easier for the incompetent man who doesn't know what to do, he just asks and never really learns . . . When I was a PC the only hope of communication was the old blue policebox . . . You walked down that street thinking 'there's a right old punch-up going on down there but they've seen me' but they too were saying 'we're having a right old punch up but he's coming down the road' and, by the time the two met, the confrontation had gone. But now its automatically presented. The car door opens and 'whoof', there's no chance for either side to speak, its 'bang', its friction.[5]

These tactics encouraged snap judgements and superficial resolutions: 'policemen like to see things in black and white. Its so much easier if you can nick somebody. You've got a result.'[6]

These points suggest that our preoccupation in reviewing community constables' tactics must be with the objects they pursue as much as the means used to pursue those objects. We cannot examine the tactics without considering the strategy. The tactics we will review suggest that community constables can prioritize crime control and act in ways that effectively achieve it. A case in point was a call at the home of a fifteen year old boy whom the officer characterized as 'a right little tealeaf' (thief). Here the officer used his 'casework' brief to maintain contact with a problem family as a device to uncover a suspected infraction. The point is not the bluff, but the fact that the officer served both ends—he maintained contact and he resolved the suspected infraction.

[5] Ch. Supt. Heath.   [6] Ch. Insp. Wills.

Bill remarks on a 15 year old named Darren who has been involved in a pre-cocious amount of thieving, aided by his very small size. He looks under half his age, and has a winsome manner. Both are useful to older boys involved in thieving, who exploit him. He crawls into premises taking advantage of his small size. He is very friendly with police. One can think him a nice lad with his heart in the right place yet he keeps turning up in trouble. The last episode was his running away from home; he was found staying on a house-boat with an older boy. He was returned home at the weekend. Bill will use this as an opportunity to get inside the lad's house on grounds of speaking to his mother about the runaway. It is a pretext because the last time Bill was in the house he thought he noticed the electric meter was not where it was before. He thinks they may have bypassed the meter and as it was two months ago the money lost could be considerable. 'Don't make it obvious but have a look at the right hand side of the hall by the door while we're in there' . . . 'Its about Darren, love.' 'Oh no, what's he done now, I can't take much more of this.' The woman is petite, pale and shaking. 'No, nothing new. Just called to see you about his running away' . . . She says her social worker has been in touch about Darren's behaviour and truanting. At the mention of social services Bill's gaze flicks toward the spot on the wall where the meter was (and the dial still is) . . . She has tried to explain to Darren that although he is very small 'he will shoot up suddenly and he'll start to be treated like an adult'. Bill suggests that his size has nothing to do with how the police treat him. 'Look, we both know he's a right little tealeaf, and he's fallen in with the wrong lads. He's too easily led. Do you know who he was with when he ran away?' 'With that Nick Low.' 'No, can't be.' 'Well, that's what he told me. On a boat on the river.' 'Nick's got a boat?' 'Yeah, that's what he says.' She continues that on past form he will inevitably acquire a criminal record and she finds it impossible to control Darren and is concerned about the older boys he hangs around with . . . The closing dis-cussion concerns whether she has Bill's card . . . He would have a word with Darren and try to find out about Nick and the boat. After leaving he remarks that the meter seemed OK. Social services probably arranged for instalment payment and the coin box was removed.[7]

The suggestion that the officer's visit was not cynically motivated but saw uncovering an offence and ongoing contact with the delin-quent and his family as being all of a piece is reinforced by an event which occurred later in the same shift. Once again, suspicion served as the trigger for an intervention that widened into the information-gathering opportunity on the boy's associates that the officer had told the boy's mother he would pursue. Some four hours after the home visit he spotted Darren near his home carrying a bulky object.

[7] Fieldnotes.

'What's he got? Bet he's been nicking.' The boy altered course but the street plan was such that he inevitably met Bill. The object was a portable stereo in poor condition. 'Where'd you get that? How long have you had it?' 'Me Mum gave it me for Christmas.' Bill left the subject; he could check that. 'You ran away, didn't you. Where did you stay?' 'On the river.' 'Who with?' 'Nick.' 'What Nick?' 'Nick Low.' 'What, the big kid with a leather jacket?' 'Yeah. On his boat.' 'He doesn't have a boat.' 'Yes he does.' Bill asked what shape it was, where he kept it moored, whether Nick lived on it all the time. The boy was confident of his ground and gave plausible replies, Bill pressing him several times for an exact description. His mother was approaching. 'Trouble?' 'No, just chatting, aren't we Darren.' 'Yeah.' 'Oh, you're having a word with him then?' 'Yes, like I said I would.' It was raining harder. 'Where's your coat?' Mrs T asked. 'You don't have your coat so you're showing out, in't ya' she jibed, as she took Darren in tow. As Bill left, Darren could be heard telling her he didn't want to go with her and was off home.[8]

In this case, then, the officer maintained a community contact which put obligations on him to intercede regularly with the family of a young offender. Such contact could yield arrests, or at least crimes detected, albeit minor ones. Neither crime control nor social service connotations unambiguously apply. This officer expressed very strong crime-oriented views on the police mandate and was critical of the public relations aspects of the role; he did not do school visits, for example, and resisted any such involvement. He was nevertheless firmly committed to the community constable's role in crime control on the basis that this was a means to discover crime-related information not otherwise forthcoming.

It is important to note here the separation between the officer's notion of the police mandate and the interpersonal skills and tactics he drew on to pursue his work. These were apparent in another incident where he was frankly dubious of the value of an intervention beforehand but demonstrated skill in prosecuting it once he was engaged. Such cases call in question just how important expressed attitudes are as indicators of officer practice.[9] In other words, it may be that low commitment is rather unimportant as a predictor of action, although it may have an effect on job satisfaction and will also be affected by the visibility of dis-preferred actions to supervisors.

The circumstances were that the officer had been asked to call on a woman who had been trying for several years to establish a

[8] *Ibid.*   [9] Fielding (1988c).

neighbourhood watch scheme with little response from her neighbours. She lived in a complex of prestigious apartments for the stu-
pendously wealthy. She had let the station know she was giving up
on Neighbourhood Watch, due to lack of response and an operation
she was to have two hours after the officer visited her. He said she
had a reputation for complaining to the station and was dangerous
because she knew the chief superintendent. She was a member of the
local Crime Prevention Panel and Police Consultative Committee.

Her discussion with Bill was a sustained and spirited attempt to disengage
from NW. She was thinking of moving, had to re-organize her life after the
operation and first priority was to get a new career started, her income was
much reduced. However, at an early point she let slip that while the flat was
on the market, interest in it stopped when people saw the view. As well as
a fine panorama one had a close-up sight of a derelict, burnt-out public
house. Steven saw that if this genuinely was an obstacle to her moving she
might still be around for some time to co-ordinate a NW scheme. Still, out
of 100 flats in the development she had only 16 members. She had been asked
by the Consultative Committee to do some research on why the uptake was
poor and had done some phone interviewing.
    She had drafted a letter to the Chief Superintendent, which she read out.
Bill knew of the letter but was curious to hear it (and reported its contents
and imminent arrival on return to the station). There were three reasons:
(i) the residents valued their privacy and did not want to know each other;
(ii) they felt the flats were crime-free and the security adequate (porter and
electronic locking) and (iii) many were not resident but lived in the country
or abroad. She contrasted the people living there to those in the successful
schemes in the owner-occupied houses adjoining. The people here kept little of value in their flats, and their cars were company-owned.
    Bill tried to fight her every step of the way. They had tried twice to pro-
voke interest by leafletting and they should try once more. If she was unable
he would do it. Also, even these residents were vulnerable to personal attack
en route to their flat from their company car, and they had recently sighted
youths suspiciously walking along the roof of nearby buildings. The most
exposed ground floor flat had been burgled several times.
    Jarvis is a highly articulate and dominant woman who spoke in steely
tones and with some force, to the point of rudeness (using easily resented
'with respect' parliamentary language). Bill knew her ways well though, for
he would not back down and tenaciously, if ponderously, kept fighting her.
It was him who first deflated the tension with a joke—a hazardous one,
about her (limb) being amputated rather than the bandage—and thereafter
they both did it, making a highly critical point, then a joke allowing the
other a rejoinder.

She had become disenchanted and doubtful that a scheme could take off. She described the occupants of each flat in her building—a drug-trafficker who was enthusiastic about NW but whom, since his release from prison, she cut dead, an aloof dentist and lawyer couple, a rich, elderly doctor, an American film producer and his wife who were seldom in England, businessmen, judges and retired couples with country estates.

Her solution was a 'federated' scheme where the two blocks would come under the two adjoining schemes of traditional working class and yuppifying owner-occupied housing. This would evade the 60% problem [the membership level required by police] and allow the signs to go up, which she wanted most, for their deterrent value. Bill pointed out that the substance of her proposal was that the residents of the luxury flats get the benefit of the vigilance of the adjoining schemes without having to do anything. She freely acknowledged this but said it would let them erect the signs. Bill came back to his own wish, again making an equally blunt rejoinder to her blunt remark, turning it round so it seemed facetious and humorous. By the end of their discussion she was saying that on return from hospital she would discuss it with him again. He had not backed down, was still talking about preparing leaflets and distributing them himself. He remarked after leaving he hoped she wouldn't give it up, because of its deterrent value.[10]

The officer then called on a second scheme organizer, this time a titled lady. After this he discussed his thoughts about Neighbourhood Watch: '"to be honest, I hate it. All this writing and newsletters, in all honesty I don't like all the preparation and paperwork. Fortunately, two of my four schemes virtually run themselves. I prefer real crime work, and doing the arrests to the paperwork."'[11] Despite this he had shown skill and a feeling of being at ease with the two upper class women.

Whatever Bill's estimation of their value, these Neighbourhood Watch contacts were facilitated by a sense of confidence and a mental agility that allowed him to anticipate lines of argument and swiftly formulate rebuttals. Bill routinely extracted the maximum from his public contacts, as may be illustrated with the following low-key incident in which he seeks to kill two birds with the same stone. He had been asked to call at a corner shop to advise the owner about a claim for criminal injuries compensation in respect of stress caused by an armed robbery. When he arrived the ten year old sister of two local 'villains' was at the shop.

---

[10] Fieldnotes.   [11] *Ibid.*

'Don't you ever go to school? You're truanting, aren't you.' 'Well, I'm going to school tomorrow. Honestly I am. That's where Mum is today, that's why she went out. Had to get me uniform. I've got to have a boater. I'm definitely going to school tomorrow.' 'I bet you can't even read.' 'Can.' 'Prove it then. You read this.' As Bill wrote out the name of the officer dealing with the CICB application for the shopkeeper he also got the girl to read out the name. She got it wrong. 'See, you can't do it, can you. You really ought to go to school' . . . After leaving, Bill remarked that the stress arose from an armed robbery 'with a shotgun jammed up his nostrils, the whole bit. But he's a bit spineless, he's let it get to him.'[12]

   This minor episode indicates the need for officers to develop a 'narrative' sense of their community contacts. By seeing people as being involved in an ongoing story with no ending, the officers construe their own involvements as having continuity rather than as being definitive. This contrasts strongly with the 'open-and-shut' perspective forced on the relief officers. Taking a micro-sociological angle on community constables' tactics for trawling for information and cultivating contacts suggests that officers must tolerate a deal of 'noise' in order to hear anything useful. To some this is an entire contradiction of the police role. A relief inspector was discussing mistakes probationers often made. 'One very common mistake is going into things in too much depth, getting involved in the rights and wrongs, trying to arbitrate something. Taking too much notice of how annoyed people are rather than the facts of the case and why you're there. Forgetting the fact that you're a policeman.'[13] While the relief role plainly differs from the community constables', taking time and hearing the parties out is known to correlate more highly with victims' satisfaction with the police than successful prosecution of the culprit.[14] The relief inspector's view obviated any need for detailed explanation of police powers, which raises obvious concern over provoking citizens, and tends to conflict with a negotiating approach.[15]
   The contrast between the view the relief inspector expresses and the narrative perspective is that in the latter the elements of the story are equally significant; one cannot know what is most salient, at least until information has been maximized. (Logically, as a story with no end, the narrative view implies that one can never know what is most salient, an implication which discourages officers from seeing

[12] Fieldnotes.   [13] Insp. Wren.   [14] Burns-Howell and Jones (1982).
[15] Norris, Kemp and Fielding (1992).

incidents as isolated occurrences and encourages them to see them as part of a continuing process.) Consequently the value of a given intervention is accepted from the outset as likely to be partial, as being one influence among many. The officers acquire a humility about any single one of their interventions but also come to recognize that any contact is unlikely to be the last. Here there are grounds for building the relationships with the public which are denied officers working in the reactive mode of the reliefs.

However, the incremental approach is not readily able to point to spectacular successes. In the policy arena, the value of multi-agency co-operation has been asserted by reference to police interventions in selected estates with severe social problems. The substance appears to be that what is most effective is the temporary deployment of teams of officers to crack down on crime problems of most concern, sometimes described as 'intensive home beat policing'.[16] Once again we are in debate about crime control and the police mandate.

Some of the more red-blooded assertions of this approach claim that it improves on an approach to community policing which has been too soft. 'Despite the increased level of policing activity on the estate and the change in style, from one of virtual non-enforcement by the previous permanent beat officers, there was no adverse public reaction. On the contrary, the police were praised by all sides. It was recognized that their efforts had been the catalyst for wider community involvement.'[17] The extract, from a West Midlands Police report quoted by NACRO, identifies by omission a critical problem for aggressive 'home beat' work. It is claimed that wider community involvement has been achieved, and that this came from identifying the police to locals as being unambiguously concerned with their traditional work—dealing with 'crime and nuisance'. It is said that, free of the fear of reprisals, people volunteered information more freely. Such reduced anxiety is likely to remain only as long as does the heightened level of patrol. Without high density patrol, crime-reporting practices revert to the norm, which in some estates means not reporting even when people are burglarized by their own neighbours (*Guardian*, 15 June, 1989).

Moreover, it addresses the concerns of one section of the community but not others. Disaffected youth, people who distrust police, ethnic minority people, are likely to see themselves as again the

[16] NACRO (1988) at 6.   [17] *Ibid.* at 34.

target of harassment, but now by a small, highly identifiable team of officers under the same 'home beat' label as the officers they have supplanted. There is a danger that the perceived message will be that policing is a sectional interest, for the white and elderly, against minorities and youth. Most importantly, then, saturation policing under the guise of 'home beat patrol' serves to undermine the developing philosophy of a community policing that seeks to reconcile and ameliorate rather than to arrest and repress. That message shores up the traditional 'crime-buster' perspective with the overtone that conventional policing has to be revived to make good the failings of community police. The potential for crime displacement is subordinated to giving people what 'they' want, high-visibility crime control, setting the stage for more resistance. It is easier than confronting what 'home beat' officers do that is effective, and learning what multi-agency co-operation means in practice. For there is little multi-agency 'co-operation' in this approach, only a division of labour in which the police resume aggressive law enforcement.

Alternative case studies exist. In the following we examine the way that a Permanent Beat Officer, Andrew, co-operates with a housing estate manager in routine problem-definition, legal advice, and a plan of action against criminal damage on the estate. When Andrew arrived at the estate office the manager was on the telephone. It transpired that the call involved a refusal by the girlfriend of a man to admit his wife (the caller) to their flat to regain her property, the man having emigrated. Once Andrew picked this up he advised at various points on the wife breaking in (to her own tenancy), which he counselled against, and on getting a court order to gain entry. When the manager, Arron, got off the telephone they discussed two matters. The main one was the theft of shrubbery recently provided for the courtyards as part of a renovation programme. When Andrew showed an architect round the previous day they noticed plants of the same species now flourishing in the front garden of one of the flats. As the architect had brought a cameraman for the report on the finished project, 'we now have photographic evidence of where the shrubs have ended up'.[18]

The second matter Andrew and Arron agreed should be dealt with was vandalism and rowdy behaviour in the new courtyard play area. Andrew discussed who might know whose children were responsible

---

[18] Fieldnotes.

and then established there was a suspect for the theft of the shrubbery.

'I'll go round to number 9 and see our friend Mills. I'll come on a bit heavy
and see how he reacts. I'll tell him I will arrest him for theft and its up to
him whether he replaces the shrubs.' '*Are* you going to arrest him?' 'That's
up to him, really. If he won't admit it, or gives me any abuse, I'll arrest him.
Let the magistrates decide if he's the one.' Andrew was fairly certain the man
would admit it and replace the shrubbery. Andrew remarked that he didn't
mind dealing with these low-key problems; at least the people were
approachable, unlike the cold and officious residents of the newly-privatized
blocks adjacent, a view Arron reciprocated.

A local alcoholic had been causing trouble by abusing shopkeepers. Arron
relayed their complaints about him; being Asian they had been abused
racially by him. However, he was reasonable when sober and in Andrew's
view the problem was partly of their own making. They gave him casual
work and then either paid him directly in cans of beer or allowed him to use
his wage to buy drink from them. 'They're on trial with me now. I've given
them notice that its up to them to prove to me that they're serious about
dealing with it. If they won't help themselves then I've told them I'm not
going to do anything.' He wanted them to stop selling the man drinks. They
would be willing to forego the custom if they wanted a resolution. If he continued to be abusive Andrew would arrest him.

Andrew and Arron discussed the new neighbourhood watch scheme. The
vandalism of the courtyards by the children was its first test and it had not
passed. Andrew was unimpressed by the scheme, as no one had done anything about the children (or the shrubbery). 'All they've done is complain to
the police without first taking any action themselves. They're there on the
scene. They can see it happening. Why don't they lean over the balconies
and tell the kids off? I'm going to see [the co-ordinator] and tell *him* off. As
far as I'm concerned that NW still has to prove itself to me.' The information about the shrubbery had not come from the scheme but from their own
investigation. 'You can't just sit and tell the police to handle it. You can't
just ring us up and tell us what to do. There's more to NW than that.
They're going to be the most effective people to see to the children.'[19]

Andrew's 25 minute visit with Arron helped him to plan and prioritize his subsequent action.

Andrew called on the 'shrubbery suspect' but he had recently gained work
after years of unemployment and was out. Nearby a front door was open
and a man periodically appeared, monitoring his son playing in the courtyard. 'That's Harry. He's a bit of a bastard but he's quite co-operative. I'll

[19] *Ibid.*

go in and have a word.' Andrew sauntered in. Harry was vaguely playing a video game and a desultory conversation ensued. Harry confirmed that all the residents suspected Number 9 on the shrubbery. Andrew went on to the rowdy children. He thought he knew who was particularly to blame after talking it over with Arron—a young lone parent with 3 children. Harry nominated this family without Andrew referring to them. Harry expressed disapproval of the vandalism but said because his lounge was at the rear of the flat he couldn't do anything. Andrew kept the chat going, urged Harry to have a go if he caught children misbehaving and to keep in touch with the NW coordinator.

Andrew's next call was a 40 minute community contact. He rang at the security door to be admitted to an upstairs flat. Andrew visited old Jim, whose front door was also open. Jim is the Tenants' Association secretary and one of Andrew's contacts, knowledgeable about local politics and active in his Labour party branch. It is a cordial relationship. The chief topic was the vandalism. Rather than 'reading the Riot Act' as he said he would, Andrew took up the issue of self-help very gently. He first checked if Jim knew what kids were involved. Jim had a new angle. 'They're coming in from all over. They come in from over the road [low-rise flats] and the W [estate]. Once they set up this play area they come in from everywhere and you can't tell who's doing what. Especially at the weekend. It was teeming.[20]

As to the shrubbery, Jim suspected the same man as everyone else. He went back to the kids, and pointed out that since the shared front lawn on the ground floor flats had been partitioned into private front gardens, the occupants spent the summer evenings sitting out there. Consequently, they were on the other side of the flat to the court-yard and could not take part in controlling the kids. Those in flats above the ground floor were reluctant to do anything because if they shouted at the kids they were ignored and if they threatened to come down the kids scattered.

A final exchange concerned problems at the Community Centre. As a result of intimidation by black youths the minister who ran it had closed its bar. The clubs that used it stopped doing so when the bar closed. The centre was declining, with a consequent loss of a focus for the community. The council had taken a line Andrew asso-ciated with the 'soft Left', that the youths be invited to work in the centre, while the Labour councillors and people like Jim wanted them banned. The minister rejected the council's line since the youths had beaten him with a lead pipe two years before. Andrew and Jim discussed the futility of the stalemate.

[20] Fieldnotes.

These exchanges suggest a misleadingly *ad hoc* character for the community contact. Because they are one episode in a continuous series of contacts they provide recurrent themes, opportunities and work for the community constable. This is conveyed by an episode some three hours after the contact with Jim.

En route to a call Andrew noticed a boy of seven urinating against the wall of an Old People's Home. Andrew dealt very formally with the boy, drawing himself up and squaring off to him. The boy's responses were minimal and meek. He established the boy's address and asked 'what would your grandmother say about this? There are old people living in there. She wouldn't like it, would she?' The boy mumbled. 'Your house is only a couple of minutes away. Why couldn't you go home to the toilet? Do you know that's an offence? That's indecency. You and I haven't gotten off to a very good start, have we? But if you can stop misbehaving you and I could be friends.'[21]

Andrew went on to ask him if he had been playing in the courtyard which had been vandalized. ' "You've been pulling up those plants, haven't you." The boy was non-committal while Andrew warned him, assuming that the boy was involved. The boy didn't deny it. "Well, I tell you what. I won't report you for indecency this time. I won't tell your Mum about it this time but next time I will. We'll keep this between ourselves. But don't do it again." '[22]

While this segment was over, the episode was not. In the following it is clear that the officer gains some purchase over a group of children by connecting it both to the information he received on the estate and by connecting it with the 'urination' incident.

Andrew walked from the precinct by the Old People's Home to the courtyard of the estate block that was vandalized. There were six boys playing there, two blacks and four whites, aged about eight. Andrew admonished them not to play on the raised beds for the new plants. The two that were walking on them got down. One boy had an iron bar. As a couple of them chanted 'he's got metal', 'look officer, he's got metal' repeatedly, this boy placed the bar in a bin. The boys were avoiding Andrew's gaze and scuffling round with their hands in their pockets when Andrew told them that there'd been complaints about them and residents were fed up with them playing destructively and damaging the plants. 'Where are you from, boys?' One or two pointed to the flats, a couple shouted that it wasn't them that had 'nicked the bushes' but someone else from a family Andrew knew.

[21] *Ibid.*   [22] *Ibid.*

As the exchange was winding down the boy earlier stopped for urinating was attempting to leave surreptitiously. Andrew used the address he had just been given by the boy urinating. 'I know where you all come from so don't think you can get away with it. I think boys from number one . . . Court had better be especially careful' he said loudly. The lad stopped in his tracks and turned to face Andrew, squinting. 'What do you mean?' 'You know what I'm talking about. Just you be careful.' And, to all of them, 'keep off the walls' [of the raised plant beds]. 'Don't suppose it'll do much good', he remarked as he left.[23]

The value of such a narrative sense is cumulative, the building-up of a reputation as being well-informed and hard to deceive. Officers can deliberately set about constructing such an image.[24] Indeed, the sceptical approach is sometimes explicitly rehearsed, as in this beat-book entry about a long-standing feud between two businesses under the 'Community Aspects' heading. 'Raynes' are always complaining that their vehicles are being "boxed in" by people using the studios. As police officers we have to be careful we are not "used" by either party, and remain strictly impartial—there are obviously faults on both sides. Mr N has suggested that yellow lines should be put down to restrict parking. He would be first to complain if they were!'[25]

The case study can be closed by completing the story of the shrubbery. After the shift Andrew discussed what to do with several other community constables. Ron suggested Andrew serve the man with a summons if he was continuously out. The problem was that a summons appears as 'process', while 'an arrest goes on your figures'. It was a problem that particularly mattered to 'the Colonel' (the inspector) and reflected the organization being geared to crime control. Inspector Adams needed to show activity and wanted his arrest figures kept up. All agreed that this could be counter-productive. It was more efficient to serve a summons; they knew the address and the man was unlikely to flee. Andrew was still reluctant and, though the sergeants pointed out that county forces routinely used the summons this way and avoided the complication of arrests under the Police and Criminal Evidence Act he wanted to try the address again. 'You've got your photographic evidence, right. And your interview with him needn't involve having a solicitor present.' Andrew was still going back to the flat.

[23] Fieldnotes.
[24] See Muir (1977) on the 'paradox of face' for a discussion of a particularly effective style.
[25] BB 4.

Two days later the community constables were swopping recent events on their beats. ' "Yeah, I arrested him and it was dealt with by a caution." Andrew had established that the man was "a bit slow. Not mad but not just thick either. And he's easily led." '[26] Andrew judged he had fallen under the influence of local youths. This moderated his attitude to the man, as had his contrition. Andrew judged that arrest and formal caution were sufficient deterrent. Mills had offered to return the shrubbery and Andrew helped him arrange it with Arron.

'He's watered the plants today and Arron's fixing up for the Council to dig them up carefully and put them back.' 'So you didn't bother with a summons' said Phil. 'No, this was better. He was frightened by the arrest and I don't think he'll forget. Its taken him four years to find a job. Anyway, if it had gone to Court they might have dismissed it. They'd see that he was uh . . .' 'Inadequate,' declared Sophie. 'Yeah, and so this has saved time waiting round for a date and going to Court.' 'And the court's time' mentioned Sophie. 'He had about a third of the missing shrubs. The Council valued them at £4 each you know.' 'Have you got a suspect for the rest then?' Phil asked. 'Yes, I do. You know that kid I caught pissing. Number one . . . Court. People are saying its him and his brother. They're the worst ones for running amok in the courtyard too. So I decided to visit the address and see their mother. I read her the Riot Act.' Unless she took control of her boys he would contact social services.[27]

It is a commonplace to say that police develop refined skills of observation, and it would be pointless to try to improve on Rubenstein's classic description of these.[28] But it is worth saying that such skills are an element in effective communication and negotiation with members of the public, too. In particular, this includes monitoring the demeanour of parties for signs of resistance and responding with appropriate means of persuasion. Another angle on this is given by Muir in his discussion of skills of 'talk',[29] which was emphasized by the community policing inspector as a key discriminant between novice and experienced police. 'A more experienced officer will talk whereas the inexperienced officer won't. He will come to a hard and fast decision and he will leave people flat. "That is the decision, that's how its got to be" and he will walk away, leaving those people thinking, "what does he know? He hasn't told us anything really." You often find that a probationer will come

---

[26] Fieldnotes.   [27] *Ibid.*   [28] Rubenstein (1973).   [29] Muir (1977).

away from a problem and not really understand what the problem was.'[30]

That is, as well as monitoring demeanour, officers need to operate with a full sense of human motives and experiences, which acts as a 'foil' for the evaluation of the performance they are watching. 'He [probationer] will have a vague idea. He will see it as a parking dispute, he won't see the background to it, the reason why. Years ago these two neighbours fell out and one of these guys who is complaining isn't really worried about the parking space, he's trying to have a go at his next door neighbour.'[31] In contrast, 'the guys that deal with these things professionally reach agreement with the people he's working with.' Note the emphasis on the officer 'working with' those whose dispute is being regulated; the public has to be carried with you. The probationer will know that at an assault involving neighbours, names and addresses should be exchanged and a referral made to the magistrates court. But 'the experienced officer would give that to the people as an option but dig into it further and try and gain common agreement'.[32]

The inspector saw a direct relation between the perceptual monitoring and motive-imputing which characterized the skilful conduct of a dispute intervention[33] and the 'powers of observation' experienced officers used in investigating crime-related calls. He recalled an arrest for burglary and intent to rape.

In the afternoon a disturbance call came out. All we got was 'a disturbance'. It didn't sound like an urgent call. The sergeant went round the block to get to the front door. I saw this little head appear out of the doorway watching the sergeant as he disappeared and he then walked off. I stopped him [and] took him back to the scene and he was very worried about me. So I thought I'd take him round the corner and see what happened. As we walk round the corner the female said 'that's him! He attempted to rape me.' Now a lot of people might have seen that the guy walked out of the doorway but would have been preoccupied with going to the address . . . But that was my perception about the way that guy was acting to the sergeant.[34]

Like the plotters in *Foucault's Pendulum*[35] the inspector was always seeking connections between apparently independent events.

Monitoring demeanour, anticipating motives, trying to carry the public with you, are then components of the interpersonal skills on which experienced officers draw. The lessons are not restricted to

[30] Insp. Adams.   [31] *Ibid.*   [32] *Ibid.*
[33] Kemp, Norris and Fielding (1992).   [34] Insp. Adams.   [35] Eco (1989).

calls where the police are arbitrating between members of the public. They also apply where police confront suspects or make proactive interventions such as street stops. The community policing inspector felt these skills related to whether people were being treated without respect for their feelings, which could 'only create resentment'. He had never suffered a complaint from a street stop because, to him, securing compliance involved looking at the situation from the perspective of the person being stopped, anticipating their concerns and doing what you could to allay them.

[If] you want to search a bloke you don't have to put your hands straight into his pockets. Have a little chat first and tell him why you are doing it. I've always shown someone my hands because there is a real fear, particularly among black people, that policemen are going to plant evidence. So what is wrong [in] you say[ing], 'Look, there's my hands,' and do it slowly, none of this [rapid hand movement], because that upsets people. I've been on drugs raids where you have other officers going 'I'm going to search you' as they're going through their pockets 'because we've got a warrant and we're looking for drugs'. At the word 'drugs' the guy is breaking into beads of perspiration, not because he's got anything but because he fears its going to be put on him. Now whether that fear is reasonable or not it still exists.[36]

The extent of the imagined placing of himself in the other person's shoes was apparent when he extended the example to police themselves.

How would I feel if my superintendent said 'Money has been stolen from the canteen, you're a suspect.' And here and now, turn my pockets out. Whereas he could have another supervisory officer present to witness fair play, and say 'this is the allegation and I intend to search you'. Explained on those terms you'd say 'we'll do it, a bit of privacy'. But the number of people I've seen in busy high streets who have been searched by police standing with their hands up, they always want to make a big thing of it. Why not talk to the guy and say 'we can do it here or just walk across to that doorway over there, whatever you like'. That costs us nothing and yet will gain us so much.[37]

Later, in response to a question about incidents he had found difficult, the community police inspector volunteered an incident from his early service where he failed, on his own terms, to use appropriate interpersonal tactics. This, too, revolved around reciprocity of communication.

[36] Insp. Adams.   [37] Ibid.

I'd had a bad day and I stopped a cab driver [who] . . . had been causing quite severe obstruction and I . . . certainly wasn't polite and I certainly wasn't professional. He had obviously had a bad day too. When I asked him to move he opened the cab door, ripped the badge off his jacket, threw it down the drain and said 'you're always picking on us, you've got no cause to speak to me like that, even though I was causing an obstruction'. He was going well over the top and really could have been claimed for breach of the peace. I learnt a lesson there because I hadn't dealt with him properly . . . He did over-react but I was sharp with him. I actually provoked the incident.[38]

Had the inspector's demeanour been correct and the cabbie still abusive, he could have brought a charge.

The case led to discussion of the subtlety of interpersonal tactics. It could be difficult to anticipate reactions, especially by those from cultures whose historical relation to the police was different. One could take the wrong tack, a compelling reason to prefer immediate micro-sociological features of the interaction to stereotypes.

At Brixton an awful lot of people, both black and white, were extremely excitable. If they just wanted to talk you'd put your pen down, let them get it off their chest. There are times equally when you can really lay down the law because sometimes people respond to authority. A couple of times I got it wrong . . . It is very difficult if you start on the wrong foot, particularly dealing with suspects. Complaints against the police reflect that. When you talk through with your complainant what the officer did, its that it was a bad reaction right at the beginning. If you look what the officer did after that they will accept, often, that he was doing it the correct way. Initial encounters are most important.[39]

In one case a youth who committed numerous offences of Taking and Driving Away was brought in by a police constable who could not get anything from the suspect. The key issue was whether he was stealing anything from the vehicles or whether it was unalloyed Taking and Driving Away. 'No one would believe that he wasn't stealing the property . . . He was joyriding and other people [were] stripping them. By building up a picture of all the vehicles he had taken we found a certain number with property recovered intact . . . Because we were able to establish that, he then told us about more crimes he had committed. That came out of establishing a relationship with the guy.'[40]

[38] Insp. Adams.   [39] Ibid.   [40] Ibid.

Officers do learn interactional tactics and ploys from each other. Take the domestic intervention. 'I went with a very much older policeman . . . and he walked in and says "I am fed up with you, you're 40 years old and you're fighting like hammer and tong. What do you want to call the bloomin' police for? Its nothing at all to do with the law, you sort your own selves out." And they were both fine after that. Now I went to one call like that and thought "I'll do that . . .".[41] It was not just learning from experience but tuning in to the expectations of others. Another discussant took up the point. 'Its partly that and partly reading the situation: "what do they want me to say to them? Do they want me to talk down to them?" You have to look at them and assess them and say what they want to hear from you.'[42] This is a sensitive interactional perspective, and best applies where a formal legal resolution is less practical than a negotiated truce. The officer tries to identify a solution implicit in what disputants are saying, to say 'what they want to hear' but in a way imbued with the manifest authority of uniform. 'It might be a couple that are very fond of one another but one night a week the old man gets drunk. They don't want to be talked down to by a younger man because they've got a son that's older than you. So you maybe have to give a bit of sympathy to one and not the other, say "I think you're being a bit unfair". Everyone's an individual and you can't categorize a domestic dispute that easily.'[43] Sensitivity was essential, as 'it could be disastrous if you chose the wrong way, it's happened to me', and there was no point in leaving without a resolution because you would create a call-back.

Community constables and their supervisors felt that their greater autonomy relative to relief officers bred discretion-mindedness and innovation. A Surrey community constable in an area with troublesome local youths persuaded a church to open a youth club 'which has taken some of them off the streets and also got him a little group that he can talk to'.[44] The dual use is noteworthy; many officers believe the real value of football matches between police and local youth is not public relations but that during the match you know where a large section of potential offenders are. The relief officer's discretion is confined by the limited purpose of each separate intervention. 'Discretion' has particular force for community constables; they felt they needed to use more discretion than reliefs, and always

[41] GD 2.   [42] *Ibid.*   [43] *Ibid.*   [44] Supt. Tate.

inhabited a grey area. 'The simplest case is where you have a punk, if I were in a car I'd arrest. Whereas what I've done is get him taken to the station, you get his mam and she knows what's happening. You see things not in black and white, there's a part in the middle . . .'[45] Another interjected,

Relief officers are very much governed by the message pad. There's a result has to go on that message. Whereas we might be stopped, 'Excuse me, officer. My little Jimmy, he's just nicked a coin out of my purse, I wonder if you could have a word with him.' Now that is an allegation of crime: there should be a crime sheet written, a statement taken from the mother saying whether she wants to prosecute. She doesn't want to know all that! 'All I want you to do is have a little word with him and put him back onto the right path.' That's how I see discretion.[46]

A third officer elaborated that 'you've got to be seen to be fair. You've not to use your discretion to let people get away with things. But they know that you're fair if they know you won't automatically stick a ticket on their car . . . Appropriate, yes. When dinner money has been stolen from the school secretary's office in theory the money belongs to the parent who's paid little Jimmy's dinners or to the school. Either way there's a loser but neither want the culprit prosecuted.'[47] Like other social institutions, such as universities and department stores, schools claim some right to regulate delicts within their boundaries. This is a significant grey area for police discretion. 'Different schools have got different attitudes, some want the culprit spoken to, some want the parents told. Schools very much regard themselves as a little society don't they, away from the outside world. Right and wrong applies but the letter of the law doesn't. We don't want to apply the law to the letter in school because kids are kids and everybody goes off the rails sometimes. So that is discretion.'[48]

Forbearance implies that community constables scale down incidents, prefer informal resolutions, and seek to ameliorate situations which relief officers may see as not worthwhile or promising a 'good collar' if left to run their course. The circumstances in which community constables refrain from conventional crime control actions are thus of keen interest. In the following incident, the constable, Rodney, encounters a scuffle which he handles in the guise of the 'stern father' and which leads to a discussion between him and

[45] GD 2.   [46] *Ibid.*   [47] *Ibid.*   [48] *Ibid.*

another community constable about the circumstances in which arresting an abusive citizen should be avoided.

Walking down the precinct towards the junction, a commotion could be heard. In the middle of the road three black youths and a tall white youth were slapping, shoving and holding the arms of a cyclist, a bearded man in his late thirties. The man straddled his bike and was almost on the ground. The youths were shouting and began kicking the cyclist, who was trying to stay upright but otherwise doing little to defend himself. As Rodney walked swiftly a bus rounded a corner and had to cross into the oncoming lane to avoid the fight. The bike had a Neighbourhood Watch sticker on it, panniers for commuting, and an Australian pennant.

As Rodney approached, the cyclist tried to get on his bike and Rodney pushed the white youth away from him. The black youths, never the protagonists, stood right back the moment Rodney arrived and kept ten feet away. The white youth attempted to strike the cyclist again, and the scuffle briefly resumed, the white youth shouting that the cyclist had run him down, 'he got my kneecap, I'm injured man' as he gave the bike a swift kick. Rodney held his right hand and squared off to him, 'pushing' him by proximity away from the cyclist, on whom he turned his back. Rodney ordered them to get to the side of the road out of the traffic. The blacks were now waiting on the opposite side of the road. Rodney asked the cyclist if he was alright. He said he was but said nothing else. He did not say whether he had run into the youth, Rodney had not seen it and the cyclist was anxious to leave. It was clear Rodney gave little credence to the youth's complaints. He had not come quickly under control by the constable's arrival. Rodney told him to shut up and calm down. 'Look, sir, I don't see any injury, all I see is you kicking this man. Keep still.' Rodney told the cyclist 'I'm going to stand here a bit longer while you get on your way' sympathetically, but the cyclist seemed not to fully take this in, replying irritably 'Yes, I'm going, I intend to get away' and cycled off. Rodney told the youth to stop bothering people and get out of the area. 'Just calm down and leave. If you've any sense you will stay well clear of me and not answer me back. Now go.'

Rodney walked a few yards down the road on the same side as the youths were now stood, by a bus stop. Another homebeat was walking his bike along the pavement. Rodney told him what had happened. Rodney said 'if you're going in that direction take it easy cause you're going to get some lip from them, they're in a mind to get in some trouble'. They discussed the youths and the point at which one should front them out. By now the white had gone and the blacks were walking away from the precinct. They all left in directions different to the one they were headed when they were crossing the road and got in the scuffle with the cyclist.

I recognized the white youth as Firkin, from an earlier incident, his previous being Drunk and Disorderly and TDA of a bus with criminal damage.

Rodney said he didn't seem drunk but his eyes were glazed and he thought he was high and looking for trouble. 'I could have come over all officious and formal and charged him with something back there.' 'Well, did he offer you violence?' 'No, he was just fractious. He could have been manipulated into an arrest. Another officer might have done that. I could easily have got him to push me.' He added, 'if he said "fuck off, man, this doesn't concern you", or words to that effect, that is, he made a direct challenge to me, then I would have had to arrest him'. The other officer agreed. 'Because the challenge is not being made to me personally, which I can ignore, but to this' [pointing to his helmet]. Rodney continued, 'its this uniform that doesn't let me walk away from things like that. Even though there are plenty of things I'd like to run away from.' For the officers, a direct challenge to the symbolic authority of the uniform must eventuate in arrest, but there was more to it. 'I could easily have got him to strike me. But what was to be gained? The cyclist had gone, no one was hurt, and the bus queues were looking on. Better to downplay it and get him off my beat.' Rodney continued on his way.[49]

In their discussion the officers were initially preoccupied with the idea of a 'direct challenge', most obviously, being hit, but including a verbal challenge to their authority. As Rodney pointed out, an officer intent on arrest (out of irritation, a desire to boost arrest figures or because it seemed most efficient) could easily manipulate a citizen so as to fulfil the legal criteria warranting a charge of obstruction or assault on a police officer. The point here is not that relief officers are not bound in the same way or might not think this way. Rather, the point is that the role requirements of the two functions place different constraints on officers which heighten the attractiveness of particular options. The principal constraints channelling action along a particular course are those of time, and those to do with how officers account for their unsupervised activities. Relatively free of the time constraint and of the need to warrant their patrol by steadily bringing in arrests, community constables are encouraged by the role to reason as these two homebeats did at the close of the incident, to decide that the best resolution was also the least visible (in a literal sense and in the sense of documented records of their actions).

Immediately following this incident the officer was drawn back to the same refrain when he noticed boys cycling on the pavement. It proved to be an opportunity to teach the boys 'a lesson' and was

[49] Fieldnotes.

couched in terms of an explicit contrast between Rodney and other officers.

One was on a BMX, the other on an adult racing bike. Rodney asked the boy on the racer his age. 'Fourteen.' 'Big man now?' 'Yeah.' 'Then you're big enough to use the public road. You take that bike on the road [a cut-throat section of inner ring road] and get it OFF THE PAVEMENT.' Rodney noticed the bike had no front brake. 'And you've got no front brake either. That's even worse if you're on the pavement. You might hit a pedes-trian. You're lucky with me but you'll come across some bloody-minded per-son or one of my colleagues who will arrest you for this. So get the bike on the road, and get that brake fitted.' 'The boy grudgingly agreed, joining his friend to use the pedestrian crossing. 'And dismount when you are on the crossing.' The boy complied while his friend cycled across. Rodney chuck-led 'that'll be ignored as soon as my back's turned'. 'There are plenty of occasions I pass offenders by, like back there in the precinct, but when some-one is cycling on the pavement they're doing so out of force of habit, don't even know they're committing an offence, so I felt I had to tell him. This boy was certainly old enough to be on the road so with the crowded pave-ment I felt I had to say something, although many times I'd pass this by.'[50]

Here the constable warrants an intervention on an 'offence' which is continually committed and generally ignored. It is worth remark-ing the tone of voice he used both in this case and the incident in the precinct. The tone was that of the 'stern father', conveying authori-tativeness combined with concern. In dealing with Firkin we hear Rodney describing Firkin's action back to him ('". . . all I see is you kicking this man. Keep still"'), and defying its author not to see the action as unreasonable. A 'lesson' is being taught. Whether it regis-tered or not, Firkin leaves the scene. With the boy on the bike, Rodney details the reasons why cycling on the pavement is wrong, on the basis that the boy is habituated to doing so. The lesson is explicit, as is the contrast between himself and his 'colleagues' who are poised to arrest the boy.

While the potential is there for any constable to act in this way, senior officers were clear that the reliefs could learn much from homebeats.

Discretion and assessment of situations. The type of policing is so different. The reliefs need . . . to understand that they should be more than just a response unit, should be understanding and sympathetic to the problems and, indeed, cautious and assess the situation before stepping in. The

[50] *Ibid.*

permanent beats certainly do that. They have that feeling of things that are on their patch . . . The reliefs are inclined to see themselves as the television image tearing around in cars, leaping out, doing the job and then clearing off.[51]

A study which used rating scales to divide officers of a London division into 'law enforcement' and 'service provider' styles found that both groups decried not using discretion and not talking to the community. 'The law enforcement group believed that they did use discretion and talk to the community, whereas the service providers believed that the law enforcers did not.'[52] The study also found that community constables' orientations were evenly spread from law enforcement to service provision. It is the role and its means of accounting for its work, rather than innate qualities of those selected, which distinguishes community policing.

Community policing presents officers with a novel problem. The challenge is not only to re-think discretion, nor only to devise new working styles and interpersonal tactics. The role also demands that officers re-assess familiar means of interpreting organizational policies and working rules, the codes and practices by which law is made operational. This was apparent in the discussion where the community constables confronted the various means to deal with the man who stole the shrubbery. It would be wrong to claim that relief officers do not also discuss how to proceed, but equally wrong to say that similar constraints applied to decisions made by relief and community constables. The knowledge about the man which informed their debate can be noted in their discussion of summons versus arrest; for example, a course of action was supported by the idea that he was unlikely to flee. The constable's eventual course of action suggests he mainly wanted to teach the man a lesson, rather than send him to court. The community policing role may encourage officers to try new tactics or exercise forbearance because their knowledge of the locale prompts them to see it as 'a community' with distinctive norms to be respected and to perceive a network among local people which rapidly disseminates every consequential action of local police.

[51] Ch. Supt. Heath.   [52] Irving *et al.* (1986) at 112.

7
Policing a Hostile Community

The police role in the community seems fairly straightforward where the 'community' comprises a mainly contented and homogenous group with a degree of consensus which identifies a few 'undesirables' (ethnic minorities, the homeless and drunks, disaffected youth) as the rightful focus of police attention. Where communities are heterogeneous, with no dominant group, and cross-cutting divisions make for high diversity, the police role is more precarious.[1] In the inner city, community policing is concentrated in areas of multiple deprivation and having high concentrations of ethnic minority population. The first half of this chapter discusses the role of community police in major police operations, including serious disorder and major raids which occurred in the research sites. The second half of the chapter examines the role community police play in the maintenance of local public order, with particular reference to relations with ethnic minority youth. While less dramatic, this latter activity has a more extensive, if more subtle, influence on the quality of life in the city.

It is worth considering in detail how community policing proceeds under the circumstances that prevail in hostile communities. It is assumed that the organization is committed to providing service to the whole community, although it is acknowledged that a common response at organizational level is to withdraw, to respond reactively only, and then chiefly to major events. It is also acknowledged that in the worst current circumstances—the *barrios* of LA, in Harlem and the Bronx, and until recently, in parts of Belfast—there is no prospect of doing otherwise.[2] But Brixton is not Beirut, and those given the task of community policing in the inner city are not in complete despair.

The sharpest challenges to community policing come from divisions in the community and from groups seldom present in county

---

[1] Banton (1964) and (1974).   [2] Brewer (1991a).

forces. The superintendent at the second research site discussed the problems that inexperienced constables had in adjusting to his area. 'I ask them, "Now, you've come down from Norfolk or wherever" and they didn't deal with any coloured people. "There was none in our village, Sir". "I thought that. You're going to talk to a group, and it is the coloured youngster who is causing the hassle, he's the one that tends to respond . . . All of a sudden there's abuse coming and they'll walk away from you. What do you do? Do you calm them?" He's in a hell of a state. He's not used to this.'[3] The superintendent added that 'it happens of course with the young whites but they've not very often met the black yob and that's the one that tends to give them more difficulty. Because they are aware, of course, of the racism allegations that will follow anything they do to this man. They are aware that they have got to treat this man with kid gloves . . . It makes their job so difficult . . .'[4] The pervasiveness of the feeling that black people pose difficulty is shown by another senior officer's comment on a planning consultation regarding a new leisure park. 'Its not just pickpocketing, its mugging, its public order and, dare I say it, we're talking about the ethnic minority who, if ever there was going to be another riot it would be a leisure centre in central London. I had to put [this] diplomatically over to the organizers . . . and then put the same views in a more politically-inclined way to the Planning Authority.'[5]

Reference has already been made to the differentiation of sections of the community. It is not simply done to separate the sympathetic from the hostile. Keeping track of emerging rivalries is a key aspect of police information-gathering. The signs of conflict on which they rely are suggested by a sergeant's beatbook entry describing developments on a community constable's beat. 'A series of incidents on the S Estate point to some underlying problems and undercurrents. They range from burnt out motorcycles, stones thrown through windows with offensive and threatening notes wrapped around them, doormats set on fire, rubbish set on fire outside doors. Two of the warring factions are the "Bashers" (I.C.1's) and the "Touracos" (I.C.3's) and PC Bundy is closely monitoring the whole situation.'[6] 'I.C.1' is a police term for 'white' and 'I.C.3' for 'Afro-caribbean'; the code is used lest citizens overhearing an officer's personal radio are offended by the free use of racial group names.

---

[3] Supt. Vine.   [4] *Ibid.*   [5] Ch. Supt. Heath.   [6] BB 4.

Conflicts such as those indicated in the beatbook seem straight-forward. But once again, an awareness of motives and the means by which people seek to play the system helps officers to find a course through entrenched and subtle conflicts. Notice in the following beatbook record that the police are proceeding against the suspected racial harassment while aware that the heightened sensitivity to racial attacks could be abused.

A case of racial harassment has come to notice in relation to the Osorem family on the P Estate and has been the subject of correspondence between the Borough Housing Department and Chief Superintendent. PC Wilk has the matter in hand; the Council are seeking evidence against the main cul-prits but witnesses are reluctant to come forward. If some concrete evidence could be secured the offenders could be evicted. Having read the correspon-dence the case does not appear to be clear-cut and there are faults on both sides. The Osorem family may be using the harassment 'angle' as a lever to obtain a change of accommodation.[7]

The desire to maintain neutrality may be motivated by awareness that both parties have committed infractions while only one side has come to the police. A community police sergeant wrote in the beat-book, 'even as I was interviewing clients at the Surgery another car was set fire to in . . . Square. This has been preceded by many sim-ilar incidents. There seems to be some "Vendetta" element and I think that the victims have a shrewd suspicion as to the identity of the culprits but decline to say.'[8]

The principal site contained a number of housing estates with high proportions of black residents. Patrols were frequent but local contacts were few, so that a good deal of the information collected was from physical observation. Comments by the few who would talk to police enjoyed high salience. 'On the T Estate in the tower block laundry rooms, traces of drugs and glue sniffing have been in evidence. Members of the "Tough Posse" gang from the D Estate have been seen frequent-ing the T Estate. The counter hand of the Fish Bar on the estate says he has seen I.C.3 youths smoking reefers in the shop but declines to assist Police.'[9] From a beatbook entry several months earlier we find that the gang had engaged in direct provocation against police, so that the beatbook entries cumulate to a narrative with only one conclusion.

On [date] a PC from the Dog Section was patrolling the estate when several stones were aimed in his direction, narrowly missing him and his animal. He

---

[7] *Ibid.*   [8] *Ibid.*   [9] *Ibid.*

was under the impression that they must have been fired by a strong catapult. There were no witnesses to this incident and no suspects have come to light. If a stone was unfortunate enough to strike an officer serious injury or worse is a distinct possibility. It remains to be seen if this instrument is used again. On Saturday WPC Shale and PC Karnitsky were patrolling and heard verbal abuse directed at them on a first name basis. As the officers continued walking, an aerosol tin landed in front of them. It had been thrown from a great height. The only group of youths on the estate who know the officers' Christian names are the coloured youths collectively known as the 'Tough Posse'. A voice was heard to shout after the object landed 'you're fucking lucky this time'. The area was searched to try and trace these youths with a negative result. The aerosol can was retained and a fingermark submitted to C3. It is only a matter of time before some officer is seriously injured. This incident was fully reported.[10]

Of the second, older gang on the estate it was noted 'there has been an increase in "walk in" thefts involving older I.C.3s in the shops on the estate. Several of these I.C.3s walk in and ask the shopkeeper for a specific article. When they are shown its location, they pick it up and casually walk out of the shop without paying. From the description given to the officers, it is likely that this group are the "MG".'[11] Research notes increases both in such blatant styles of theft and shoplifting accompanied by verbal abuse and intimidation.[12] In that shops in the area were often run by 'Asians' the incidents involving young blacks testify to multiple divisions in the community. As a community police sergeant put it in a beatbook entry concerning the emergence of the 'MG' gang on an estate where there had previously been only one gang of black youths, 'my main concern is that now there are two identifiable groups on this estate . . . they may decide to rival each other and gain themselves kudos through notoriety.'[13]

One must consider how realistic a grasp of the other's perspective can be gained when contact is minimal or hostile. How sensible was it, for instance, to approach a youth club on a 'black' estate as an 'ideal' source of participants in an identity parade? 'There's no hassle about it and they get paid for it, but all I got back was "the police are now trying to stitch us up".'[14] The visit had been 'set up by the inspector . . . who knows the community youth leaders down there because he has quite regular contact there, monthly meetings, so I would have thought that he was a person they could trust'. The constable seemed to find it hard to appreciate the concern that people

[10] BB 2.   [11] Ibid.   [12] Hibberd (1990).   [13] BB 2.   [14] GD 1.

have about appearing in identity parades, or that the inspector's contacts were superficial and that 'community leaders' may themselves be remote from local people. Indeed the more aloof the local people are from police the more likely they will also be remote from these 'leaders'.

Another instance of a routinely difficult matter complicated by race was the involvement of bystanders when police were conducting on-street interventions.[15] Discussion revealed some attempt by community police to respond to the problem.

Some people had just been searched for drugs and there's several teenage mothers and simply because these other coloureds were getting searched they were ranting and raving because 'my son or my daughter is going to get a bad impression of the police because you are doing this all the time'. Not the fact that there's been a complaint [of drugs] to the police. We tried to explain that it wasn't the fact that these youths were getting searched that their kids were going to have a bad impression. It was because of the mothers' opinion.[16]

Another homebeat recognized the women in question. 'The two women he is talking about live on my beat. Her attitude when I first started working there was one of extreme hatred but she's quite mild towards me now. She speaks to me, her boyfriend speaks to me.'[17] He argued that the essence of the matter was doing something that did not come naturally to police, explaining what you were doing.

If you are stopping somebody they know its not just picking somebody off the street for the sake of it, and you can explain . . . Police officers feel quite objectionable [sic] towards displaying to people why they are doing things. Quite often an explanation can go a long way to allaying distrust and fear. There are a lot of young blacks who cause problems but that percentage is still very small. But there are quite a lot of young blacks, and perhaps justifiably so, who are very frightened of the police. I don't think the situation is helped when you've got young police officers who behave towards them as if they're shit. That's a very valid complaint.[18]

When the discussion moved on to why youths were ill-disposed towards police it took a conventional turn which left scope for their own mission but did not exaggerate the hostility. ' "You can have perfectly good relationships with all kids and different backgrounds but it seems once they reach senior school age something happens

---

[15] Southgate (1986).   [16] GD 1.   [17] *Ibid.*   [18] *Ibid.*

which puts them not against just police but against society in general. I don't think its just us." "Its authority." "At that age they get rebellious and don't do as their parents tell them."'[19] This is a familiar line of speculation, where resistance is construed as a 'stage they're going through'. What is significant is that the officers do not see the problem as a 'blacks versus police' one but rather as a particular stage of development which the youths were going through. This gives them something to work on, so that a role opens to them in trying to bring the youths through that stage to a better relation with the police.

But the 'difficult' stage was perhaps more typical of their relations with blacks.

At the moment it's very popular to be an unruly West Indian. Don't get me wrong. I'm not having a go at the West Indian community. You get white kids now using the West Indian drawl and all that rubbish, and you know as soon as you've spoken to them you're going to get trouble with them, because that is popular. It used to be the Teddy Boys at one point, before that it might have been the skinheads. At the moment its popular to be a stroppy West Indian youth whether you're black, white or whatever.'[20]

Like the point about 'being at a certain age', the attribution of resistance to a widespread attitude encourages officers to see it as temporary, merely a matter of fashion and style rather than of deep, politicized hostility. But this 'eternal recurrence' point was not enough justification for one, who continued ' "you've obviously got to balance that against other factors. There is immense unemployment amongst young West Indians, and extremely grotty housing conditions. They go to schools which give them a dead-end education." ' It is not merely that one is policing a 'hostile community'. Circumstances are more fine-grained; where there are few consensual values it is hard to anticipate on which issues and policies each group will grant or withhold approval of the police. Officers had to be alert to divisions and conflicts in all spheres of community life. Thus, a beatbook entry which warned that the local newspaper distributors were members of the SOGAT Union and had stopped handling Rupert Murdoch's newspapers, over which a local shut-out might arise, went on to detail that the homebeat had 'good rapport with the older employees (ex-National Service types like me!!), but received some stick from the younger skinheads';[21] the two groups

[19] GD 1.   [20] Ibid.   [21] BB 4.

kept their distance in the depot. The situation the community police face is volatile; yesterday's ally may desert police today, groups formerly opposed may coalesce on one issue, a trusted spokesperson may turn out to have no legitimacy, or lose it by contact with police. The circumstances are open to manipulation, mundane events are liable to be treated symbolically and all police action has high visibility. Long-term planning and initiatives may always be subverted by events.

Unlike strategic planning, whose long-term perspective often appears to defeat police, reaction to specific threats can be planned. A contagion model informs the exercise. Senior officers have to be involved because the spread of disorder does not respect divisional boundaries and requires intelligence of developments outside the station's jurisdiction. While local knowledge was relevant, response 'would also be based on developments in other areas. Now if you think in terms of public order situations and there is a mini-riot, shall we say in Tottenham or Brixton or anywhere which involves ethnics, it would become necessary to ensure that the deployment of men covered the points where you might have a similar problem.'[22] In reacting to civil unrest, this chief's first step reflected the emphasis he placed on community constables. The response would not immediately be in terms of Police Support Units but 'deploying the walking manpower to the beats, where those things were likely to occur, which would not necessarily be your high priority beats in terms of crime'.[23] The rather military terms of this response were misleading, though. The chief was very conscious of the need not to escalate by giving the riotous 'ethnics' something to respond to. One did not necessarily rush relief officers onto the estates. 'In [notorious local estate] your strangers from the relief . . . might cause more problems than not having men. You would direct your homebeats to the [estate] at the appropriate times, and maybe specialist officers.'[24]

But there were detractions to the gradual approach.

About the time of Scarman I was a superintendent, aware of the need being pushed out through the force for not causing confrontation situations and having this mob run from [fairground] to a point where we should have gone in and crushed. But, 'hold back, we're not going to create confrontation'. They then went on the rampage and smashed 33 shop windows. I forever since have regretted that I took that position. We finished up with riot damage, claims and everything.[25]

[22] Ch. Supt. Heath.   [23] *Ibid.*   [24] *Ibid.*   [25] Ch. Supt. Heath.

In fact the unpublished Association of Chief Police Offiers' 'Guide to Public Order Policing' (*Guardian*, 11 September, 1991) grants considerable discretion to the commanding officer on the spot. It warns police to expect criticism for going in too hard, too soon, and equally if the response is slow and disorder is allowed to escalate. When rioting broke out on Meadow Well estate, North Tyneside, neither the strength of community spirit nor Northumbria's tradition of community policing could check it. The chief constable admitted control had been lost but said it reflected a 'contain, not confront' policy which avoided injuries but ceded control of the estate to rioters for five hours (*Guardian*, 11 September, 1991). Some 200 youths aggrieved at the death of two local car thieves in a police chase lured officers into the area by setting fire to shops. ' "We fired the shops because we wanted to get the law on to the estate . . . so we could take out a grudge on them. Not just for Dale and Colin but for years of getting heavy with us" (*Guardian*, 11 September 1991).' Power and phone lines were cut, barricades built and scanners monitoring police radio were used. Rioters firebombed buildings while police gathered strength. ' "That was when people suddenly started getting this feeling: we can do anything. We had the run of the estate. It was a feeling of power." ' Even where co-ordinated community-building efforts have been made there is no evidence of their having any effect against disorder. In 1992 there were disturbances on a 'model' estate at Stockton-on-Tees. Community workers had overseen self-help initiatives backed by the council and police. A credit union to see off loan sharks had been set up, a local football team was thriving, and £1 million had been spent renovating houses and starting a warden scheme. There had been a particular effort to maintain traditional beat policing (*Guardian*, 16 June, 1992).

Clearly one must not overestimate the role accorded community police, either in decisions about whether to conduct operations in 'sensitive' areas or in the operation itself. The potential for major operations to provoke disorder in hostile communities requires senior officers to monitor reactions closely. Chief Superintendent Heath was discussing a drugs raid on a pub frequented by blacks. 'You had to be mindful of the sensitivity of the area, you had to have your evidence before you went in.' In such an operation 'there was a certain fear by the police that we'd have trouble' but the success of this operation encouraged others. Quality information was essential so there were no complaints.

They had been dealt with fairly, the evidence was there, no question of planting. On the deal being done, the observation officers inside would wait until that person left, a bleep was transmitted to an officer on binoculars with camera equipment. They relayed to the SPG units positioned away from the sensitive area. The description was given and the direction they were heading, and all the roads being blocked at a discreet distance. It worked beautifully. We had 33 arrests . . . Going in armed with that information and dealing with the licensee and his wife and the dealer in a very, very sensitive area, ethnic sensitive area, and no complaints at all.[26]

The operation, like others, took place against the awareness that such action could trigger disturbances. 'You were conscious that riots had occurred. Do you say "we'll let that place carry on dealing"? No, they're offending the law. Scarman wasn't saying you should not arrest people for that. You've got to weigh it up, the pros and cons . . . The critical thing is the quality of the information from the observation . . . We had fellows sitting there with bleepers from totally different areas of the Met. Not local, no way.'[27] Here was an exception to 'local knowledge'; it may supply the name of the pub and those involved but after that it was important to keep those who are identifiable at a discreet distance 'because of recognition dangers'. It is one of the ways in which the essence of community policing is betrayal. It is not just the police who betray; the popular community bobby who was exposed would also discover the limits of the delicate relations garnered on the street. Further, the decision to proceed did not rest on the interpretation of discretion; to the chief, the 'law was being offended'. The critical matter was whether, on their own terms, an effective operation could be mounted. There was little question of whether proceeding would alienate a dangerous section of the community.

A similar case reveals how the differentiation of the community is used to pursue desired police objectives. The superintendent at one of the research sites had led a major raid against an estate where residents were suspected of involvement in international drug smuggling. Relations with the local council were not close and consultative meetings were often conflictual. Nevertheless the raid shows how, even in a community whose representatives were distant from police, the role of community representatives can be important. The case also shows how the police managed community involvement of a very direct kind by playing on divisions in the community,

[26] *Ibid.*   [27] *Ibid.*

particularly inter-generational divisions. Knox Pool had been under observation for six weeks because 'I wanted to go back to source. Knox Pool is international. But because of financial restraints I was forced to raid on the evidence we had.'[28]

Having worked as a complaints inspector and conducted many 'single house drugs raids', the superintendent was keenly aware of the need to manage the problem of malicious complaints, put up to impede or overturn prosecutions. This is where the community representatives came in. 'I've often thought "if only we'd had somebody with us they'd have been a marvellous witness". The raid was on the Friday and on the Tuesday I telephoned Godfrey, the consultative group secretary and said "could you meet me in the police station at 6 o'clock Friday night to talk about a sensitive matter; don't ask me any more".'[29] The representatives agreed, and arrived at the appointed time.

I said 'I'm going to tell you something on 2 conditions: (1) you agree to be my prisoners, you don't leave my side and (2) you'll have a phone call to your families and that's it, otherwise I'm not going to risk. You're not going to risk this thing blowing, because we've got a lot of money invested, trucks lined up and the thing is "jacked up".' And they agreed. Once they had done that I told them everything. We then had a discussion on the merits of it. I told them what to expect.[30]

Mention of a discussion on the 'merits' of the raid suggests that the representatives were not supine, although by then it is difficult to think what they could have done to stop the police action if they had thought it ill-judged. As will emerge, other representatives could have been contacted to attend, and there was considerable negotiation about this. The point at which the representatives could have blocked the raid would have been prior to, not during it, and the superintendent had arranged their arrival for immediately before his officers went in.

We were down in the yard [the 2 representatives and himself] when X gave the go-ahead. Trucks came, lads in the back and sledge hammers and God knows what else. So you'd all the doors open, they're of steel, they're made to withstand police entry, literally. Even the inner flats are made to withstand police entry. Never seen anything like it. But once the truck came I said to Godfrey, 'you can do what you like, other than going into the premises' at that stage, because of the danger. In fact they had a totally free

28 Supt. Vine.   29 Ibid.   30 Ibid.

hand. I left them because I wanted to do other things. They saw the drains coming up and the blokes coming down and its been a great bonus to us.[31]

The representatives had been able to see enough of the operation to vouch for it having been properly conducted.

This proved to be of signal importance, because there was considerable criticism of the raid in the black community. 'Its been a tremendous bonus. It's taken a lot of flak. I've had some flak that has been easily answered by them. The [ethnic minority paper] did an outrageous article on the raid that has been answered by the chairman and the secretary of the Consultative Group, I am now convinced that if it hadn't been for those two I'd still be writing replies.'[32] Anticipating likely reaction in the Afro-caribbean community, the superintendent had effectively co-opted into the police effort two community representatives likely, as we will see, to be most credible to the older members of the black community. But it is not all a matter of clever, tactical manipulation. As the superintendent maintained, there was risk, particularly as his officers were conducting their raid in a hostile community which, even if uninvolved in drugs, would be quick to find fault with any deviation from correct procedures. One could not guarantee officers' behaviour in a large, exciting operation in a hostile area, and if there was a lapse he had put community representatives on hand to witness it.

It could have gone the other way. By God, you're taking a hundred police officers, there's always one who is going to possibly misbehave. It doesn't matter what control you've got on it, he over-reacts and gets hit or something. This is always a fear . . . Misbehaviour normally is attitude. This is the problem with many police officers. Very often they'll over-react, often verbally. I have more trouble in my complaints investigations from that than the main complaint. Nine out of ten [complainants] say 'if he'd just been a bit different'. So there was a gamble involved because we really did open ourselves up.[33]

As suggested above, a good deal hung by the choice of community representatives. The superintendent made the contact initially, and this appears to have been crucial because his offer to choose others if they wished was not taken up. By choosing the chair and secretary, two officers of the consultative group, he was likely to secure the involvement of 'responsible' individuals, although, to this officer,

---

[31] *Ibid.*   [32] *Ibid.*   [33] *Ibid.*

his fairness could be seen from his not having chosen 'right-wingers'. The involvement of the representatives

has given us a lot of credibility although, of course, within the consultative group, a certain faction are saying 'Oh, they're the wrong people to have gone.' But we sit back on that. I said 'I don't argue.' It seemed to me the secretary and chair are both socialists, lefties, but objective. One man is a teacher round here, a marvellous man. We couldn't ask any more, he was very objective in his reporting. Looking at that point, we didn't choose two right wing, I chose the secretary and chairman. They asked me 'What if we had a resident, a youth leader?' I said, 'Send who you like, provided they kept to my terms.' I'm not going to risk the job blowing for a phone call being made. 'Provided you kept to my terms, you could have sent anybody, it was just that you were the two we had direct contact with.' It was most successful.[34]

As I have noted, the police are well aware that their consultation and community contact is selective, that they can never embrace 'the full spectrum' of views, if only for the obvious reason that the full spectrum includes offenders. This example suggests that, in co-ordinating a major intervention with local representatives, police will prefer those with highest credibility in general society (the case made the national press), those closest to established credentials, knowing that the truly alienated—the young, street people—will be alienated within any community. Their constituency can be ignored, provided it can be bifurcated into, say, 'respectable' and 'disreputable' Afro-caribbeans, or 'youth club youths' and 'deviant youths'.

However, these fractions of a hostile community are not the only divisions police managers need to bear in mind. They also have to look to the sensibilities—'morale' was the superintendent's term—of their own ranks. First, the raid had been good because of the close involvement of senior officers, an emphasis we saw at the principal research site. The ranks 'don't expect you to go around picking up drugs and arresting people, they just want you to be interested. We're like children and any job's the same, isn't it, just to show some interest in what they're doing.'[35] However, the superintendent's innovation was less welcome.

While I know they were delighted that Knox Pool was done, because it had been tried before and abandoned, so our credibility went up, many of them decried the presence of the consultative group, because they don't know

[34] Supt. Vine.   [35] Ibid.

what the consultative group is, although I have actually said to [Police Federation] reps and inspectors 'will you please tell the men what the consultative group is'. But now I hear comments how great it was because they've seen the newspaper articles, they've suddenly realized there's good in this for us as well as a knocking shop.[36]

In other words, the flak-taking role of the consultative group had helped to convert those whose strong sense of police ownership[37] was offended by intruders.

At the close of the account the superintendent suggested that the elements I have been discussing—managing a new and major community involvement in hostile conditions, building across-ranks integration and heightening police awareness of 'positive' elements of community involvement—probably exceeded in value the direct gain from intervening against the drug scene. Such things had to be put in the balance because the operation had been very costly.

Quite honestly, successfully or otherwise was a plus, because we had made a move on something that we've been told for four years was too expensive, couldn't be done. That involved a decision on my part against my hierarchy, because I was asked [about] the Special Patrol Group, 'Can you afford them?' I said 'Yes, of course I can.' I couldn't. The cost of that was about £140,000. The easy way out would have been to have said 'We've only got X amount in the kitty, tell the lads what we'd love to do.' But somebody somewhere has got to say what your priority is. It's bad management, of course. To hell with the budget. To hell with the management. To hell with Area. This is sufficiently serious to go ahead and face the consequences afterwards.[38]

Again, a senior officer towards the end of his service, free of the need to ensure that no controversy endangered the next career move, had been able to experiment with an unusual interpretation of the community policing function.

The superintendent saw two particular problems in policing the inner city, both relating to social change. One was change in the attitude of the public, which was more critical and whose esteem was more explicitly central to performance assessment. The other concerned the organization's response to change, which was left confused after the Tottenham riot, in which police constable Blakelock died. He addressed these problems from the perspective of the ranks.

[36] *Ibid.*   [37] Holdaway (1983).   [38] Supt. Vine.

Many senior officers don't realize how difficult the street is now, and its bloody difficult. You have a public now much more important than they were when I was a PC. They're much braver and will take us on, and query, and attack. I didn't have that as a PC, my uniform was a definite protection. These lads nowadays don't have that and find themselves in tremendous difficulty. They also worry about backing from the force. They make much of Tottenham. They don't fully appreciate all the problems behind Tottenham. Our boys saw senior officers there who weren't trained; why need they be trained, this had never happened. Now we have a vast training programme for that. At the same time they're trying to keep the public quiet, the consultative group, Scarman etc. I don't think we know what to do with this situation. Whichever way senior officers went wouldn't be right.[39]

The Tottenham riot was a case of policies based on public consultation being misapplied and too long adhered to after disorder was manifest.

The poor old chief superintendent found himself in tremendous conflict. He had been brainwashed so much into public consultation that he took the 'softly softly' approach . . . They had this information beforehand, some evidence to react to. You really have got to react to it, you need a brave decision. The consultative group, the whole community know you're a policeman. I think it was sheer inexperience, the change in society . . . Tottenham was a disaster of leadership . . . The troops themselves, the sergeant or inspector, went away from their prearranged spot because of a call somewhere else and not knowing the overall position, and that made things worse . . . You're back to discipline, training.[40]

Thus, dealing with serious disorder not only needed accurate information but an adequate diagnosis of suitable tactics with no hostages to fortune in the shape of set policies, plus decisive leadership and strictly marshalled, closely-instructed action by the ranks. 'With my SPG (in a disturbance elsewhere), they never moved without first consulting me. That's why we were so effective . . . Tottenham, they didn't want any policeman to get injured. And you can't do it![41] The chief superintendent at the main site also stressed decisiveness but suggested that the potential of escalation called for caution and close supervision.

Take the X Estate where there is a history of confrontation, from nothings, absolute trivia, but if it's not handled correctly it can lead to bigger things. Your PC, all he can see is that somebody has committed a criminal offence and it is his job to deal with that. He would probably call for some assis-

[39] Supt. Vine.   [40] Ibid.   [41] Ibid.

tance . . . You need the inspector or sergeant to say 'get the man, take him out, we're not going to be soft, we've got a job to do'. But, as Scarman suggested, it should not be at the expense of public order. Do you hang about? No, you get that individual out and you get the policemen out and that's the end of the confrontation situation. The inspector has got to be that tight. Similarly he needs to be able to assess whether it would be right to go in strongly or send a reliable, steady PC who can do it a different way.[42]

Keeping the lid on a divided, hostile community took a calm, restrained and deliberate style.

Is he prone to panic, to bluster and go 'bull at the gate' to any situation? Or to evaluate, to assess . . . Some of the PCs see [it] as weakness . . . Because they . . . want to be able to get in and take out those troublemakers or criminals . . . But you've got to have that commonsense which says 'if we do that, what's the result going to be and how long are we going to have to live with that?' I'd rather see a sergeant or inspector assess a situation than the bloke who goes in, causes a bloody riot, and somebody has to deal with the aftermath.[43]

A feeling was general in the principal site that, should there be further rioting, it was very likely to occur in their area. It was a matter of proximity to major riot sites, ethnic composition on a number of grim and poorly-maintained council estates, and the uneasy relations between key ethnic groups in the area. The division had a record of serious public disorder. As the community policing inspector said, 'the elements that would contribute to a feeling of public disorder which we witnessed at Brixton are also in this area'.[44] However, like his community constables, he felt that 'because of the work of the homebeats, the intelligence we are picking up, we are able to monitor situations as they arise'. This was crucial because 'there was a lot of rumour and rumour can actually bring about public disorder'. The example he gave concerning a notorious local estate vividly conveys the trivial beginnings from which serious disorder can spring. This has been remarked before, classically in the published accounts of the events that 'triggered' the Brixton riots. What is especially notable in the present case, however, is the role that the community constables had played in averting disorder.

A publican near the D estate had a lot of scaffolders, who were erecting scaffolding on blocks of flats on the estate which is neighbouring D, commenting one lunch-time, 'We've had a visit from the Council. They've been told

[42] Ch. Supt. Heath.   [43] Ibid.   [44] Insp. Adams.

by the police there's going to be a riot here and we've got to clear up our sites and remove all the scaffolding poles and bricks and debris so that it can't be used by rioters.' What had actually occurred is that the Council were worried, we [police] were worried, and we were told to tell [scaffolders] to discreetly look round some of the sites, because, although at the moment there is no tension, if somebody were to engineer a situation of confrontation we really don't want that ammunition there. [We advised] if you are going to tell people to clear up a site, will you do it on the grounds that its dangerous because of the Health and Safety at Work Act, not because of a riot. So that went in to the Executive level of the Council. By the time it got down to the manager or whoever was actually doing the job it was 'move this stuff, there's going to be a riot'. In the space of about three hours that rumour went from the pub to the local people, the Neighbourhood Watch contacts, who were ringing up various people, their contacts for our division. One went to a homebeat officer, two came to me, another went to our District Information Officer, connected to the Youth and Community Section. All these rumours came together, and it looked as though a rumour heard by me was being confirmed by each of these other people.[45]

In this tale of Chinese whispers we have an initial concern of the police about what may happen in the event of a riot being converted into ostensible evidence that a riot was imminent. But instead of this chance transmission through tiers of council officers to workmen and so to publican and so to local informants and finally back to police, leading to a police riot in a new and farcical sense of the term, we have a community policing section able to stall the process short of disaster. The first step was to trace the course of the rumour, to ensure that it was not valid.

We went straight down the Estate, it was a Friday afternoon, a pay-day, and the workmen went home early because they'd been paid off at lunchtime and told to go by their boss, who had picked up the rumour, there's going to be a riot, and he said 'clear the site and get out, don't want you involved'. We started delving. I went to see my mate at the school, deputy headmaster, who is dealing with kids who would possibly be involved and from his enquiries it led back to the pub. We went back to see [the other informants] and it all came back to the pub. Went and saw the licensee [and] it came back to the scaffolders had been told to move because there was going to be a riot. It connected to somebody with the scaffolding company who said, 'Yes, somebody came round from the Council.' So we got that rumour and we're going to knock it on the head.[46]

[45] Insp. Adams.   [46] Ibid.

As we learn next, disaster was plausibly imminent because the community was 'jittery' and it would be a short step from the communication network already transmitting the rumour to contacts who might make the rumour a reality. The second step was to deflate the rumour by making public its status, using the widest possible network available through the community policing contacts.

We then put all the homebeats out on the estate and went round putting the rumour right, and people were breathing sighs of relief and the tension went and in about five hours cleared up. Had that tension been allowed to go on somebody would have made that rumour a reality because people were jittery and all you need is an instance where a bottle gets smashed, start ringing the police, the police have heard the rumours so they are going to react, so we are going to send a DSU instead of a local bobby in a panda or homebeat officers. Because that turns up, that reinforces people's ideas that there's going to be a confrontation and if they came across a group of lads who were hanging around doing nothing and there was a confrontation it all blows up, people getting nicked, bad publicity, people from other areas saying 'riot's going to happen at the D, let's get down there, let's go'. Now that is something which the homebeats here were able to do.[47]

The major drug raids we have examined provide only a limited early warning role for community police, providing basic information. Indeed, in these operations the community police are kept clear lest the very identifiability on which store is set in routine beatwork should give the game away. But where civil disorder is possible, community police contacts on the estate, and with those in regular contact with fractions of the community who may participate in disorder, come into play. While it is easy to criticize reliance on contacts with 'respectables', these may be adequate to calm those with whom police have no direct relations.

Local Public Order

We have been considering the contribution community policing can make to policing serious crime and public order incidents. Of course, community policing normally operates at a more mundane level. One of the community constables' working codes was pragmatism, which may be why they often derided the rigidity of 'policy'. This involved negotiating discretion by 'taking people as they come', starting from the 'people' and not the law. Police constable Dick

47 *Ibid.*

Dyer was assigned to the D Estate, the 'worst' cluster of tower blocks on the division. Touted as the likely scene of the next urban riot, it had a nearly all-black population and was the scene of numerous assaults on police and inter-gang combat.

An 'industrial area' is on Dick's beat, consisting of workshops under the arches of a railway viaduct given over to car repair premises. When he joined the beat he had gone into each workshop to introduce himself. He was met, at best, with a grunt. No one said hello and some looked right through him. Most of the people at work were Rastafarians. 'Now, unless they call for me I don't bother. I just walk through every now and then.' He suspected their involvement in the numbers of stolen cars regularly found abandoned in the area. As Dick walked past, the mechanics looked out with sullen glares, mouthing things to themselves or ostentatiously turning their backs on him. Rounding a corner Dick encountered an abandoned car. Its licence plates had disappeared, leading him to suspect they may be in use on a 'ringer'. The car had been stripped of many of its parts. This conveniently left the engine block and chassis numbers visible and Dick radio'd a check on them. The car was stolen.[48]

The officer could recognize a hopeless situation in which there were no grounds to attempt to cultivate any relationships. However, the same attitude was struck towards the 'yuppie' tenants of privatized council apartments and towards a local bank which had shunned the officer's attempts to make contact. A response would be made if called for, but there was no point in pursuing proactive work where contact was unwanted. On the estate, the officer sought to cultivate local youths, as early as possible, recognizing that having one or two contacts in a group of fifteen could be enough to tame conflict.

This perspective applied to an incident in which a youth worker had appealed for Dick's presence when several youths were 'sacked' from a job creation scheme in a youth and community centre. Dick had not been told they were being sacked, only that their pay was being docked for non-attendance. Dick and the youth worker had been verbally abused and a plate had been thrown at the latter; Dick spent time with her afterwards until her fright subsided. Calling at the centre the next day he almost immediately raised the situation.

He told her that 'to be quite honest I felt somewhat set up for that'. He was looking for an excuse for his presence that might mollify the youths when

[48] Fieldnotes.

he encountered them subsequently. 'I think I've lost credibility with them, and there wasn't much to start with.' He was going to tell them he was only there because she'd asked because of the short pay. She had thought it over and come up with an idea. 'That bloke [one of the researchers] that was with you, can't we say it was for him. You know, getting a look round.' 'Yeah . . . Yes. That's good. That's brilliant.' 'That way its completely not to do with you.' 'Yes, I like it. Thanks. We'll do that then. I'll put it round when I see them.' She said that she had been very anxious indeed. 'What did your boyfriend say?' 'He told me I shouldn't go in to work. He didn't want me to come. But—I don't know—I didn't like it but I just had to. But I thought I was going to get a smacking.' 'Yeah, I felt a bit nervous myself. But you know it was all just verbals. Calling us names and that, well, its not nice but that's all it was.' 'Yeah, but for a few minutes there . . .' 'Yeah, I know. Have any been in today?' 'Yeah, a couple of them and its been the same—calling us names.' She had seen some of the boys who had said hostile things but it hadn't gone any further. One of them had even been fairly friendly. She was somewhat relieved but wanted to see what happened next. She thought it was important to take the initiative again after a day to cool off, and her co-worker suggested they press ahead with a football match. 'Some of them are even asking for cricket but football's hard enough to get together!' She asked what had become of the arrangements 'your lot' offered to make for football and Dick reminded her that last time no one had shown up, which put him out, having got a team together and booked a field. 'Well, Gary [co-worker] is after you now.' 'That's fine. I'm pleased to support it. I don't mind if I can play football on the job's time' he quipped, taking his leave.[49]

The officer was clearly prepared to offer the youths a further chance and to make efforts on their behalf, despite the events of the day before and the failure of the last football match.

His efforts were concentrated on this age group because their elders were inaccessible. The local scene included two major youth gangs, whose older members derived from a multi-racial gang, 'Rampage', which had been dominant until five years before. 'The Tough are all·black with one or two exceptions.' They were fifteen to eighteen, involved in streetcrime, and it was from them that verbal abuse and any conflict with police on the street came. Members graduated to the MGs who were in their twenties, all black, and involved in 'the more lucrative kinds of crime—burglaries, handling and drug-dealing'.[50]

They gave police no trouble, being aloof and scrupulously well-behaved on the street.

[49] *Ibid.*   [50] Fieldnotes.

Burglary, 'mugging' and autocrime in the prosperous areas adjoining the estate had increased. This beatbook entry shows police beginning to surmise as to the culprits.

PC Masters reports to me that there has been a gradual rise in I.C.3 suspects taking part in 'theft person' offences, which has contributed a rise in major crime this month. Such offences have been occurring on the . . . Estate, where previously there have been no such offences. Bearing in mind that there is a bridge in . . . Road, leading into the D Estate, it is a reasonable assumption that the offences may come from the D Estate or . . . Road area. This is further supported by recent friction reported to me by PC Ayre [District Dog Handler], between groups of coloured youths on the D Estate and groups of white youths in the area of . . . Road. Could the two be connected?[51]

The prospect that resistance to the egress of black youths from the estate by groups of white youths could provoke racial confrontations posed particular concern. The beatbook logs dates and places where the groups of white youths appeared. It does likewise with groups of black youths, e.g., 'a group of approximately 20 I.C.3 youths sitting on the wall by the bus stop at this location' and 'upon PC Gann walking past there has been deliberate eye contact but no verbal abuse. When PC Gann is approximately 50 yards away, verbal abuse is forthcoming.' A sense of events moving steadily toward disorder is conveyed: 'although this situation may appear vague and non-specific, several officers have mentioned an increase in potential confrontations with several groups'.[52]

As traditional white working class housing opened to ethnic minority occupants by tenancies falling vacant on death, others became involved in tension with the groups of youths.

PC Gann informs [sergeant] that the majority in this block are old established residents. Recently a coloured family have moved in. Other residents started complaining to this family about the loud playing of music. The daughter has retaliated by continuing the music and bringing home a large group of young men to wait outside the block, presumably to intimidate the white residents. This has resulted in minor disturbances (plant pots being broken, etc.). There is now a general feeling that residents will take matters into their own hands. This situation is potentially volatile.[53]

The overt hostility of the 'Posse' and serious criminal character of the 'MGs' put them out of the community constables' reach, height-

[51] BB 2.   [52] BB 5.   [53] BB 4.

ening the importance of any slender and strained contacts they managed to establish. Despite the plausibility of Dick's feeling like the
victim of the 'workshop incident', he had to restore the credibility
which had been impugned by his siding with the centre against the
sacked youths. We have already seen that he looked for ways of
denying agency in the incident. On one of his returns to the estate
the following day he spotted two black youths by a tree, one seated,
the other leaning on the tree. The sitter [Paul] looked about sixteen
and the other somewhat younger.

'How are you Paul?' He made a restrained but not hostile reply. 'Now look,
I just want to explain what I was doing there yesterday. Because that was a
problem, wasn't it?' The boy grunted. 'I expect some people are feeling
pretty resentful about what happened. What happened was this. You know
that some people haven't been showing up for the work?' Paul demurred
from confirming this and traded a remark with the other youth. 'Well, you
know that it's been happening, don't you? And you know that they've been
getting short pay as a result.' Paul suggested that just because they were late
a few times didn't justify firing them, in a pained tone of voice. 'Look, I
know that it looked like a set-up but I want you to know that I wasn't told
they'd been sacked; I was called in because of the short pay. I'd been told
there might be some problems because of that. She thought there might be
some aggro. You know what women are. They do get frightened. They're
not like us, not like us big strong men are they, Paul?' Paul smiled weakly
at this. 'Yeah, alright man.' Dick continued that that was why he came and
he was as surprised as they were to find that they'd been sacked. 'You don't
have to believe me but that is the story. That is why police were there. I
wanted you to know that that was the situation.' Paul looked balefully up
at Dick, who said 'I'll see you around' and departed.

Out of earshot he remarked 'You'd never believe it but that's my best contact among the youth on this estate. Its funny how it came about.' Paul's
brother was a well-known drug-dealer and burglar and Paul himself was
involved in an assault on a PC on the estate. When Dick entered Paul's block
once, Paul nearly ran into him coming down the stairs. Dick remembered
his name and asked where he was going. Paul was amazed Dick knew him
and they struck up a conversation. Dick had played on this to build up a
contact. At first when Paul was with other blacks he was embarrassed by
Dick greeting him but latterly the other youths had grudgingly started to
reply.[54]

Dick had carefully made himself accountable to Paul, a youth with
whom relief officers were unlikely to have other than adversarial

[54] Fieldnotes.

contact. He had done so with a view to Paul relaying Dick's account back to his 'constituency', the others associated with the workshop. In the extract it can be noted that Paul is sufficiently sure of his position with Dick to tackle the centre's policy, confirming the existence of a basic reciprocal relationship. Significantly, Dick does not directly defend the centre's policy which Paul has criticized, but seeks to emphasize his part as 'honest broker'. He also gives Paul the real reason for his presence, rather than the justification worked out by the youth worker. The recourse to a 'males together' closing comment transparently seeks to affirm a bond between officer and youth.

The contrast between relief and community policing is sharp in this example, where a white constable seeks to justify to a young black male his interceding in a violent assault by several black male youths on a white female. It is also worth noting that Dick explicitly acknowledges the tenuous basis of the relationship, initiated purely because of Dick's memory for names. Dick's willingness to justify his actions to the youth is easily construed as betraying weakness, a construction many relief officers readily put on community policing. But Dick is acting tactically, pursuing longer-range motives which lend an instrumental, even devious, quality to his attempted relationship-building. Without a knowledge of the history of his relations with this youth one sees only a constable apparently ingratiating himself with a known delinquent. Forbearance is plainly an important technique if one accepts the community constable's reasoning that it is only through a developed relationship that crime-relevant information can be gained.

It has already been noted that police on the estate had to negotiate the ambivalence of the youth and community workers, the overt hostility of black youths and the growing confrontation of white youths with blacks, against a backdrop of sharply rising street and residential crime. As early as a year before, the beatbook revealed their containment tactics were part of an orchestrated strategy, which hinged on the collection and collation of crime-relevant information. The preamble to the key entry is a brief account of an incident revealing a simple but compelling source of leverage possessed by the community constables, who had a vital role in the strategy. Their essential role was to 'keep the lid on' until sufficiently incriminating information was in hand, and the account shows 'local knowledge' in a new light.

'At the last Police/Workers meeting, certain members of this

"Tough Posse" group actually were waiting outside as police entered the Community Centre, and directed verbal abuse at them. This group is reluctant to do more than direct verbal abuse at officers, because the officers can identify them by name.'[55] From this, the entry details recent instances of abuse, including obscenities directed by name against specific officers, before commending restraint in the use of resource charges so as not to enhance the prestige of those youths involved in confrontations.

It should be noted that such verbal abuse is only forthcoming when this group outnumbers the police present. Arrests may be effected, but at the risk of officers being assaulted or the incident escalating. As soon as assistance has been requested, the youths quickly disappear into the estate. An amount of verbal abuse in the course of everyday duty . . . is to be expected. If we are to maintain 'credibility' on this estate, this group of petty-minded youths must be dealt with *effectively*. Offences of threatening behaviour and breach of the peace are short-term and non-effective remedies which may only give prestige and acclaim to those arrested.[56]

This is certainly unconventional thinking, at least as regards customary responses by relief officers to provocation. However, such tactics make sense as part of the strategy then described.

I have been informed of the way it is proposed to deal with this problem, in particular the D Occurrance Book and Incident Report writing and the aid proposed from C3, with an eventual view to arrest for the more serious public order offences. Such a remedy takes time, both to accumulate evidence and for any public order offence triable by indictment to come to court. Any trial will be contested, with the political campaign supporting the defendants, Ms Mary Knoll [community worker] being a member.[57]

Thus, community police were being used to befriend the younger, unaligned blacks, 'cool out' the gangs, and collect information as evidence by compiling detailed incident records focused on the estate and conveying forensic material for analysis. The entry closes with the statement that 'with the summer approaching—hot days, longer days and more youths on the street, confrontation in this estate is a distinct possibility. We must ensure that we have a good intelligence system and the necessary resources to deal with any possible situation effectively.'

It becomes less tenable to maintain a bipolar view associating relief policing with crime control and community policing with social

[55] BB 5.   [56] Ibid.   [57] Ibid.

service. Indeed, the reliefs are marginal to this strategy of ensnaring the members of the black youth gangs in serious public order charges, while the community police are central. It is worth noting that the effort to play to the sympathies of the older black residents also focused on community police efforts, notably contacts made in regular patrol by homebeats, the police surgery on the estate and efforts to start neighbourhood watch.

Forbearance, then, is something which can be indulged with a view to a longer term strategy which preserves law enforcement values. It is also valuable in situations where police are threatened and outnumbered. Officers in such circumstances have to directly confront the dilemma of the crime control versus befriending, social service approach. In this station the view was that, while befriending was a valuable device, officers should remember that citizens have expectations of police which ultimately revolve around law enforcement. The doctrine presented community police with sharp dilemmas, as they usually patrolled on foot and alone, and in areas where they were sometimes the only white face.

To examine their tactics in such cases we should note the background to the next incident, given by a beatbook entry. 'One continuing problem is the meeting of black males (mainly Rastafarians) in the area around . . . Close. In August, arrests were made of the occupants of a van involved in the sale of drugs. This practice has grown recently and PC Todd has been told the van will sell "whatever they require". The Crime Squad have been fully informed concerning the increasingly blatant sale of drugs (predominantly cannabis) in this area.'[58] In the period of eight months between this entry and the fieldwork the van had been busted, but many still congregated in the area. The fieldnote describes an incident arising from obstruction of the pavement and enables examination of the officer's negotiating and proxemic tactics. These are used in pursuance of his conviction that, no matter how much tact one uses, citizens expect police to act in role.

Trevor walked towards the rear of [railway station]. On the edge of the W Estate, between the back of a parade of shops and the Church of the Nazarene, he encountered a group of blacks and their cars parked on a wide area of pavement by entrances to the Rich site. There were four cars parked on the pavement, eight Afro-caribbean men in their twenties, three Afro-

[58] BB 2.

caribbean women and several young children and babies. The women were stood in a close group by an 1100 [car] in which were two of the children. Next to it was parked a grey Cortina, behind it a new Vauxhall. At the road-side was a Capri with three of the men working on its bodywork. Another pair stood by the Cortina and the rest sat in or stood beside the Vauxhall.

As Trevor walked up he remarked 'We can't have this; they're blocking the pavement' and his arrival was greeted by alert stares from the men and more surreptitious looks from the women. Throughout the following exchange the women remained in their cluster and, apart from getting the children out of the 1100, played no part in the incident. 'Hello, lads. You know I'm going to ask you to move these cars. You're blocking the pave-ment. What're you all doing here, anyway?' A man with close-cropped hair, wearing a designer vest and gold jewellery, approached Trevor from the Vauxhall. Trevor paused between the 1100 and Cortina. A Rasta with bon-net and sunglasses approached Trevor from the Capri over the road. A Rasta with waistcoat approached Trevor from the Vauxhall [hereafter 'Vest', 'Shades' and 'Coat'].

Vest squared off to Trevor. Shades was by his side. Coat stood behind Trevor. The others moved in about ten feet from this group but waited and watched. I stood behind Coat. In a plain, neutral tone Trevor again asked 'Why do you want to put the cars up on the pavement?' 'Why you harass-ing us, man?' demanded Vest. 'I'm asking you to move the cars off the pave-ment, that's all. Why are they up here?' While Vest looked the most hostile he was also the most prepared to parley. Coat, Shades and the rest were silent.

'We're selling a car, man' said Vest by way of explanation. 'That's no rea-son to park up on the pavement. There's a car park over the road. Why can't you park in there? You still have your meeting or whatever it is here.' Trevor used a slightly pained tone, as if to say this is just a silly, minor nuisance. 'There ain't no spaces man.' Shades spoke: 'You just harassing me, man. You keep 'em moving on. Why you want a move me?' Trevor repeated, 'Come on, lads. I'm asking you to move the cars.' While the tone was not proactive, it was an order, not a request. There was no direct verbal response to this. Instead, Vest, Shades and Coat circled round Trevor and he simply looked back at them, without blinking or averting his gaze. While Vest's features were animated by the angry dialogue he had already had with Trevor, Shades and Coat kept their most severe look on.

Their attempt to spook him now took another turn. Shades and Coat were very close to Trevor, Vest about two feet away. Vest now pointed at me. 'Who's him? You police? Hey, man, is he police too?' he demanded of Trevor. Coat was next to me. I said I was not police but was with the officer today. I looked at Coat and he turned his gaze to Vest. Vest said 'You have no right. You can't just come up here and tell us to move our cars.' 'I just did', Trevor stated, in a tone like 'whatever will they come up with next'.

Throughout this stage of the incident Trevor made no attempt to compromise his request and little attempt to explain it. He stated what he wanted, did not deviate from it and ignored all attempts to draw him out.

Trevor turned very slowly to face Vest's car, whose position meant it would have to be moved first. His movement caused Vest and Shade to step back and turn half round off the track of their previous movements. The circling behaviour stopped. The officer wasn't moving and this appeared to confirm that the initiative was his. Consequently, Vest's movements became quicker, more agitated. Scowling and muttering, he broke the confrontation and hussled back to the Vauxhall. Two of those from the group of onlooking males got in the car, loudly slamming the doors. Vest started the engine and drove it fast off the pavement. Coat got in the Cortina and moved it. No one moved the 1100.

A space was easily found for the Cortina. The women returned to their group, clustered round a tree with the children. The onlookers returned to the Capri at the roadside. Vest had not parked but kept the Vauxhall running as he watched Shades approach Trevor. Shades got very close and Vest and Coat came up to Trevor again. Vest and Coat stood behind Trevor while Shades argued with him. His patois was thick but Trevor picked up enough to respond to. He said it was a reasonable request, that other people might like to use the space but were put off by the cars and that there was not going to be any further action once the cars were moved. 'Why do you get so uptight when I ask you to do something? There's nothing to it. No one's ticketing anyone. There's no problems. You get annoyed at me before I even ask you to do something.'

Shades and the others had noticed another vehicle on the pavement. It was a flooring contractor's van, parked well out of the way near the building site but undeniably on the pavement. Trevor muttered 'I suppose I'll have to do him now.' With several others calling out about the van, Shades acted as spokesman, asking Trevor what he proposed to do about the van. Trevor walked up to the van. Vest got back in the Cortina. Trevor ostentatiously wrote the van's index number in his notepad. Shades walked up. 'You got to move that van, man. If we were white like him be, you would have left us. You take him number.' In an exasperated tone, Trevor replied 'I'm *going* to move it, what do you think I'm doing!' Shades, more diffidently, repeated that he better move the van and went to the 1100. The Vauxhall was reversed swiftly back to where Trevor was finishing his note but there was no more dialogue with Vest.

Trevor approached four whites having a break from the site. As he did so a Rasta at the wheel of a red Mercedes drove past, turned round and drove back towards the group Trevor had encountered. Trevor asked one of the men if he knew where the flooring contractor was working. This man took Trevor to the site entrance and pointed out the foreman who should know. The foreman didn't know where the contractor was but a lad helping him thought he did—the 16th floor of a tower block. Trevor decided a long search to give the contractor the unwelcome news that his van had to be moved was more than proving his fairness to the Rastas was worth. He asked the lad to tell the contractor if he saw him to move the van, and left. As he did so the workmen said he'd chosen the right guy for directions as he had a beautiful body and Trevor quipped 'I'll be back with a fiver in half an hour then' and all had a laugh.

As he walked past the group the red Mercedes was parking. It was a legal space but its position was such that it might be clipped by contractors' lorries using the site. Trevor said to the driver that it might not be safe to park there. The Rasta jumped out and demanded to know why Trevor was hassling him about parking. 'What you hassling me for, I haven't done anything wrong.' 'No, no. You're getting it wrong. You accuse me that I'm hassling you before we've even spoken. I was telling you for your own good that it might be clipped by vehicles from the building site and you might want to move it . . . Just keep an eye on the car.' The Rasta lifted his shades and said 'That's all right, man'.

By now Shades was standing with the Mercedes Rasta and Vest had reversed back into earshot and gotten out of the car to take part. Vest and Shades reiterated their objection to being moved but Trevor maintained the line. 'Why do you get upset before I've even spoken to you? You know I was bound to ask you because we've had this problem before. Its not as if its a big deal. Why don't you just park the cars over there and have your meeting. No problems. Why do you have to get uptight before we've even discussed it?' Shades lifted his sunglasses, looked into Trevor's eyes and said 'Well, right then'. It signalled the close. Vest got in the Vauxhall and gunned off the scene. Shades went back to rubbing the Capri's bodywork and the Mercedes Rasta went with him.

Out of earshot, Trevor remarked that the Mercedes looked in awfully good condition for its age. He had noted the index number, suspecting it had its plates changed. He radio'd for autocrime squad but they could not be raised. He also wanted to advise them that dealing may have been resumed there. Trevor remarked that, presented by a group of blacks on the pavement, most officers would turn a blind eye and hurry past. But they knew who he was and his point of view and he was not about to just walk past. He would not avoid his duties because he was a beat officer.[59]

Minor though the incident was, it is the sort in which insensitive action can easily escalate into physical confrontation. There is danger when a crowd takes sides; it is a common 'trigger' to public disorder. Yet audience members can be used to explain what police want, and conciliation may be more acceptable if done other than by

[59] Fieldnotes.

police.[60] In light of this it is worth noting that Trevor achieved his objectives: the cars were moved, he was not compelled to follow through the *quid pro quo* of moving the contractor's van, and he had the opportunity to chastise the Afro-caribbean men for their attitude. Yet he achieved these things with minimal cost to himself, and without calling back-up, a measure that at the early stage of the confrontation could have seemed a necessary option to a relief officer.

Trevor felt he was able to be firm with the group because he recognized them, and knew that the spot had been used for drug-dealing and that the men would have an interest in compliance due to the suspicion that subsequently fell on congregations of black people there. From the first he had ensured that residents knew he would not compromise his 'duties' as a policeman simply because he was a beat officer. But the account of the incident suggests the influence of events on a much shorter time scale. Trevor had begun the contact with a command, albeit a civil one, instead of 'turning a blind eye and hurrying past'. In the verbal confrontation that followed he maintained his position without deviation. He used plain language (rather than 'legalese') and a tone of voice that conveyed a sense that the obstruction was so easily solved that it simply was not worth making a fuss. When the talking ceased and the men circled Trevor and the observer he literally stood his ground and by the deliberate placing of his body made it impossible for them to further impinge on his personal space without assaulting him. His slow move to face the car not only meant the circling had to stop but visibly reinforced the request he was making, as the car was the one that would have to be moved first.

The incident indicates that, at the most tangible level, community constables are not confined to a repertoire of forbearance and passive information-gathering. They also use firm tactics involving personal resolve and fortitude. In this case it was done in such a way that the matter could simply be classified as the routine maintenance of civil order. A more pugnacious response could well have seen several arrests, gaining an enhanced activity record but at the expense of court time, police time spent at court, and sections of local public opinion.

Community constables felt that they had special advantages in calming down and moving on youths on the street. 'As far as the lads

---

[60] Field and Southgate (1982).

on relief are concerned, its just another group of blacks roaming round . . . You get all this spitting, etc., but as soon as you pick one out, if you actually got to saying "Hello Des, how's things tonight" and he's with a group . . .'[61] The point lay in the power of the 'name'; community constables were able to identify 'their' people, and thus 'they lay off because you know them. As soon as you know them and have any conversation, they are identified and have to come into order because they are not just anonymous and drifting around.'[62] Most important, however, was the constables' recognition that their greater local knowledge helped them to control their own reactions in close contact with large groups of hostile people.

When you go into a group like that, you have got to keep hold of your own feelings as well. When I first went up to a group of ten coloured youths, the adrenalin was going and you're watching for the old knife that might come out, and you tend to go in a lot harder than you should do. If you go in very, very low key, you can walk through them and have a chat with them. If they don't want to hang around they'll go, otherwise they might have a chat with you. Some [officers] almost psych themselves up when they go in.[63]

The terms of reaction to this suggest that the low-key tactic does not diminish the constables' 'crime-mindedness'. They were asked what motivated them to intervene in large, hostile groups. 'It's my beat and my area and I want my area to be good . . . Now if they are causing trouble then I have to stop the trouble because it reflects on me . . . You feel like "I'm going to keep this lot under control because I don't want all the hassle of reporting crimes right, left and centre. That is my motivation for going in there and just having a word with them.' Another added, 'You can't gain respect by walking away.' As Muir demonstrated,[64] the role is one of building, and managing, one's reputation.

Any befriending element in the role appears to be instrumental, a practical tactic. Nor were these constables a skim of the most liberal and racially-enlightened. When one suggested that it was not hard to find common ground with young blacks he was forcefully challenged, leading to a forthright expression of how difficult at least one other constable found it.

'We've all been teenagers. The biggest difference between us is the colour but at the end of the day their feelings can't be that different. They're not

[61] GD 1.   [62] Ibid.   [63] Ibid.   [64] Muir (1977).

aliens, they're not from somewhere else, they still live in [X].' 'That's naive, actually. I mean you're totally different. You're an owner-occupier, you're earning maybe £20,000 a year and, as a teenager, you were never living in central London nor were you ever walking around in, let's face it, gangs of criminals a lot of the time. You might like to call them the same, a few you can talk about, but a lot of these groups of lads, there is a culture of crime there and you can't get away from that and to suggest that we're all of that same culture is absolute rubbish.'[65]

As the constable who emphasized similarity protested that he did not mean we were 'all of the same culture' the critic confessed 'I think they're totally removed from when I was young and I think it is bloody hard work getting to talk to them'.[66] However, he did have a way of confronting the problem. 'If you go in on a nice relaxed level you can put any situation right.' A sense of humour helped a lot. Another agreed but 'sometimes it hasn't even got to be humour. Even in a group you can find someone who's got a peculiar hat or something, "Oh, that's a great hat", you know. Even if its not particularly funny, they're taken off-guard and it just defuses. Or at least gets them in some sort of conversation with you.' There was mileage in getting petty offenders to see the consequences of their actions from the perspective of the other. 'You've got to say "Look, there's a couple in there and you're sitting on their wall. How would you like it if they sat on your wall?" Obviously if that approach doesn't work you've got to use other means. If that means arresting them you've got to do it. You can't be seen to back down in the end because they'll just do it again and again.'[67] Patience was essential because the ritual element in the abrasion of youths against police meant the same 'lesson' had to be endlessly repeated. 'It's a power struggle, that's what I found. You'll slay it one night and then they'll come back another night and this will just go on and on.'

The relevance of a firm approach to community policing is that the public have certain expectations of the police, just as they associate other public agencies with characteristic actions. Whatever the legal weight given to the argument that law enforcement is essentially a vehicle for the overweening goal of securing public tranquillity, most police and, arguably, most citizens, associate the agency with law enforcement and crime control. People turn to the police because they want help with such matters rather than because they want counselling or befriending. Consequently, people expect the

[65] GD 1.   [66] GD 1.   [67] GD 2.

police to perform certain duties. The 'in' that police have with 'respectable' inner city residents soon evaporates if police interventions prove ineffective. The words 'inner city' appear in the previous sentence because residents in such areas are likely to be subject to intimidation by neighbours who do not align with the police. In poor areas, the 'rough' and the 'respectable' are immediate neighbours, and the consequences of a failed attempt to control crime can be enough to stifle further co-operation. This beatbook entry describes a juvenile reported by a neighbour who had watched him systematically remove the beading surrounding the glass above a fire escape, presumably to provide a means of exit from a block he was subsequently seen breaking into.

The local community are becoming aware of Doug Brock's reputation as the local regular burglar, and it is apparent after talking to the informant with reference to [the breaking of the window] that people may adopt a retributive method in dealing with him, rather than refer their observations to us. He is a serious threat to our getting people on the estate to come forward and give us information, and the ability for police to deal with it promptly and efficiently to gain the public's confidence.[68]

The informant was later severely beaten by an associate of the suspected burglar, who was acquitted of the burglary attempt the informant reported. With public confidence having such significance the investment of time which community constables can make may be more important than the direct return from their interventions.

In the following case a community constable takes considerable pains over an unpromising theft of tools from a house undergoing renovation by an all-black team of builders; he also spends some time discussing the morals of builders with the man in charge.

About £2,000 worth of builders tools have been taken. Six working on site, in charge is Jeff Queen. Initial contact was with three men working in the hallway. They were sarcastic and their manner could have been construed as offensive. 'Man in a blue suit to see you, Jeff.' 'You better talk to the boss cause I don't like to talk to the police' (laughter), 'you here to arrest us, man?' 'Yes, I'm here to arrest you for the theft of your own tools!', Andrew joked back. Before it could be misconstrued he added, 'No, no, I'm only joking. I'm here to see your governor about this.' Queen emerged and took us to the cellar where the tools had been in a strongbox.

There was no headroom and Andrew and Queen squatted by the box as he got the basic details into his notebook. Some tools had initials on them but no serial numbers were kept. Andrew pointed out this was a serious drawback. Eventually, Andrew said it was a bit cramped and they went to the front room. Queen had brochures for the missing equipment from which he laboriously gave Andrew model numbers. Andrew said there was a second hand tool shop nearby and Queen could go there and see if he recognized anything. Queen volunteered that they'd also dealt with some shops over the road and he could ask there too. Andrew agreed. When Queen got beyond the information in the brochures, Andrew said he should get his list together and ring it in. He gave Queen his card, with the case number 'for the insurance' and his telephone number . . . Queen seemed pleased with the card, and asked Andrew if he wanted to see the back route out. Andrew said he thought they would have taken things out via the front as that's how they came in, but agreed to have a look. Andrew asked Queen if he'd sacked anyone or if anyone had quit. 'I don't have any grudges against me. We have asked some people not to work here again. But I don't think that's it.' Andrew didn't pursue this.

In the backyard, Andrew repeated that he didn't think they would have bothered spiriting things away over the back fence, which adjoined a railway line. The rest of the conversation was non-specific to the theft; Andrew referred to it as 'philosophizing'. Queen felt people's morals had changed. A few years ago, though people were always coming round sites with stolen goods to sell, it was a matter of pride to refuse. Now it was different. Andrew asked again if his insurance was all right but it was not this so much as 'the way things were going' that bothered Queen. Andrew established it would be several weeks before Queen could secure the front door properly. Queen said this time he would keep a list of the serial numbers. Also that he would make some enquiries, and Andrew said he would now do so himself. On leaving, Andrew gave one of the men directions to the second hand tool shop and called on several neighbours but none had seen anything.[69]

At the point of contact Andrew had to negotiate entry with several men whose sarcasm thinly covered the edginess in their attitude to him; he joked mildly and did not rise to their mocking expression of stereotyped 'hostile' attitudes. When it emerged that there were no serial numbers and that even the model numbers would have to come from catalogues, his handling of the call began to diverge from expectations based on the approach of relief officers. He patiently waited as Queen laboriously searched for model numbers, and helped him to comb through the catalogues. He further advised that

[69] Fieldnotes.

Queen could ring details through later, and took care Queen had full details on how to find him, even detailing his location in case Queen wanted to see him rather than telephone.

A further sign of Andrew's thoroughness was his agreement to look outside, although he thought it unlikely to yield clues. It may be that Queen made the suggestion because he wanted to chat to the constable. If so, Andrew readily participated in his 'philosophizing'. He checked the insurance position more than once and made sure Queen knew the procedure. Finally, he engaged in local enquiries, despite the burglary being 'stale'. Relief officers did this only when a burglary had just been discovered. In all, Andrew spent nearly an hour on the burglary report, conducting it in such a way that there would be more involvement required of him subsequently. Because of the emphasis on crime-relevant activities among the community constables, the most distinctive characteristics of their practice, relative to relief policing, lie in information exchange, tactical planning and the investment of time in investigations. But their efforts in respect of information exchange and tactical planning rely on the co-operation of other functions, whereas the investment of time may yield benefits in improved public relations regardless of its outcome.

Community contact can support strategic decision-making, by affording a clear idea of the reaction of different groups in the locale, as in a case in the second site where a superintendent attended community meetings which helped him establish that the majority would support police intervention against disorder on a housing estate. To further illustrate the differentiation of the community and exploitation of its divisions, the case may be taken of a young black man requesting advice after an attempted burglary of his flat. A female community constable was asked to call.

James had been to visit his mother and returned at 1.30 yesterday morning. On arrival, a 'half-caste' and a black youth were kicking his door in. Two other black youths stood watch. He gave chase but they ran off in the direction of the flat of a man he named as 'Sonny' and he lost them. Sonny was instrumental in bringing the block into disrepute, according to the victim. Sonny was a Fagin character who organized younger blacks into gangs committing burglaries in the building and dealing drugs. 'I know he's even sold them to children.' Sophie [the WPC] said that that was objectionable. James continued that, ever since Sonny had moved in, the building had gone downhill. 'Just about all the white families moved out. It used to be a good building, clean and quiet.' He was fed up. He was going to move back to Tooting to live with his mother. The proceeds of the burglaries were used to buy drugs. It incensed him that people like himself had to save to buy things which were then sold at a fraction of their value because they were stolen . . .

. . . Sophie got James to give a full physical description of the four people he chased off. He did not react to the 'racial' element of these descriptions, e.g., in describing the hairstyle. Sophie referred to his own extremely close-cropped hair, almost a skinhead style, and he joked about it. He also displayed no hesitation in describing the 'half-caste'. Sophie was particularly interested in what the 'half-caste' wore but did not mention the apparel she was interested in. [She was trying to confirm a description of a suspect reported by someone else but did not want to contaminate the informant by mentioning the detail she was after; this incident is more fully discussed below.] The descriptions James gave were practised and as though said by a police officer.[70]

These notes are from the early stage of an intervention for an apparently straightforward police matter which evolved into a lengthy (and useful) 'community contact'. From James' responses Sophie formed the impression that James was not hostile to police and may indeed be favourable toward them. The willingness to castigate a fellow resident, regret at the departure of white residents, attitude toward burglary and drugs, joke about the hairstyle and manner of giving the descriptions, were all drawn on. Sophie also knew James was a student. It is worth noting the relevance about the mention of children and drugs. In this area, as in most, the principal illegal drug was cannabis. Many police are ambivalent about it being illegal and classified as dangerous, and the community constables were aware that many otherwise 'respectable' pro-police local people were users. Consequently, they emphasized dangers of young children being sold the drug, as frequently happened (even one 'joint' at a time). This often registered with those who would not condemn adult use of the drug. At any rate, Sophie drew on a number of signs to conclude that James was a useful contact, especially as he lived in a building that had become notorious. While the incident is fully discussed below, it can be noted here that later in their discussion it emerged that James was interested in joining the police. While James was very much a willing informant, Sophie used his interest to extract very detailed information, which ultimately led to the arrest of certain of his neighbours, an outcome which posed obvious dangers to James himself. Information is valued more highly the more

[70] Fieldnotes.

directly applicable it is. James not only offered clear, authoritative information about crime in his building, but this information related to a criminal matter Sophie did not disclose to him and was already investigating. James' interest in the police was a further bonus.

Aware that some members of the public do not accord police legitimacy, and that these groups are not confined to known offenders, officers learn to differentiate sub-groups in the community they police. Elaborate typologies exist which label citizens according to the degree of trouble they cause police. But some categories, notoriously blacks, are simply based on gross characteristics of physical appearance and ethnic origin. Community constables are in a better position to differentiate members of such groups according to the degree of their support for the police. Officers who can do this may draw on a further tactic, by exploiting divisions within a hostile community.

8

Local Knowledge and Informants

The insistently practical focus of police interest in information prioritizes short-term content with a direct pay-off. The kind of thinking that could inform local crime pattern analysis is relatively marginal to this approach. But the community constables' local knowledge offers a promising base for crime pattern analysis, and their beatbooks include tables to be used for the purpose. Among the descriptive entries in one book it is reported that 'a reprobate called Mann was arrested for drugs following a search of . . . House. Mann later admitted that the flat is regularly used by up to fifteen youngsters (need we say they include Renny, Villey and other "old faces"?) for smoking cannabis.'[1] In another case a Permanent Beat Officer with 'an unrivalled knowledge' of an estate whose residents were troubled by youths from his beat had been able to identify a badly decomposed body as that of an elderly resident who had threatened to throw herself in the Thames. Again, there is a contrast with information-handling on the reliefs. While crime collators draw information together, its use is haphazard. Some officers regularly visit the collator, others do not. Some shifts receive information from collators when they parade, others do not. Some information is passed from uniform to detectives but much rests with those who originally collected it. Rivalries based on rank and the perceived status of different units obstruct the transmission of information to those who might act on it. Another reason that there is little alternative to low-level information-gathering of the sort done by community police is that collated crime information is not kept in a form enabling crime pattern analysis. The crime reporting system may be sufficient to provide a Home Office statistics return but inadequate to support pattern analysis for operational decision-making.

Increasing the information available to police enables community

---

[1] BB 4.

policing to enhance responsiveness to local concerns, here the rowdiness associated with illegal gambling.

Trevor Todd learned that a grocery on his beat was accepting illegal bets. People were aggravated by the types who were using this facility. Next door is a pub. People . . . would come from far and wide, using that pub, getting into fights, upsetting people who lived in the area, and staying all afternoon causing more problems . . . As a result of observations by PC Todd and another homebeat we managed to get a warrant in conjunction with the Customs and Excise, raided the place and put a stop to them.[2]

The inspector encouraged such activity: 'officers are expected to display initiative, get into the problems on their beat and either do something about it or report them.'[3] A community constable had uncovered 'child abuse cases where he's picked up information, looked at it and thought "yes, there's something wrong"'.[4] The officer passed the information to social services, a referral facilitated by the routine contact with other agencies.

A superintendent confirmed there was little alternative to low-level information-gathering because collated crime information did not enable crime pattern analysis. '[Our] crime reporting system . . . provides a Home Office statistics return to headquarters and that's really all . . . Which in terms of operational decision-making is meaningless. The present crime reporting system has no ability to tell me the scale or even the nature of the problem. If someone asked "Where are most of your burglaries?" I would have to send somebody to search manually.'[5] The superintendent had heard of the success of a property marking system in Wales and wanted to try it. 'I . . . had to go to the collator and say "Tell me what the burglary is." I had to send it back twice because it came back with a list. That doesn't tell me anything.' He needed local knowledge to decode the statistics.

I then had to ask 'How many of these happen in the village and how many to outlying houses? How many of them are tuppence ha'penny and how many are significant?' There was no way he could tell me the nature of the house that was being burgled . . . Even with a relatively small number of burglaries I was knocking somebody off for half a day just to get basic information . . . In crime the information is very difficult to come by. In crime your analysis is on the basis of 'How good is your memory?' You read the

[2] Insp. Adams.   [3] Ibid.   [4] Ibid.   [5] Supt. Tate.

crime book everyday and think, 'That's the third one I've read there, maybe there's something worth investigating.'[6]

A less obvious benefit of improved information is a better grasp of the offender population. Criminologists have long argued that police tend to return to the 'usual suspects'. One problem this causes is allegations of harassment. Another is that, because of the parleying which takes place around offences taken-into-consideration when suspects are prosecuted, objective involvement, and thus any sound basis for crime pattern analysis, becomes impossible to establish. The reasoning supporting such unimaginative targeting is apparent in a relief inspector's remark that,

so much of the crime on our division is going to be committed by a small number of people and it is important to know who they are and where they hang around, so putting yourself in the right place at the right time and recognizing thieves who hang around is important. You're going to pick that up partly by poking your head into the chargeroom and having a look at the prisoners in there. You can pick up a little bit from the collators' records. Its quite hard to recognize people from photographs anyway. It's also largely a matter of confidence in your own reactions.[7]

Significantly, the only locations mentioned are police locations, and the approach involves a passive 'recognition' strategy rather than active community involvement. Such reasoning leads police to the same suspects again and again, and the negotiating process surrounding dealings with 'the regulars' renders surreal any attempt to derive an accurate picture of local crime.

The community constable's way of working may seem indulgently slow to relief officers. The teamwork and closely-reasoned analysis of a criminal situation associated with the myth of classic detective investigation[8] is seldom manifest in any uniformed police work. Its elements existed in community policing, as in this aide memoire.

I gleaned some useful information from the Security Guard guarding the . . . Storage Premises. My informant tells me that the main bugbear on the site is a car breaker's business—they are coming and going day and night, with vehicles on 'hook wagons' and could be the ideal 'cover' for conveying stolen property in and out. One adjacent firm has had petrol siphoned and have taken to parking under the eye of the security guard's office.[9]

---

    [6] Supt. Tate.   [7] Insp. Wren.   [8] Manning (1982b).   [9] BB 4.

Rather than the classic 'jigsaw approach' to detection, information use is typified by this extract about a court duty by one community constable on behalf of another. 'Edwina explains she wasn't the arresting officer, but took it on from Al because Rains lived on her beat. In fact, she knew he was using the car daily, but hadn't had a chance to nab him for it. She had written the file and was aware of the other cases that could have been entered on [the police file prepared for the court].'[10] Here a community constable had information 'filed away' with a view to prosecution at a later date. The information was simply that the youth had often been seen driving despite disqualification; officers often memorize the details of disqualified drivers on their beat.

The community constables were also versed in the idea that local knowledge helped them identify pro-police residents who could aid surveillance and observation.

Two streets on the beat were plagued by autocrime, chiefly expensive cars whose owners were using trendy restaurants. Initially, using her background in surveillance, she set up an observation. It was fruitless, but she had developed a relationship with a tenant who let her flat be used as a look-out. Sophie tried another approach. Every shift she walked the streets in question at least three times. There had been a marked reduction in autocrime. 'Now they're lucky if they see one [theft from vehicle] a month.'[11]

It is worth noting that the unsuccessful observation was turned to advantage by cultivating the lady whose flat was used for observation; people willing to accept such demanding intrusions on their privacy are likely to oblige by maintaining a watch after police have left. When this happens the courts encourage it; a 1991 Court of Appeal judgment held that, in appropriate circumstances, a trial judge is entitled to rule that police should not have to answer questions designed to find out the location of observation posts (*Regina* v *Hewitt*; *Regina* v *Davis*; *Guardian*, 4 March, 1992). The prosecution requested this because of the risk that those who co-operated would suffer reprisals, that they would lose the chance to use the premises again, and that others would be reluctant to help if they knew the precise location of their premises would be disclosed in court. The defendants argued that without knowing just where the posts were it would not be possible to ask the police relevant questions in cross-examination. The Court of Appeal determined that the

---

[10] Fieldnotes.   [11] *Ibid.*

detection of crime called for this increase in the anonymity granted to police action. In that respect there was no essential difference between police informers and the providers of observation posts.

Community policing is seen as a means of penetrating the apathy that inhibits greater public assistance. 'The homebeat has to act as a link, liaison, and gossip. Ask people to come to you and they'll never come, knock on their door and you'll find out things . . . We have murder enquiries: papers, press, television, posters up—nothing! And that's where it all comes from, knocking on the door. You go to them and they'll talk.'[12] There were examples of citizens proving helpful provided they were given a familiar contact.

A NW person, because I pop in on a regular basis, gave me some information which led to a good chap being arrested without any previous, a handler, and that led to three other burglaries being solved with the goods we found. That was purely that he happened to look out, take a registration number. That information would have been lost had it not been that he knows I come round regularly, and 'I saw this car moving suspiciously at four a.m.' I knew there were no deliveries that morning.[13]

It is not so much that constables must hone their persuasive conversational tactics; they simply need to be regularly available. 'It's because we represent a big organization, don't we. We are just a faceless mass until they get to know us.'[14] Nor do constables have to cultivate vast numbers of contacts; the helpful are never more than a fraction of those routinely greeted on the street. Asked how many people offered 'useful information', one homebeat said 'since I started (six months before) I'd say you could go to about ten regular people'.[15] A more experienced homebeat confirmed 'that's all you need'.

Community constables are well placed to grasp that short-term gains are not the only yardstick of success and that information should not be taken only at its face value. Direct, short-term uses of information are, of course, easy and must be tried initially in case a desired end can be straightforwardly obtained. But community constables are aware of the 'jigsaw approach' to solving a crime by accumulating apparently discrete units of information.

A van parked by a building site on corner. Bill knew the youth in the van, 'He's one of the few youths on the beat who doesn't have a CRO number.' They had a friendly relationship and chatted about the health of the youth's

¹² Insp. Sharp.   ¹³ GD 1.   ¹⁴ Ibid.   ¹⁵ Ibid.

dad and sport. However, the youth came up with some information Bill later identified as useful, drawing on it on the next call [a burglary investigation]. It was an instance of things clicking into place with other details one had gathered while the informant might not even know it was significant. It was the name of the punk youth who had recently moved into the end house of the road, and the fact that it was a house where glue-sniffing was taking place which directly adjoined the trendy shops on the edge of his beat. The house was behind the newsagent at which Bill was about to investigate a break-in. He also told Bill that the entry to the newsagent was by a ladder, which was left in the courtyard behind the newsagent. Bill said it was worth collecting all the fragments that came your way; they might not connect up at first but later they could fall in with something else. Bill did not show the informant that he found this information specifically useful. The youth said his appointment to the Special Constabulary was coming up and Bill congratulated him.[16]

There is a similarity between this perspective and that of the ethnographic researcher. Bittner identifies the key point as the parallel with the ethnographer's analytic brief.[17] The goal in accumulating information incrementally is not to have the fullest possible description but to create the basis of an interpretive scheme that will allow one to select salient information so that, in future, the irrelevant is disregarded.

No matter how rich such factual knowledge of an area and its residents is, it can never encompass more than a fraction of reality. Many places have not been visited and most persons are not recognized. Though interest is directed to the accumulation of factually descriptive information . . . the ulterior objective is to be generally knowledgeable rather than merely being factually informed. That is, patrolmen seek to be sufficiently enlightened to be able to connect the yet unknown with the known through extrapolation and analogy . . . to reduce the open and unrestricted variety of interpretive possibilities that baffles outsiders to a far more restricted range. They always have, as it were, something to go on.[18]

Local knowledge is not a jumble of unconnected facts but a scheme of interpretation. The officer 'employs typifications without sacrificing interest in and respect for individual variation. Every person and every event is always run as a particular instance of a class, i.e., neither merely unique nor merely a type.'[19]

Much has been written about the police use of classifications and typologies of citizens; it is an essential element in their working

---

[16] Fieldnotes.   [17] Bittner (1980).   [18] *Ibid*. at 91.   [19] *Ibid*.

codes.[20] Exercising 'judgement' is a universal work-related skill, applying as much to workers whose efficiency is enhanced by anticipating the alignment of components on assembly lines as to those whose notion of the 'ideal' social worker helps select candidates for training. Typologies reduce the need for judgement to a minimum. In work covering as broad a range of behaviour as policing, the need for categories is especially compelling. The risk in such attempts at data reduction is justified by the fact that most work is routine and the categories, supported by training and occupational culture, are usually borne out. To police, the range of their legitimate concerns seems very wide. The impetus to their development of selective categories is strong. But the inherent dangers of stereotyping can be overcome when one's knowledge base is detailed; the extra information can be used to define the limits of the application of types. It may be no more subtle than knowing that this particular 'black youth' is a committed Christian or that the local vicar has a fondness for strong drink.

Versions of the idea about the accretion of information manifest in Bill's contact with the youth were widespread among the community constables. In this case the information joined what the constable already knew about the layout of the premises and he immediately called on the newsagent to look at the ladder and rear courtyard. Despite the officer's self-conscious description of the incident as a case of the 'jigsaw approach' it is hardly a profound instance. The officer already knew about the ladder; the 'news' in the informant contact was that 'punks' were squatting nearby. This was hardly subtle or obscure information. Indeed it was information the officer acted on immediately (he went to see if the corner house provided any special degree of access to the rear courtyard). The idea of the 'jigsaw approach' was plainly current among the community constables but it would be unsafe to conclude that it was practised widely or with much refinement. This should not be taken as a criticism. We have already noted that direct, 'easy' applications of information must be tried in the interests of efficiency. There are real costs in forbearance. While you wait to gather all the jigsaw's pieces another unit may jump the gun and have your prisoner.

The significance of the myth of the 'jigsaw approach' in the culture is, then, its simple existence as a symbol of a way of working

[20] Manning (1977).

and of justifying work. It forms an icon of community policing's essence in explicit contrast to the relief mode of work ('fire brigade policing'). Further, it taps into the approach of the most powerful, mysterious and status-filled of policing's branches, criminal investigation. Recall that in the principal research division, community policing assignment was an established route to a plainclothes posting and enhanced prospects of transfer to CID. Recall also the antipathy customarily prevailing between reliefs and 'homebeats'. Recourse to the myth not only depicts homebeats working in a way characteristic of the high status detective but rehearses their claim to eventual transfer; the incidents they retail to the fieldworker they can later present to an appointments board. All of this is separate to the actual promise of a 'jigsaw approach', and none of it undermines its value. Indeed, it heightens its value by reinforcing the myth while lending reflected status to the undervalued community policing function. These 'within-job' overtones of laying claim to the thoughtful, calculating 'jigsaw approach' do not debunk it but rather reinforce its appeal. It must be obvious that the approach is also useful in warranting interventions and contacts which do not yield anything of manifest, immediate use. Misused, the tactic forms a helpful 'easing behaviour'. There are, then, several reasons for valuing the 'jigsaw approach' beyond the practical benefit of the rare cases where it is done and succeeds.

If the approach is rare in complete form perhaps its components can be identified and whether community constables have some of the required abilities can then be considered. Maintaining the jigsaw analogy, the principal of these elements is the capacity to perceive the 'big picture'. Detectives and investigation-minded constables need an imaginative sense of the complicated schemes from which illegal profit can be gained and of the complex human relationships that accompany them. They must be alert to this while examining and seeking to connect the small details which are usually the only apparent signs of what is afoot. Establishing the significance of a detail requires a dense but flexible interpretive frame, where many small signs are collated but the character of their association is not so rigidly construed as to blind the investigator to other plausible connections and interpretations.[21]

There were fieldwork incidents which plainly did attest to such a

[21] Fielding 1984.

competence. In the following case, the constable draws on background knowledge to form the hunch that the motor scooters are 'wrong'. The incident is not a complete narrative; before it extends the background knowledge the constable has of the two 'little villains' and beyond it lies some unknown but plausibly nefarious outcome. The officer may perceive what he thinks as an intuition, but behind 'intuition' lies creative inference. The motor scooters present the officers with a puzzle to be solved but also offer an excuse to be exploited in order to warrant another in an ongoing series of fishing expeditions.

Walking down a residential road Bill noticed two identical new motor scooters outside a house. 'I've seen them buzzing around. Think I'll go in and find out about them.' He rang the bell and was answered by a ten year old girl. 'Is Dee in?' 'Dee, it's for you,' leaving the door open. Dee came downstairs, drying his hair. 'Let the officers in, girl' he motioned. 'Have a seat.' Dee is a short, well-built white youth. His brother, slightly older, was making telephone calls. 'To what do we owe the pleasure?' 'Just curious about the scooters.' 'Company-owned. Pay for themselves in cheapness to run and they get round town very easy.' 'Company-owned?!' Bill couldn't believe these two. The older replied. 'Yeah, its my company.' 'What, building trade?' 'Yeah, well, more in the nature of cleaning. Its office and site cleaning's the game.' Bill left it.

The manner of the two was that of respectable citizens. Bill asked if they'd had more trouble 'with over the road', motioning to the blocks of flats opposite. 'Not lately. But, see, I can understand a bit of fighting, that's fair enough. But it's the vandalism. When are they going to do something about it. It's disgusting. The vandalism's just sick. I think they're mental.' Bill agreed that there was something pretty stupid about people who spray-painted their own names, indicating to one and all who was responsible. The girl played round his feet. Bill asked Dee if he was getting on OK. 'That gap in your teeth makes you look well-hard.' 'Yeah, and it wasn't no fight neither. Just the nerve at the root.' Bill grinned: 'Any trouble, you know we've moved' [the police station had relocated]. 'Yes, you're at . . . now, in'cha. Twenty seven cells.' 'How'd you know that?', Bill wondered. 'We have our sources, eh. Must keep informed.' The elder brother offered tea, Dee said there were only two cups, was told to go upstairs for some. Bill said 'Never mind, we'll make it easy, we've got things to do.'

Outside the door Bill remarked 'The bloody cheek, you've got to admire it, "company vehicles"! Those two are right little villains.' They had a garage over the road where they kept stolen goods. The blacks with whom they were co-operating had fallen under suspicion when the goods that the two brothers had stolen were re-stolen, and the result had been a serious fight between the blacks and the brothers. Bill had arrested Dee for this and autocrime in the past. The reason they mentioned vandalism was because the blacks were mainly responsible for it, and their own windows bore evidence of having been sprayed with various insulting messages. 'Fancy them coming on like that with the tea and the "company vehicle". They're well involved with crime.'[22]

The officer's remarks suggest that by the close of the incident the scooters had become a more complex puzzle, to be checked further. The details he gave of the history of tension between blacks and whites involved in theft and handling indicate the knowledge base to which subsequent action by these individuals would be related; it gives an idea of the character of inferences made in the officer's effort to understand their motives and method of operation. The scooters and the talk of the company challenged the understanding he had arrived at and posed both an information deficit (what were they up to in their site-cleaning activities) and an item of news to be reported to other officers. The sense conveyed is akin to a narrative competence, where the 'big picture' is kept in view while maintaining openness over considerable time to information which may or may not fit as details of the big picture. Informing the continual attempt to 'think' the details into the big picture, is the officer's knowledge of the ways in which gainful crime is pursued, and understanding of the relationships of those involved.

An under-remarked but highly important source is the informant. The value of informants is dramatically understated in this beatbook entry under 'patterns of crime': 'The outstanding matter was the murder of a . . . youth, NIXON, by another coloured youth . . . called CLORE. It is pertinent to note that information gleaned from one of his informants by PC MOUNT enabled CLORE to be arrested within a few hours of the murder. This underlines the value of local Home Beat Officers' knowledge on the subject of criminals and informers.'[23] The same beatbook recorded that another community constable received information concerning the identity of 'youths making a nuisance of themselves with air weapons', and this resulted in three arrests.

The community constables confirmed that much of their information came in such ways. Neighbourhood Watch was less likely to yield actionable information about culprits than were individual

informants. The key motive behind informing was revenge; information flowed from grudges: 'it's usually for no other reason.
They've had an argument with someone. Its basically just internal
arguments from which you get information.'[24] Particularly with gang
members, it was important to frequent the community centre and to
convince users over time, who had 'to have a lot of confidence in you
to keep it quiet and not reveal where you got it'.[25] Building trust
mainly took time rather than other demonstrations of trustworthi-
ness. 'Just time really so they can trust you properly. Definitely when
I first came on this beat I wasn't getting anything.'[26]

It also involved a degree of contact with the discreditable which
was not normal among uniformed police. One of the research team
had been impressed with a community constable's rapport with a
group of white youths all of whom had previous convictions. 'I do
find that I can talk to people on my beat who have got previous like
TDA where a normal relief officer wouldn't really want to talk to
them, he wouldn't want to be seen to talk to them. I don't know if
you remember that, but I actually arrested those people the next day
for TDA and robbery.'[27] So, while the officer had achieved a rapport
the researcher found impressive, he had been engaging in a tactical
contact, perhaps fishing for more information. Of course, even in a
contact that the officer might perform for his own motive, there can
be some benefit to the member of the public. The officer had known
something was afoot but the gang member had later asked who the
researcher was, as part of his own information-gathering.

Revenge may be a key motive for informing but there were
others. 'That's [revenge] another kind of approach, another way
information is obtained. Another way is that they want to tell you
something because they think they'll win you over, which will win
them a favour at a later date. Maybe you'll give them special consideration. Or they just want you to be their friend. Win you over
so that they feel you will be indebted to them.'[28] This list of reasons
reflected the consensus emerging in the discussion that, while revenge
was important, 'they've all got different motives'. Informant contacts
could, of course, compromise the officer's official role and status. 'In
any relationship when I go out there I make sure that they know that
I am still a policeman. In the end, maybe the biggest stumbling block
to community policemen is that you are a policeman. As I explained

[24] GD 2.   [25] Ibid.   [26] Ibid.   [27] Ibid.   [28] GD 2.

earlier with this person [local informant] who talks to him [PC] and says "he is doing so-and-so", so he [PC] tells another officer. Give it someone else and then you don't look to be the one who shopped them.'[29] All discussants agreed that they practised this tactic: 'there have been instances where I don't want to be seen as the arresting officer because it could muck up other jobs. So I ask someone else.'[30] Aware of the potential motive of offering information to curry favour, the police constable has to have implicit personal boundaries on what will be conceded. Favours could be 'cashed in' at any time: 'you'll be indebted to them in some way and that stands them in credit, whatever might come along at a later day.'[31] One can also cultivate contact with citizens who may be hostile or reserved when they, themselves become victims of crime. As one officer remarked,

he becomes the victim of the crime . . . Not usually but it does happen. You have a victim and he becomes an informant. Basically, I was the bloke to talk to. You've got to be a regular customer to talk to. You're the listener. If he wants to tell you all, you just listen. As long as you've got some knowl-edge of what he's talking about. You've got to know about what he's try-ing to get across, and the more you show an interest the more he will. And also, let him know the results of what he tells you . . . Act on the informa-tion and inform him of the outcome.[32]

The art of cultivating and maintaining informants emerged as a key and sophisticated skill. Information given was not a 'one off' but part of an ongoing relationship; this was necessary, because this rela-tionship acted as a control which regulated, and so made predictable, the consequences that could flow from giving the information.

Anybody will give you limited information but when it comes down to the nitty gritty, where there is a possibility they may have to stand up and be counted, we're on a different ball game. Then for them to come forward with information they've got to trust you entirely. I've had information which has been put to good use where arrests have come up purely because they trust me and I've only got that because I keep going on a regular basis and they tell me things in confidence and believe that I will keep their confidence. And this is what you've got to do because the minute that some-thing gets out which puts them on the spot you've lost it.[33]

Constables become the guardian of secrets, usually and simply the source of actionable information. They must then have evidence of the offence independent of the information source, and protect

[29] GD 2.   [30] *Ibid*.   [31] *Ibid*.   [32] GD 1.   [33] *Ibid*.

sources from the culprit's surmise as to their identity. In this work, community constables strongly differentiate their approach from other police; it is a source of pride as well as information. 'I've got pure information where they tell me things and trust my discretion as to what I do with it. They can rely on my discretion and totally trust that the information will go in the right channels and will be dealt with properly which no way would any other PC. Some of the people I know, they would never get anywhere near them.'[34] Indeed, it appears that community constables are trusted this way in specific contrast to other police, or the organization as a whole. '[I]ts lack of trust in the police—a general lack of trust—and it takes that amount of visits and total confidence in the officer to get that information out of them. They just wouldn't get it out of a casual visit, they've got to have more than that.'[35]

The emphasis on trust did not blind the constables to the 'low motives' which inspired the granting of information so generally guarded. 'Some of the greatest informants are the people who are committing the crime. That's the motivation,'[36] a reference to giving information for reasons of self-preservation. This interpretation is supported by the fact that rivalry was mentioned as an *additional* reason for this group being a possible source. 'I think jealousy as well. If you have something on someone, if you have a group of younger ones on the estate, for instance.' The self-preservation was referred to as 'you back off me and I'll give you something more important'.[37] The community constables saw the informant's motivation as a universal of policing but also felt they were uniquely in a position to capitalize on it because of long-term local assignment.

All policemen are detectives to a point. But then again you can say anyone is an informant. Provided you ask the right questions, and he's willing to answer them, anyone is going to become an informant. That's the distinction between the relief and the homebeat. You're always in the same area and see the same faces, you deal with the same people and can follow things up. On relief they work a fire brigade service, so the detective side is reduced.[38]

Seeing this contrast to the reliefs inclines community constables to maximize their use of crime collators' files and other official records; being assigned long-term, time invested here is more likely to pay off, and the beat area helps them to reduce the frame of relevance to rea-

[34] GD 1.   [35] *Ibid.*   [36] *Ibid.*   [37] *Ibid.*   [38] *Ibid.*

sonable size. In the following there is also a hint of team spirit jux-
taposed to the self-interest of the reliefs. ' "It's important to see the
addresses and who their associates are and those sort of records."
"Input is just as important. Giving information to the whole police
station, where inevitably people like to keep things back to themselves. That glory which goes against the teamwork spirit . . .".'[39]
The community constables felt it necessary to check the collators'
records regularly, as a resource for cultivating informants. 'It's
through the record sheet, collators' information and also crime
reports. Crime reports are very important. For instance, if you have
an arrest for a burglary, in your mind you've got an idea what other
burglaries on your beat will fit into the same pattern.'[40] This emphasis on records led the interviewers to ask if the main source of information was paperwork rather than contact with officers involved. It
was a matter of personal relationship and distance between functions.

'You can easily find out as much in the canteen. It's not supposed to happen like that but it does.' 'You won't find out from the CID, that's for sure.
I was there yesterday and looked through the Crime Books and got phoned
up at home by one of my NW co-ordinators this morning asking about an
aggravated burglary and I didn't know anything about it. You feel such an
idiot. You'd think that just a word [from CID] that some old bloke was
beaten up and robbed on your beat last night!'[41]

But with informants, constables have interpretive work to do.
Informants inform for a reason, as Becker's classic analysis of 'moral
enterprise' suggests.[42] The arrests appendix of a monthly beat return
includes the entry 'LAGRANGE, Mark . . . Arrested sus/burg. Gave
info re drugs.'[43] Determining how best to play information received
is another working requirement which is facilitated by a subtle and
extensive understanding of possible motives. It may be that the person informed against is acting, or threatens to act, in ways counter
to the interest of the informer; revenge is a most tangible and regular motive. Such a motive requires that careful interpretive work be
done by the officer in order to avoid manipulation and action unwit-
tingly prejudicial to an innocent who has been set up.
A problem in discussing this is our image of the informer as
the seedy marginal character of popular crime fiction. The stereotyped informer apparently scrapes a livelihood through the trade in

[39] *Ibid.*   [40] *Ibid.*   [41] *Ibid.*   [42] Becker (1967).   [43] BB 4.

information. In practice the line between the casual but informative community contact and the regular informer can be hard to draw. This is especially so if we accept that 'payments' can be in kind (even mere reciprocity in the provision of information); 'paid informers' could include more than those kept happy by cash. To get an idea of the breadth of informants and the manner of contact with them we refer to an episode taking place in the yard of a small garage workshop where three black mechanics were working.

. . . One of them, a tall, burly man, the foreman, approached Bill [the officer]. 'How are you, Winston? The family?' 'Yeah. About that matter.' 'Yes, have you got something?' Bill and the man became *sotto voce*. 'Him?', eyes darting at me. 'He's all right, with me.' 'We can't talk here but I got something. Obviously it'll have to be a phone call.' 'Have I got your number here?' The man gives Bill the work number. 'I'll speak to you later, then.' 'Yeah.' 'Thanks.' Bill walks to the bay. A man is welding a fan mounting. A few pleasantries, then some conversation about the man's teenage son who has been in trouble. 'Of course the thing about it is that he's still a juvenile. When he hits 18 all this will be wiped off his record.' 'Yeah, but its such bother. It's getting me down. Why does he want to go on like this.' The mechanic sees the boy's trouble as serious while Bill is trying to say there is no lasting record. Bill left, greeted the third mechanic, working on a car in the street—'All right then?' 'Yeah, all right' comes a bewildered reply.

Departing, Bill remarked the nature of the foreman's information. A friend of the foreman is a partner in a drug-dealing network. The partners quarrelled, with mutual accusations of a rip-off. The foreman's friend told him he was looking for ways of getting even. He was prepared to leak information as to where the dealing was taking place in order for there to be a raid. Information given by the foreman had already been acted on once. The information was an address and a raid occurred but everything had been cleaned up. The foreman had subsequently contacted Bill to confirm it was the right address but the dealer had got the wind up. The foreman had now been given another address but didn't want to be seen with Bill in case it got back to the dealer he had been talking to police . . . Bill doesn't try to copy the manner or accent of his black informants, who are in any case all in their forties [he is in his twenties], but simply banters in the same manner as with a titled NW co-ordinator. His tone is sincere.[44]

The garage was (marginally) off Bill's beat. Apart from his general 'crime-mindedness', his interest is perhaps explained by a beat-book entry suggesting that some of those involved were residents on one of his 'problem' estates. 'It would appear that youths in . . .

[44] Fieldnotes.

House are committing robberies, autocrime etc. in order to fund drug-taking habits. PC Davis has established that a flat on the estate has been raided by the Drug Squad, which resulted in one arrest and a small amount of resin being discovered. The officer's informant says that dealing is continuing, and the situation is being monitored.'[45] Thus, the fact that the garage was not on his beat had not prevented Bill cultivating two of the mechanics, and in this contact he seemed to be starting to work on a third. The foreman's motive here is plain enough (as presented)—to assist his friend to revenge the 'rip-off'. In the case of the second mechanic it appears that Bill had been acting as an informal advisor on the law; there was no sign he was getting anything back, but the role he had adopted provided an obvious opportunity to cash in on any feeling by the mechanic that he should reciprocate the 'favour'.

This feature implies that the parties are involved in a relationship of negotiation where a close check is kept on a tit-for-tat form of exchange and on the equivalence in value of each *quid pro quo*. This heightens the interest in motive already prompted in officers by the need to avoid being manipulated by one side in a dispute.

But a big source of my information comes from people with grudges anyway. You can't be naive about why they are telling you.' He mentioned a feud between two local women. One had won some money and left it in the keeping of the other while she returned to her flat for something. When she returned the other woman was unconscious on the floor and the money was gone. When she came to she said she had been assaulted but the first woman still held her responsible. The first woman freely admitted the money had come to her by illegal gambling but told the police she wanted to see retribution and would help them any way she could to implicate the second woman in drug-dealing. She knew the woman was thus involved and suspected her of stealing the money despite her injury. Dick, and Rick Morrow, were waiting to cash in on this.[46]

The scruple of officers in exploiting such circumstances should not, then, be over-emphasized. Their interest in exploiting the opportunity available did not, apparently, extend to checking the accuracy of either woman's allegations. The woman who initiated contact held the reigning version because she had come forward, and had done so with information police could use. The 'check' on the allegation would take the form of a search for drugs at her opponent's premises.

[45] BB 4.   [46] Fieldnotes.

Simple deception is also an available technique in dealing with informants.

Bill and [another officer] were discussing the fact that, while low-level adult drug taking was virtually ignored, they were worried about the increasing amount of children with drugs. They discussed a recent coup they had achieved as a result of information gained by Bill. Bill had arrested a kid for possession of a small amount of cannabis in a joint. The kid's older sister, one of the girls who hung out at the stable [see above], took it up with Bill. 'Why did you bust him for one spliff?' Normally I'd just crumble it up and send them on their way with an informal caution if it was an adult. But it was a kid. I don't agree with children being given drugs. She said 'You shouldn't be busting the kids then, but the dealers'. 'Well, no one will help us identify the dealers. We can't get their names. But we did do *one* recently.' 'Was that in . . . House?' she asked. Of course I said 'yes' but in fact the raid had not been there. So I stored that away and went on listening. 'Oh yeah. Was it Phil Brown?' 'Yeah, that's right', I says, hoping I'm not showing out. Bill now had name and address. A nice bit of bluff, the other officer thought. A couple Bill had earlier pointed out on the street were duly busted.[47]

Occasionally a community contact will yield not only a directly usable piece of information but the prospect of an ongoing relationship valuable to the police. Such contacts rely on informant motivation beyond that of the grudge. They rely on values in the form of a pro-police attitude. While the white middle class can reasonably be counted on to hold police in positive, or, at worst, neutral esteem, this is not the expectation in black neighbourhoods. We have already examined Sophie's dealings with a young black student, James, whose flat had been burgled, apparently by neighbours. The call on this occasion was for police advice in light of an attempt at burglary which he had foiled by returning home. After discussing the deterioration in the tower block after burglaries drove out the remaining white tenants—graffiti and the smell of urine in the lift and corridors suggested its decline—Sophie asked James for the name and address of the 'Fagin' character suspected of organizing the burglaries.

Sophie asked if the flat would be in his name [Sonny, the suspect's] and James thought that he was down as a tenant but the flat was originally in the name of the girlfriend, a Carol de Franc 'but he calls her Yvonne'. James added that the names could be checked 'on the electoral thing' and Sophie confirmed this, saying she had a friend in the evictions unit of the council

[47] Fieldnotes.

who helped her on such address and name checks. James continued that it was common knowledge in the building that Sonny was responsible for the crime there. James had previously been burgled and lost most of his few possessions. For a while afterwards Sonny had gone out of his way to be pleasant to him. He had taken to coming to James to borrow or lend items like foodstuffs and cooking utensils, until another youth told James that Sonny was establishing when James was at home with a view to breaking in again and clearing the place out . . .

By now it was clear that James was not only a forthcoming contact who was proceeding regardless of any prospect of retribution from Sonny and his associates, but was seemingly knowledgeable about, and interested in, police procedure. Sophie asked if he could give addresses on the associates he mentioned, particularly one he described as a half-caste.

He had seen the 'half-caste' before and, though he did not have the flat number, he knew the youth lived on the seventh floor of the building. After he was burgled he suspected the involvement of the 'half-caste' and James would chastise him when they saw each other. The 'half-caste' responded in a sneering, sarcastic fashion. James did not have names or addresses of the other youths but knew they were associates of Sonny. James continued to be clear and direct in his manner and displayed no evasiveness.

Sophie examined the door but gave no advice on strengthening it. James had already secured it with a new bolt and there were a couple of sliding bolts on it too. In any case, he said he wasn't planning to remain long. 'With idiots like him', jerking his thumb in the direction of Sonny's flat, 'there's just no hope. I'm going back to Tooting to live with me mum.'

It should be noted that the purpose of the call had been conveyed to Sophie as responding to a request for crime prevention advice following an attempted burglary. While the discussion took place in an entrance lobby thick with wood shavings from installation of the new door, Sophie had given very little advice. What she had done was to pump a willing informant and, as noted earlier, she did this without revealing that she was trying to connect what he said with fragmentary information already circulating among the community constables. Having gotten what she could, she made a cursory examination of the door and started to leave. At this point there was an important shift of topic.

Sophie was wrapping up the discussion and confirming the notes she had made in her pad about the suspects when James said 'There is another thing, actually. This has nothing to do with this thing, OK. What it is, I've been thinking for a while now of joining the police. When I finish at College.' James looked at his feet and didn't seem to have said all that was on his mind. Sophie encouraged his interest, saying had he obtained any particulars and he could get them from the station. James said that he had got some forms and that he had been invited to go to Scotland Yard to see the video on recruiting coloured officers. ['coloured' was the term Sophie used throughout the interview and he fell in with her usage].

He then seemed hesitant. 'What I really wanted to ask you about is this. I've had some convictions. I was stupid, it was when I was young, you know. I wanted to know if this would prevent me coming in.' Sophie delicately probed the nature of the convictions. 'It depends, I think. I don't really know myself.' [Her tone suggested he could confide in her.] 'What were they, if you don't mind me asking: were they just driving or were they [pause] anything else?' 'No, they're all for driving.' Sophie said that she understood that these were condoned nowadays if the person was otherwise fit. 'I was stupid, you see. It was for failing to stop after an accident and for failing to give my name and address. Only what happened was I did drive back and I offered the other driver my details and he said he didn't want to offer me his. So I drove off and then I got called to court and got convicted of not giving him my details.' Sophie said that it sounded like the sort of thing they would not hold against him.

He wondered if there was much of a delay in applying and, in light of his studies, when he should apply. She said she thought there was a bit of a delay but wasn't sure how long. 'Yes, I suppose they've got to do their checks on you and everything like that.' Sophie confirmed this and since he had raised the issue, she remarked that the kind of thing they want to know is where you live and who you associate with. 'You know, if your uncle is a criminal and you live next door to him they might not like it. They like to check your associates and who your neighbours are.' 'Well, that's all right. Like I said, I'm not going to be living in here. I'm going to be living with Mum.' 'Well, anyway, the police have lots of section houses and you could live in one of them.'

Sophie suggested that he ought to consider beginning by joining the Specials [she had done so herself]. That way you gained experience of the work, there was a good refreshments fee, you could decide if you liked the work and liked working with police officers. Further, it would prevent the interview panel asking most of their standard questions because you would already have experience of the shift system, basic law—'cause as a Special you have just the same powers as I do'—and you would know whether you liked having police as your social life and so on. She encouraged him to think over the Specials. He thanked her and she left.[48]

---

[48] Fieldnotes.

I have suggested both that these contacts can be regarded as relationships of negotiation where there is a degree of parley between
police and public, and that until the topic shift Sophie was proceeding instrumentally, in pursuit of her own ends. It may seem that the
negotiated element here is slight, and it is noteworthy that it was
James who initiated the topic shift. From Sophie's perspective it may
have seemed that the scope for crime prevention advice was limited,
that James had secured the door and, his having been burgled before,
that he knew the essentials of what to do. Indeed Sophie may have
reasoned that the best form of crime prevention 'advice' here was to
get as much information as possible about the suspected burglars in
order to arrest them and prevent further burglaries. We should also
notice that once James had shifted the discussion to his interest in
joining the police Sophie proved a more than willing informant. Her
response to his worry about having a record was an encouraging one
and she patiently went into some detail about the recruitment procedure. She also broached the idea of section houses, perhaps anticipating that the police would take a dim view of James living with
his mother in what some regarded as a black ghetto. She drew on
her experience as a former special constable, and interposed the issue
of a police social life, a demerit to some who consider joining, adding
self-disclosure to the detailed information she offered James in reci-
procation of his detailed statement about his neighbours.

But the clearest sign that she was particularly forthcoming because
James had been a very helpful informant comes at the end, in the
detail about the interview panel. This was a piece of detailed, 'inside'
information, but more significant, it is a piece of information construed and presented very much from the perspective of the ranks. It
is said as if from one organizationally-adept peer to another; interview panels, like annual appraisals and other dealings with senior
officers, are partly about catching you out. They ask awkward questions, serve as a filter to desired rewards, and you have to play the
system to get what you want.

Of course, Sophie would also know that the force was keen to
recruit black constables, but her detailed and willing career counselling was set on course by James' unusually forthcoming attitude.
He gave every sign of being prepared to stand witness if police proceeded against his neighbours, and the general unwillingness to do
this was a continued refrain among local police. We have remarked
on the constables' use of the tactic of exploiting divisions in a

hostile community, when available. While the main device appears to be the exploitation of interpersonal grudges, community constables can build a knowledge base which allows them to sub-divide groups seen as generally hostile by relief officers. In areas of ethnic minority concentration there is frequently an inter-generational basis for this, with respectable 'elders' as concerned as are the police about the ways of the younger generation. But here was a young black man with some knowledge of law and plainly pro-police attitudes, a good contact who had already demonstrated his potential value.

9
Information Exchange and Teamwork

We have been examining community police work very much as an individual enterprise. There is some warrant for this. In the main, community constables do work alone; patrol is usually solo. But it is to be recalled that much of their effort is justified by its relevance to the collection of information. Like community police, organization theory emphasizes the centrality of information to organizational performance. The chief superintendent at the principal site saw community police as unusually inclined to planned, proactive policing, information exchange and co-ordinated action. He also gave them prime role in gaining information for tactical planning, including a collating function. 'The system of intelligence is that your neighbourhood watches, local authorities and outside organizations feed back through the homebeats and they liaise with the collator.' Equally, when the chief wanted information 'I'd go direct to the homebeats or the Detective Chief Inspector.'[1] It was 'a daily occurrence' for constables and sergeants to proactively initiate an operation.

An example, the homebeats came to my chief inspector about a 'drinker' that was going and they felt it had to be done. There was no way that a couple of PCs could do it. You have to have somebody in there, so ultimately that would come to me. I then got coloured officers from elsewhere and put them on the premises so that we know exactly what we're going into. That originated from the beat officer who when I did that raid ultimately was part of it.[2]

The initiative from the community police led to a co-ordinated effort involving different units.

This brings us to questions of co-operation and information exchange among the community police, and between them and other

---

[1] Ch. Supt. Heath.   [2] *Ibid.*

units, such as the collator's office, the reliefs and the detectives. It is clear from beatbook entries that community police see a need for co-ordinated work, as in this under 'Commendations, recommendations or requests': 'More uniform and plainclothes patrols [on a particular estate], use of mansion rooftops (the owners and caretakers are most co-operative in this respect) for surveillance, we have to be several moves ahead of the villains,'[3] and this under 'Special Constable Patrols', '"Specials" to be used to the full, they must be made to feel "Special", their enthusiasm must be guided and channelled'.[4] Beatbooks serve as a repository of information that may later prove useful, such as the news that office premises had been sold to a property company owned by the Collator's office 'Target Criminal of the Week'.[5] The news was followed by details of his convictions and the specialist unit which had targeted him. Both this concern for the free-handed collection of information, and the 'big picture' idea derived from the jigsaw puzzle version of investigation, suggest that officers cannot always act alone on information.

Community constables have already worked elsewhere in the organization, at minimum, on the reliefs. They learn that information is a closely-guarded resource. Career advancement is facilitated by 'good arrests', even in times that have seen more graduate entrants and a steady sophistication of specialisms. You may be lucky with a good arrest that falls onto your lap but the surer route is to develop 'local knowledge', a compendium that includes knowledge of crime patterns, individual offenders, tea spots, the character and predilections of local police officers, in short, the host of resources and constraints Rubinstein tirelessly documented.[6] Any expectation that officers will co-operatively exchange information, let alone sources, must negotiate the fact that officers are competing for a valued commodity. The exchange of information between constables only reflects the haphazard nature of information exchange higher in the organization. A relief inspector typified this as 'very variable' among inspectors.

There's not a lot actually. There was an inspector's handing over book, blank pages on which you could write information for other inspectors. I always wrote up but I don't think everybody did. That was one of the things that I found unsatisfactory about the shift changeover: the fact that a bloke comes on and you're off. You have very little time to discuss things with

³ BB 4.   ⁴ *Ibid.*   ⁵ *Ibid.*   ⁶ Rubinstein (1973).

him. You can't book on the overtime a half hour briefing, which you might easily spend.[7]

Such practical reasons for failing to maximize the gain from information are added to intra-organization rivalry, classically between CID and uniform. 'It's still a divided force: liaison between CID and uniform, there are exceptions but generally its pretty poor. The DCI or DI may occasionally pass down to uniformed relief inspectors things he feels are important or set up particular operations or comment on your deployment or discipline, unfavourably, but I didn't find there was much productive exchange.'[8] Also asked about the volume of information from CID, another relief inspector said there was 'not a lot, if the truth must be known'.[9] Liaison between reliefs and external bodies was even more haphazard. 'None with police committees, no. Neighbourhood Watch only in as much as [CP inspector] would occasionally remind us the importance of responding quickly to calls from members. Occasionally you would meet members of Neighbourhood Watches who made themselves known to you when you went to a call and obviously you chatted to them.'[10] There is a hint of favouritism in the remark; Neighbourhood Watch members were a group to stay on the right side of, and, instead of a source of information to seek out, they would receive a chat if they happened to be present at a call. The interviewer pressed: were they a source of information? 'Only through the homebeats . . . If the homebeats passed on anything to the reliefs then you got it.'[11] So did the inspector make an active effort to get information from the homebeats? 'I had an idea . . . You get the PC from each homebeat to come [at beginning of relief shift] and give a quick run-down on what was happening on his beat. That happened once or twice but it was more an idea than a practice. Occasionally . . . the homebeat sergeant or PCs would address the parade and ask for co-operation.'[12]

Some inspectors made more regular arrangements for community constables to attend relief briefings. The arrangement had proved useful. 'I had a few doubts when [name of inspector] started doing it but after a while I realized that he was right. It does work.' 'So there are occasions when information does come out?' 'Oh yes.'[13] This was plainly an inspector who could see the value of

[7] Insp. Wren.   [8] *Ibid.*   [9] Insp. Sharp.   [10] Insp. Wren.
[11] *Ibid.*   [12] *Ibid.*   [13] Insp. Sharp.

co-ordinated effort but who could not alone secure conditions that facilitated teamwork outside the usual avenues of relief policing. He explicitly saw relief officers as lacking the opportunity to take on 'projects' of their own, which conforms with evidence that police constables often commenced shifts with specific goals in mind but were diverted by incoming calls.[14] 'You can encourage PCs to develop specific interests. This was something early on I had a plan for trying, the PCs suggesting 20 important topics, like child abuse, minicab firms, street traders and get each PC to have one that he would be the relief expert on. But it was a "pie in the sky" thing. I never tried it.' The fate of 'graded response' and 'targeted patrol' innovations suggests the obstacles to a more proactive or specialized relief role.

Competition was most acute between uniformed and detective officers. We have been looking at the matter from the community police perspective, but the rivalry is mutual. CID officers think community constables should bring more information into the station. A mid-ranking officer remarked, ' "there is a real communication problem . . . They [the community constables] don't spread information and are, therefore, not credited with the work they do".'[15] It is a clear case for some form of enhanced liaison. There is evidence of community constables being under-utilized as a source of information on serious crime. 'There's been a murder on my beat on a Saturday night and nobody saw fit to ask me as the homebeat my knowledge of local inhabitants round there.' 'Did you have any information about it?' 'I had a reasonable idea. The woman was drunk and she was strangled and she lived [in] a flat where the local drunks lived. It was a simple case of supplying the names of people who frequent that place. Nobody asked me if I knew anything like that.'[16]

When crime-relevant information was to be exchanged the community constable had to decide to whom to transmit it and in what form. This depended on the seriousness of the suspected offence. 'It depends on what kind of information it is and what it can lead to. If it's low-level it will be the uniform unit. If it's high level, CID.'[17] On the uniform side it was less likely to go to the next rank, sergeants, or the same rank, a relief constable they might know. 'No, I would probably see the chief inspector of operations. Because at the

---

[14] Burrows and Lewis (1988).   [15] Irving *et al.* (1986) at 111.
[16] GD 1.   [17] GD 2.

end of the day the sergeant has to go to him anyway.'[18] While informal exchanges cannot be ruled out, the hierarchical form of the organization clearly regulated initiatives by the community constables. In CID the information would go to a detective inspector or detective chief inspector, and would be taken in person. The constables greatly preferred face-to-face exchange 'to explain it all, if you give it to him in note form it doesn't cover everything'.[19]

However, we are chiefly examining relations between nominal peers, not hierarchical relations, with their obvious tensions. Relief and community constables are on the same rung but there is a pronounced rivalry between them. Despite this, some community constables did do as they were supposed to by sharing information across the divide. In one case a complaint from the public was first negotiated by a community policing sergeant, who explained why it would be hard to respond to at that time, and second, conveyed to a relief sergeant placed to act on the matter. 'I had occasion to visit a Mr Wowre from . . . Crescent after receiving a complaint about coaches and HGVs using . . . Bridge which is the subject of a weight limit . . . I will be mentioning this matter to PS Frank to employ his street duty officers on this if he thinks fit.'[20] The information gathered by community constables, McConville and Shepherd found, was useful mainly in facilitating operations conducted by other officers. '[T]hey were able to facilitate the arrest of an individual sought by the police through their knowledge of the individual's habits and routines, and could provide officers with "safe houses" from which observations could be conducted.'[21]

In its most basic form, information exchange between relief and community police simply involves posting notices for the general information of a section. An example is drawn from one of the beat-books.

PC Till issued a special request for attention of Reliefs as follows: 'TO BE BROUGHT TO THE ATTENTION OF EARLY TURN AND LATE TURN OFFICERS FROM MONDAY UNTIL THURSDAY. Disturbances at . . . College. Over the last two weeks groups of I.C.3 youths have been forcing their way past Security Guards into the College. They then proceed to run amok, and make for the canteen where there is a large amount of cash. May extra attention be paid to the College over this week at lunchtimes and at about 4 p.m. If called to the premises and no substantive

---

[18] *Ibid.*   [19] GD 2.   [20] BB 4.
[21] McConville and Shepherd (1992) at 142.

offences are obvious, then Police have a power of ejectment for persons causing a disturbance on Local Authority Education Premises under S.40 of the
Local Government (Miscellaneous Provisions) Act 1982. As you would be
acting officially, the little blighters come into play for Obstructing Police and
Assault on Police!!! . . . RESULTS: Extra patrols maintained and no renewed
disturbances.[22]

The fruits of co-operation seem obvious. But notice in the following
example that this was done with a sophisticated appreciation of
organizational and interpersonal obstacles to its being effective.
'Another procedure Sophie employs as a homebeat is to liberally
write messages for the relief officers in the parade book. This means
the message gets read out when they parade a Relief, getting round
the problem that entries in the collators' records and crime books are
not consistently read by all relief officers.[23]

During the stage of fieldwork where relief officers were accompanied there were few signs that such efforts were reciprocated.
Perhaps more characteristic than Sophie's careful action was this
instance of a major operation where neither community nor relief
constables appeared to have any clear idea what was happening.

I mentioned that another officer (Izzy, a relief WPC) pointed out a jewellers
suspected of receiving stolen goods and other infractions on the beat. 'I suppose I can tell you this, we are watching a jewellers on this street and there
will be a major crime observation and operation on it, but that's way above
me, I'm just aware of it.' We had just passed the jewellers Izzy had indicated
but the interesting thing was that Rodney said the place in question was
'Goldfinger, we know the brothers who run it, they're from the East End
and have plenty of previous.' Goldfinger is at the opposite end of the
precinct to the jewellers Izzy mentioned.[24]

The information deficit and lack of follow-through when information was actually released between functions was a common complaint among community constables.

The need to constitute a team with some notion of functional integration was recognized by most community police. 'The next stage .
. . is developing the team, that there will be some officers who will
recognize the need for crime prevention but don't feel inclined to do
it and others who know there is a need to arrest people but have
never felt great crime busters [who] would like to do crime prevention, mini-surveying or have the contact with people.'[25] But at the

---

[22] BB 4.   [23] Fieldnotes.   [24] *Ibid*.   [25] Insp. Kaye, Surrey.

main site the feeling was current among community constables that a promising system was not working as it should despite exceptional resources and management support. The attitudes and contingencies that gave rise to their feeling can be explored by returning to the case of the information Sophie had got from James. After an hour's visit to a minister involved with a youth club, and a period of patrol, Sophie had returned to the station canteen.

Sophie discussed passing the information gained from James to another officer to take action. She felt it was necessary to pass it on rather than act on it herself, as long as it was the right officer. She didn't want to pass it to someone who was going to let it go stale. If no one acted on it, she would act on it herself. However, she had to go onto the estate every day, and she 'didn't want the fingers pointing, the lip-sucking [a hissing sound understood as an insulting gesture], the missiles thrown and general abuse' that she thought would arise if she was seen to take a role in executing a bust in the building. Conferring with CID, she discovered that the autocrime squad had arrested 'Sonny' for cannabis that very morning.

She wanted to pass the information to a sergeant she trusted, Chris Trout, on the Plainclothes Autocrime Squad, but, unfortunately, she had heard that it was disbanding as of today. (Sophie and Trout had worked together before and she was intent on giving him the information and not CID, despite Trout's overt brief being autocrime and the imminent disbanding of the squad.)

After refreshments she radio'd Comms to establish if the squad was still around. Comms said they were meeting at the canteen at 1430. Despite that morning's arrest she thought they would want her information, particularly if 'Sonny' was still being held for questioning. She nevertheless thought it was unlikely he was in custody as he would have been bailed for drugs, unless it was a large amount. The other problem was that it was supposed to be an autocrime squad yet Trout was hauling in drugs arrests. Her information, likewise, was on burglaries. You could only use TICs on offences the same as those of the original arrest. However, they should still have the information, she felt. 'We might as well take a walk for 20 minutes. Let's go down to the river.[26]

The officer's sense of thoroughness would seem to account for her wish to pass on the information, along with the availability of a trusted former colleague. She used the time by the river to look over some old boats which Bill had told her his errant juvenile (the 'right little tealeaf') had been sleeping in.

[26] *Ibid.*

Sophie returned to canteen to pass the information to DS Trout and the squad. He and two others were there, a young PC and a young WPC. They were pleased to receive the information. Sophie gave them all the details in her notes. Trout was especially interested in the 'half-caste', who sounded like the person wanted after another PBO had given chase to a bagsnatch suspect. The suspect ran into this estate and disappeared. He was wearing a red zip-up hooded jacket at the time. Sophie knew this but had carefully avoided planting the idea when the informant failed to mention it. Trout mentioned that Sonny's flat had been 'a dump—foul-smelling and disgusting'. Sophie got from him the man's actual name and told Trout the name the informant knew him by. The WPC commented that she heard the girlfriend call him that. 'Oh yeah. I thought she was saying 'bunny', remember Sarge?' Sophie went on, 'Now, this Carol de Franc? Something like that.' Trout gave her the correct spelling and Sophie told him she was told the woman was called 'Yvonne'. Again the WPC confirmed this, 'Yes, he called her "Von".' The correspondence confirmed the credibility of Sophie's informant. Trout thought it would be best for them to call on Sophie's informant. They discussed if she thought this would be OK. She had said he 'wanted to come into the job' [join the police] and they didn't want to queer his pitch in the estate. Sophie said he didn't seem uncomfortable at having her there this morning and she thought it would be OK for them to visit him. Trout particularly wanted to seek further information about the 'half-caste'.[27]

Sophie had carefully constructed a detailed note of the information received from James. She had accumulated several details that allowed her and the crime squad officers to corroborate their identification evidence on the suspected burglar and others. Importantly, Sophie had mentioned James' career interest as the discussion came on to her informant. Having already been able to gauge James' information as highly credible the officers were minded to take his interests into account in deciding further action. James was 'Sophie's' and she was invited to represent his interest. They gave her the decision as to whether it would be all right for these other officers (in plainclothes) to visit him.

This etiquette serves to establish some of the conventions of information-handling among officers, and that information-handling is sufficiently consequential to have generated a set of norms informally regulating the conduct of those involved. It can be seen as a negotiation, just as was the original contact of community constable and informant. But it must be emphasized that it was an unusual episode. Such exchanges of information between officers in different functions

[27] Fieldnotes.

were seldom encountered in the fieldwork. The 'information' that community constables garner is often vague, merely a hunch and some possibly-relevant details which are held on test until confirmation comes their way. They may be disinclined to share it in case it does not pan out, and only rarely is this information sufficiently 'firmed-up' to pass to another. The suspicion remains that rivalry continues to account for some of the disinclination to share. It is relevant that Sophie knew Trout; she confided that she felt sorry for him, a hard-working and effective officer whose career had been blighted by a run-in with a 'high riser'.

One consequence of the chief superintendent's keen support of the community constables was that they had their own offices within the station. They had staked out territory as their own and this helped to promote a team ethos which was amplified by the fact that they always worked the same hours (unlike the reliefs). All this produced conditions favourable to collective planning of operations, information exchange and a degree of co-ordination uncharacteristic of normal police work. While relief officers generally form plans to pursue specific matters on a shift, the timing of demand and its lack of predictability mean these are almost never followed through.

However, supervisory approval for teamwork was limited by personnel and overtime constraints. Three community constables who initiated an observation were given four hours to show results, when such efforts normally require longer. If immediate supervisors discourage planning and proactive operations then the chances for co-operation with specialist units seem even worse. A respondent raised a problem with street robberies, which required an effort co-ordinated with crime squads. To proceed they needed approval of the community policing inspector and detective inspector but it was refused. What was being spoken of was a considerable operation, involving both surveillance and Special Patrol Group units to 'snatch' suspected offenders. Further, while a respected community constable might individually receive the co-operation of each, 'there's a problem as well with a lack of co-operation between the surveillance unit and the SPG. Neither knew what the other was doing. Once again there's the lack of communication . . . nobody took the other unit into their confidence. We are talking about confidence and they tend to be their own separate unit and don't want anybody to give too much away.'[28] Asked if their experience of similar

[28] Ibid.

operations offered them scope for playing a liaison role, they remarked there was always a rivalry, partly because of the need to establish 'ownership' if the operation succeeded. 'They have the information from us. We are setting up observation posts and of course they were very pleased that we could get involved. When the actual operation was over the units that needed us at the time, we never had feedback from them . . . The people on our beat, through the NW in my case, that put themselves on the line by letting us use their place for the observation posts, asked how it went. We could only give them limited information.'[29]

The experience with burglary screening offered a further story of rivalry and guarded relations.

When they suddenly realized we were getting lots of arrests, the CID saw that by taking the burglaries back it would automatically give them the arrests we are bringing in. And obviously it didn't work because they didn't have the same contact with the community and were still hoping we would pass information. Because we were a bit disappointed that liaison didn't take place . . . I now feel disinterested in doing it. I won't get too deeply involved in case the same thing happens again.[30]

So planning does not just run into problems of supervision, co-ordination, and co-operation with specialist units, but confronts the vexed working relations flowing from the performance measure of arrests, which makes related units rivals instead of teams. Now homebeats screened cases, with those above the threshold passed to CID, and those below it 'written off'. But the homebeats could not get information about the outcome of cases passed to CID, cases they themselves had initially investigated. 'The burglary was reported by me as going over the [threshold] so its a CID matter. Within two days I found that the suspects had been named on the Crime Sheet, but even a month afterwards there wasn't even an entry by the investigating officer. Six weeks later a note came back saying can I deal because he's on a murder enquiry. That typifies the reaction we get from CID.'[31]

The problem of achieving working relationships with other units amplifies the importance of good working relationships within the community police section. As earlier observed, the homebeats latterly saw reduced backing both by their inspector and senior management. They linked the lack of support at the top with their own inspector's

---

[29] Fieldnotes.   [30] Ibid.   [31] Ibid.

increasingly frequent relief assignments. 'There was a time, two years ago when we first set this system up, when if you got a good arrest he'd know about it. Recently you don't see him from week to week . . .'[32] This was a real loss; the inspector was 'very important because he's the only one who can recognize what you're doing', 'at the end of the day he's going to get us what we want'. Because advancement is gained by positive achievement bringing one to the notice of superiors, the homebeats came to feel their new senior officers could hardly see to their own advancement by pushing the same thing as their predecessors and this not only affected their commitment but that of the homebeat inspector: 'If you are interested in making a career in the police force you've got to push the popular things and the unpopular things you push under the carpet.'[33] Another communication problem involving management was that senior officers had great difficulty in gaining information about circumstances as perceived by the ranks.

When senior officers come round to the stations and get the person on the beat's impression—you know, morale—the day is set up months in advance and it's put on the jungle drums . . . the whole station is given a once over with some paint, all the files on top of the cupboards are put in the cupboard, all the troublesome people are given the day off. They'll push the people in front of them they want them to speak to. They go back thinking 'what a wonderful place to be'.[34]

To the community constables these communication problems were tied to the transfer system; an officer with continuity would gradually develop an accurate knowledge base. 'Perhaps you could have the inspector promoted to chief inspector and superintendent, still on the same division so he's got a broader idea of the problems of the area.'[35]

The obstacles to the planned, proactive approach which the community constables wanted to pursue speak to various characteristics of the organization: problems of supervision (including the use of 'their' inspector for other duties), problems with specialist sections, policy changes, and problems arising from promotion and transfer. The use of terms like 'planned' and 'operations' in the discussion of the initiatives the constables wanted to pursue suggests that these were major incidents, perhaps because co-ordination ususally occurs only in such cases. But community constables deal with the

---

[32] GDI.   [33] Ibid.   [34] Ibid.   [35] Ibid.

maintenance of routine civil order and low-level law enforcement. The level of incident dealt with is less important than the fact that, as a by-product of the way community policing was organized, there was sufficient spirit of shared endeavour to give rise to co-ordination and exchange of information.

For example, take a stolen vehicle crime which costs insurance companies millions a year. 'Ringers' are stolen vehicles given the identity of a written-off machine. Insurers often sell written-off vehicles to scrapyards to recover some of their costs. The wreck is bought and its chassis number and registration document transferred to a stolen vehicle of the same make, giving it a 'clean' identity. The insurance companies effectively pay for the original write-off and the stolen vehicle. It is a long-established means of moving stolen vehicles into the marketplace (*Guardian*, 9 August, 1990).

Before leaving, Bill spent half an hour trading information and making a telephone call following up a beat crime another officer informed him of. It was a complicated inquiry regarding a 'ringer' and it seemed that before the switch [of licence plates] the car had been re-sold, bringing another set of owners and garages in on the act. When he was finished another officer took up with Bill the prospect of some tactical planning. He had seen three Minis on their beats in convoy and, on checking, one of them proved to have been totally demolished at the front, whereas the Mini he had seen was perfect. Either it was a legitimate re-build or the plates had been switched. The drivers had records, he knew, and the officer was suspicious. 'They're well-tasty and well-active. It's worth giving the ringer a pull to see the serial on the engine block.' Bill agreed and they discussed when their shifts next coincided to go after them.[36]

As Burrows and Lewis showed,[37] such ideas are not exclusive to community constables, but relief officers are seldom able to put them to effect. It is also worth noting that the information being acted on was unsophisticated, amounting to a sense of puzzlement about the condition of the car and the knowledge that the drivers had criminal records. It is simply that the relative autonomy of the community constables gave them sufficient time to act on the hunch, and to do so without involving their supervisors. Free of the demands of reactive policing, the officers could contemplate an operation that involved both of them being present at a prearranged time.

Commenting on planning, this chief superintendent's initial line is that planning is information-based and deployment is rational. 'The

---

[36] Fieldnotes.   [37] Burrows and Lewis (1988).

role of a chief superintendent, it's strategy and it's not just that man's idea of how policing should be carried out. The problems [are] identified by research, by analytical study of statistics . . . That information having been obtained you then rely on your inspectors, particularly, and sergeants and chief inspector of operations to direct and ensure that deployment is according to the problems.'[38] In the statement quoted above, we see that the chief superintendent's role immediately becomes one of relying on his inspectors, even sergeants, to deploy according to need. However, in the following example we see that the structure of the organization is not attuned to these types of specific and varying demands for particular concentrations and modes of policing. It is not hard to imagine how a sergeant wanting more constables to meet a specific 'problem' would regard this as being anything but determined by him; if this is not the business of senior officers, what is?

The chief had discovered that deployment was not always according to need. 'That is not always, surprisingly, carried out. We did a statistical examination of the patrol system and I eventually put up to do away with it. Because [our] policing was based very much on the beats, what was the point in having patrols? Did you have enough men surplus to be able to put on patrols? The answer was no.'[39] It emerged that, far from assigning constables to the patrols featuring the most 'problems' (public demand), deployment was 'by the number'. Thus

we carried out an analysis to see how those patrols had been used, in relation to the problems, and we found that the patrol most often manned was number one, next was number two and next was number three. As opposed to looking into the problems on the division . . . The point being that it was numerical, start at the top and work your way down. Valueless! So it was important to get the problems over to officers posting men and set them out in some form where they could see what they were rather than having to read reams of paper and analytical appraisal. So we designed maps for . . . recent crime and trends.[40]

Whether a planning awareness was simply at a crude state of development, or whether those responsible were blinded by irrelevant paperwork, the point is that this straightforward idea was a big innovation. The lack of planning in the ranks, then, merely reflects similar deficit at the top echelons of the local organization.

[38] Ch. Supt. Heath.   [39] Ibid.   [40] Ibid.

Planning appears to be a relatively marginal aspect of routine policing. Certainly there are operations which are elaborately planned, with observations being kept and expert officers applying a particular expertise, but in the main the organization's customary mode is reactive. Furthermore, the organization is powerfully inclined to inertia, to press on with an established procedure simply because it is established. There is little planned action, deployment is not attuned to variations in demand and change is hard to achieve, even for commanding officers.

10
Conclusion

This book has emphasized the distinctiveness of the community policing approach in the primary research site, with its generous establishment, emphasis on crime control, and career advantages. Perhaps what appeared as an advantageous approach could instead be the victory of the crime-busting ethos of the ranks, thinly disguised as community policing? Scepticism is valuable, but here a search for the hidden agenda misleads us. First, we have profiled many interventions by community police, and not all emphasized crime control. But there were signs that certain elements of crime control—planning, acting on sound information, teamwork—were facilitated by a community policing approach. Second, we have the officers' testimony to a mixed role, a preventive focus on crime control plus a realistic grasp of what kinds of social service police can best perform. The primary agencies for social service already exist. If community policing consists in ghosting Neighbourhood Watch newsletters, counselling the vulnerable on their troubles with officialdom, and running youth clubs, community police should be replaced forthwith by trained youth and community workers. But there remains room for an active construction of the police mandate, and the ground for it was laid long ago, in London, when the preventive function of the then 'new police' was emphasized.

The point is *not* that community policing routinely and generally delivers what is promised of it, but that, under some circumstances and in certain respects, some community police did deliver. We have examined community constables on permanent beat assignment, what they do and how far their practice exemplified the ideas of community policing. With commitment to 'sector policing' now widespread in British forces, such findings have much to say to those who seek to apply an approach so closely informed by community policing ideas. Just how far community policing can be taken by some advocates is revealed by Figure 10.1. It can be propounded as

Figure 10.1. Contemporary models of urban policing: a comparative analysis (with acknowledgements to C. Murphy, Ministry of the Solicitor General, Canada[1])

Philosophy	Conventional policing	Community policing
Police mandate	Control of crime: – response, deterrence, apprehension – Law enforcement – Crisis response	Community order, peace and security – crime control as a means – Preventive as well as reactive policing
Police authority	– Authority from law – Agency of the criminal justice system	– Authority from society, community granted through law – Agency of local government and community
Police role	– Legally defined/limited by law – Distinct and separate – Professional crime fighting – Law enforcement officers – Crime alone	– Socially defined, expanded role – Legal and social agencies – Peacekeeping professionals – Crime and social problems that impact on crime – One of several agencies of order
Community/police relationship	– Passive role – Supportive and adjunct to police	– Active role – Policy – Shared responsibility for crime and order – Community as client
Politics	– Police must be apolitical – Police alone manage mandate – Separation of police and political issues – Fiscal accountability only	– Police as political: mediate interests – Responsible to community and political representatives – Policy and operational accounting
Organizational structure	Bureaucratic: rigid, formalized, paper-based, rule-oriented, standardized	Non-bureaucratic: corporate, flexible, rules to fit situation, paper where necessary, collegial atmosphere
	Centralized: centralization of all management, support, operational and authority functions	Decentralized: decentralization of authority and management functions to meet operational requirements, organization driven by front end and community-based demand
	Hierarchical: pyramid, multiple-rank levels	Flattened rank structure: additional rank at operational level
	Specialization: specialized and varied police functions to increase efficiency	Generalization: limited specialization, support generalist constable, patrol-based
	Closed organization orientation: distinct from environment, resistant to environmental influence, internally-defined agenda, means over ends	Open organization model: interact with environment, open to change, sensitive to environment, product-oriented effectiveness

[1] Murphy (1986) and (1988).

Figure 10.1. Cont.

Management policy	Conventional policing	Community policing
Communication	– Top down – Command oriented – Formalized policy	– Interaction between ranks – Consultation – Minimal formalization
Authority	– Rank-distributed and based – Promotion: longevity and merit	– Knowledge, contribution – Promotion: value to organization, performance-based
Control	– Disciplinary, rule-oriented – Punishment-centred – By the book	– Involvement – Reward-oriented – Job satisfaction
Leadership	– Authoritarian – Reactive	– Managerial – Participatory – Delegated – Proactive
Productivity and efficiency	– Quantitative – Internal measures	– Qualitative – Product oriented
Operational strategies and tactics	Orientation: crime oriented, reactive incident specific, response based, police based	Problem solving: community defined, proactive/reactive mix
	Calls for service: rapid response, mobile based, full patrol response, little call screening, load shedding	Differential police response to calls for service, call screening, call analysis, load sharing, inter-agency referral
	Criminal investigation: specialist function, large caseload, follow up investigation entails little patrol involvement, centralized	Criminal investigation: limited caseloads due to case screening and enhanced role of constables in preliminary investigations, decentralization of some CID services to support patrol teams, more analysis of crime problems, better case management, enhanced community-based information and intelligence
	Patrol: calls for service directed/reactive, shift-based, random assignment, primarily mobile, rapid response and random patrol, crime-focused, constables as call takers and responders, passive supervision and direction, crime prevention as a specialized function	Patrol: emphasis on patrol, team policing, territorial, beat ownership and responsibility, mixed patrol response (car, foot), generalist constable with broad functions, criminal investigation for some crimes, problem and crime analysis-oriented, proactive and reactive mix, crime prevention a basic patrol strategy
	Product/purpose: the control of crime and enforcement of law	Product/purpose: the provision of police services in order to support a safe and secure environment

a total approach to policing which transforms the entire police force and has managerial, legal and political implications. However, that is not the agenda of this book, nor could it be in an ethnographic study of selected working groups in close focus. However, the ambit of Figure 10.1 does help us to grasp the breadth of the macro-level variables that exercise influence on the micro-sociology of community policing practice with which we have largely been concerned.

Contrast to established practices has always provided the principal means of establishing the character of community policing and Figure 10.1 expresses this in ideal-typical terms. Several points are highlighted. First, under 'philosophical' considerations, community policing is seen as explicitly political—officers 'mediate interests'. They are responsible to community and political representatives, and are bound by 'policy and operational accounting'. Regarding organizational structure, the trend in conventional policing is to specialization, whereas community policing promotes generalist patrol-based skills. This heightens the importance of community policing to trainers, as a model and first posting. Looking at management policy, communication in conventional policing is from the top down whereas community policing seeks interaction between ranks (beat officers become experts on their beats relative to supervisors). On the evaluation of service, conventional policing uses 'internal', quantitative measures, whereas community policing uses qualitative measures which are 'product-oriented'.

In operational strategies and tactics, conventional policing is crime-oriented and incident-specific while community policing pursues 'problem-solving' on a 'community defined' mix of reactive and proactive modes. Relief response is marked by 'load-shedding' because there is little call screening, whereas in community policing calls are analysed and there is 'load-sharing' due to inter-agency referral. Community police engage in criminal investigation, have more opportunities to analyse crime problems and gather information, whereas reliefs refer these matters to detectives. Random assignment impairs teamwork in conventional policing, while in community policing the patrol emphasis facilitates teamwork. Also, when detailed information is collected it becomes worth trading, enhancing information exchange. In conventional policing, crime prevention is specialized whereas in community policing it is a basic patrol strategy. Relief officers also have clearer priorities and are tied to central control through the despatcher, while community police must decide whether the best response is crime control, social service or both. Community police face more choices, have more autonomy and discretion, and correspondingly less guidance, while being more open to public pressure and scrutiny.

While Figure 10.1 highlights contrasts in ideal-typical terms, and is speculative and suggestive rather than empirically proven, I earlier argued that, if community policing was to be shown to have a distinctive effect on police practice, it would be necessary to examine decision-making by relief and community officers. Contrasts in practice were then explored in terms of making community contacts, information-gathering, interpersonal tactics and the achievement of order and crime control in hostile communities. Different styles were also seen as resulting from the organization's processing of service demands: how the organization classified the demand and which of its units it deemed most suitable (CID, relief or community police). If community police are only passed demands for which a legal remedy is unlikely one would expect them to have a different approach and to employ discretion less legalistically.

Differences between relief and community policing practices were therefore apparent, but periodic reference was also made to the idea that relief and community officers' different organizational location afforded different means of *accounting* for their action. Differences of autonomy, supervision and shift times, joined differences in style in making community police differently accountable. Indeed, we may view the numerous typologies of officer 'styles' in the policing literature not as guides to action but as guides to accounts of action. The 'account' of an action and the 'reason' for it are logically distinct. The crucial matter is whether those representing a given type act consistently to type over time. There is little point in typologies unless they let us anticipate officers' action. Methodologically, this implies the importance of sustained observational data to augment interviews or activity surveys. Even so, the problem of determining officers' reasons for an action will always be with us, so let us accept that what we most reliably have is an account of the action, albeit one mediated by the observer's knowledge. This does not mean we are left without a grasp of officer decision-making, because we have acknowledged that the organization makes different types of accounts available to different units. In this sense the means of accounting for or legitimating action prefigure action. An influence on the decision that is made is thus the form of account that will later be available to justify it. An organizational feature again affects decision-making.

When sociologists construct theories they increasingly acknowledge the need for closer fit between the 'micro' and 'macro' domain.[2]

[2] Knorr-Cetina (1988); Fielding (1988d).

Despite seeing action as the basic social unit, Parsons' analysis of 'acts'[3] and 'structure'[4] arguably left 'interaction' behind, making a rigid theory of social order which neglected how the relationship of behaviour and organization was mediated. Turner argues that, rather than action and behaviour, social *inter*action is the most basic unit of analysis.[5] It involves three interrelated, dynamic processes: motivational, the process of mobilizing interactive behaviour; interactional, the process of mutual signaling and interpreting with symbols; and structuring, the process of repeating and organizing social interactions in time and place. Thus, 'just how people signal and interpret is related to their motivational energies; in turn, motivation is circumscribed by prevailing structural arrangements as well as by the course of signaling and interpreting; and the structure of an interaction is very much determined by the motivational profiles of individuals as these affect their signaling and interpreting activities.'[6] Resulting models concern how variables influence each other across time, involving feedback loops, lag effects, and reciprocal causal effects.

Let us consider the elements of a broad comparison of officer decision-making in such terms. At the 'macro' level, our account would include (i) the constitutional 'mandate' of police, (ii) the law regulating police work, (iii) administrative regulations, (iv) function to which officer assigned (relief, community policing), (v) accepted practices in police culture, (vi) local variations of those practices, (vii) local supervisory officer policies. At the 'mezzo' level, the bridge to process variables includes: officers available; their individual capacities and characteristics; equipment; local shift system; availability of overtime payments, allowances and bonuses in kind (e.g., training courses); the system of appraisal, performance measurement and promotion locally in use. 'Micro' variables would cover (i) officer character and orientation (motivation, 'types'); (ii) officer specialist knowledge; (iii) officer sense of back-up and teamwork; (iv) spatio-temporal dimension of incident (where on beat, when on shift); (v) presenting problem of incident; (vi) parties present; (vii) disposition of parties; (viii) nature and quality of interaction (condensing detailed features noted by observation); (ix) immediate citizen-perceived outcome; (x) immediate officer-perceived outcome; (xi) inter-officer discussion prior to paper processing; (xii) paperwork in station; (xiii) effort of other officers

---

[3] Parsons (1937).   [4] Parsons (1951)   [5] Turner (1988).   [6] *Ibid.* at 16.

affecting case; (xiv) longer-term outcome and any continuing involvement of initial officer. While this model offers some necessary dimensions in comparing the two types of patrol work it condenses
decision-making at incident level (point viii of the 'micro' list).
Considerations at this level are shown in figure 10.2. This sketch of

Figure 10.2. Incident description model for decisions at reactive incidents

1. Officer disposition variables (spatio-temporal variables, officer personal
   resources)

2. Mode of input to organization (999; local station phone; on-street request
   for assistance; event in progress)

3. Information available to officer from initial contact

4. Interactional features
   a. Course of action description
   b. Dialogue description
   c. *In situ* option points (as action unfolds)
      i. Nature of option
      ii. Explanation of option by officer
      iii. Negotiation over this option
      iv. Degree to which officer indicates preferred option
      v. Quality of officer elicitation of further information pertinent to
         decision
   d. Change in officer demeanour

5. Closing negotiation of what officer will do
   a. Explanation of decision by officer
   b. Expressed satisfaction/dissatisfaction by citizen(s)
   c. Discussion of further action between officer/citizen
   d. Explanation of decision/situation by officer to other officers
   e. Explanation of decision/situation by officer to observer

6. Any role of back-up/other officers/supervisors

7. Paper work decision-making
   a. Informal discussion with other officers
   b. Advice-seeking from other officers
   c. Informal discussion with supervisor(s)
   d. Advice-seeking from supervisor(s)
   e. Formal paper work
   f. Discussion of paper work
      i. Other officers
      ii. Supervisor(s)
      iii. Citizen(s)

variables associated with decision-making suggests that research evaluations based on time spent in various activities or comparisons of crime statistics before and after community policing, are unsatisfactory, just as, one hastens to add, would be an endorsement of community policing based purely on a qualitative study such as this. I say more about the research agenda below.

The pessimistic research evaluations of community policing engender suspicion of the motives of policy makers in their sustained enthusiasm for this apparent panacea. Further, because 'community policing' is an umbrella term for several related programmes, it is sufficient, for some critics, to show that one element does not 'work' and thus dismiss the whole enterprise. Such use has been made, for instance, of critical research on Neighbourhood Watch.[7] Neighbourhood Watch is characterized as involving 'low take-up rates, weak community penetration and limping, dormant or stillborn schemes'.[8] There is little reason to doubt the findings of this careful, multimethod study. But its extension from Neighbourhood Watch to community policing in general is more dubious. ('. . . Neighbourhood Watch is used as a way of looking at police-community relations and the state of contemporary policing in Britain.'[9]) In asserting that Neighbourhood Watch 'encapsulates the thrust of the police approach and epitomizes the promise of a new age of policing', McConville and Shepherd are referring to the official recognition that 'impositional policing' has both limited effectiveness and qualities that alienate the public. While agreeing that Neighbourhood Watch represents a tangible icon in the 'discovery' that the public still has a part in social control, Neighbourhood Watch is but one part of community policing and, on McConville and Shepherd's own evidence, it is not the central part. Like the public, police see intensive patrol and a stronger preventive emphasis as the central component of community policing. 'CP is about emphasizing and encouraging the development of preventive and non-conflictual aspects of policing and giving them more status than they currently have . . .[10] Neighbourhood Watch should certainly be read as an element of that more preventive emphasis but the very limits of public involvement in it show that people still look to the police to effect control in the community. It is unsatisfactory to assess community policing solely on the basis of Neighbourhood Watch.

[7] For example, Bennett (1989).   [8] McConville and Shepherd (1992) at 115.
[9] *Ibid.* at 1.   [10] Weatheritt (1987) at 8.

Yet few studies have focused on what community police actually do in long-term beat assignment. The most detailed account appears as a sub-theme in a book about accountability for routine police work.[11] Further, researchers have not pursued the argument that the key to determining the 'effectiveness and efficiency' of community policing has still not been turned because the successes of community policing lie in the realm of forbearance—offences scotched at the planning stage by low-level arrests, crime information passed to other functions for prosecution, the diversion of potential offenders by making it apparent that their activities were known to police, the scaling down of potentially riotous situations.[12] It is easy to make community policing look slipshod and inconsequential by assessing it on measures designed for high-activity, short call-duration motorized patrol.

But measures of community policing's less visible activities can be devised. The 'beat crime book' could be revived, with a requirement that officers report when they have used discretion to avoid arrest and indicate likely charges had this not been done. Officers could issue numbered chits as warnings to those 'advised' as they intervene on patrol. Community constables could take on the crime collator role for their beat, and set themselves quotas for crimes cleared. On patrol, officers could routinely issue keyholder cards for premises fitted with alarms, the number distributed forming an index of activity. Time spent on non-law enforcement calls could be measured; more ambitiously, officers could write or tape summaries of incidents for periodic vetting. Officers could help residents mark their property, as some already do, and the number helped could be tallied. Official enthusiasm for community policing could be conveyed by changing the requirement that chief constables should have served at senior level in another force, a policy which may limit their knowledge about the community their force serves.

Community consultation could be developed at beat level, with feedback on the officer's efforts and a requirement that detectives attend so they can hear what enforcement the public wants rather than letting social service demands dominate meetings, and so detectives can share their problem-solving perspective with patrol officers. Crime patterns and tactics to deal with types of offender could be discussed. In Halifax, Nova Scotia, where the whole force received

[11] Grimshaw and Jefferson (1987).   [12] Fielding *et al.* (1989).

training in community policing, three impact measures were used: officer satisfaction, crime data and calls for service, and community satisfaction. Local media could be monitored to see whether community policing policies are commented on by citizens.[13] Official evaluations should also accept that there can be no universally-applicable measures of community policing. Variations between communities require locally attuned measures. For example, in one Canadian town with a largely elderly population, neighbourhood police stations were set up, using volunteers recruited from the elderly and a community constable for liaison. Low crime rates meant the station's chief role was not operational assistance but counteracting fear of crime and providing information.[14]

Few analyses have taken issue with the *philosophy* of community policing. Indeed, the editor of a generally pessimistic book about community policing begins his collection with the words 'there is no real alternative to a community-based approach to policing'.[15] One of the few who has challenged the philosophical underpinning of these schemes is Mollie Weatheritt. In Wilmott's book she identified the problems community policing was meant to address and evaluated its effectiveness in achieving programme objectives. Her conclusion: 'whilst community policing ideas have been useful in stimulating debate and action, answers to policing problems cannot be found embedded in community policing philosophy nor in the practice to which it has given rise'.[16] However, this analysis is based on an empirical review of programmes tied to a particular policy context. Such effort is informed by the attempt to evaluate policing in terms of its final objectives.[17] But, as Smith points out,[18] many aspects of policing cannot be analysed in the language of objectives, especially the symbolic elements and those objectives about which there is no consensus.

Even discounting this point, Weatheritt's review of the empirical evidence can be read as highlighting the ambiguity of the evidence rather than its proof of community policing's failings.[19] The 'evidence' of community policing patrol ineffectiveness amounts to one study conducted in the United States and not replicated here. In an

---

[13] Loree, D., Canadian Police College, Ottawa, personal communication, 28 Feb., 1990.

[14] Clairmont (1990).

[15] Wilmott (1987) at 4.

[16] *Ibid.* at 19.

[17] Lubans and Edgar (1979); Goldstein (1979).

[18] Smith (1989).

[19] Weatheritt (1987).

earlier study Weatheritt[20] reported a re-analysis of police data from the 1981 West Midlands foot patrol experiments which revealed increases in recorded crime in the test areas, but the officers were both unclear about their new objectives and unwilling to carry them out. In the absence of sound comparisons of foot and car patrol, she reverts to the plausible hypothesis that the likelihood of foot patrol officers spontaneously encountering a crime are low.[21] But the point about community policing patrol is that it should involve increased information-gathering contacts with the public, not just walking around. The forms this can take are illustrated throughout this book and amount to more than the 'essentially symbolic' role accorded to community patrol by McConville and Shepherd.[22] This is not to deny the symbolic assurance given by foot patrol nor its value in balancing the excesses of the 'impositional' style in urban 'strategic locations'. The clearest message from Weatheritt's reviews of patrol is that an adequate assessment of their effectiveness awaits a detailed study of how community police go about their work.

Leaving to one side the questions begged by assuming that community policing effectiveness can be measured as in the studies to which Weatheritt refers, there remains the matter of community policing philosophy. How is it possible for Wilmott to see no alternative to community policing in the same volume as his contributor Weatheritt can see in it no value at all? Perhaps this comes about because of imprecise specification of the term 'community policing'. For it is not the philosophy but the practice which Weatheritt finds wanting. The 'philosophy' she highlights is little more than abstract statements of policy, as in the writings of ex-Chief Constable John Alderson. But it can be argued that the relevant 'philosophy' lies in jurisprudence, particularly its development in common law. The connection of community policing with that stream of 'philosophy' is direct and worth more serious consideration than it has received.

One certainty does mark this field, that policy makers come back again and again to the appeal of community policing. Its current manifestation is the enthusiasm for 'sector policing'. Here, the idea is that, far from a flop, community policing is so grand that the whole of relief policing is to be discarded in favour of geographically-based community policing. How can such a discredited method remain so

---

[20] Weatheritt (1986).   [21] *Ibid.* at 15.
[22] McConville and Shepherd (1992) at 36.

appealing? Let us turn to another notable critic of community policing, David Smith. His chapter in the Wilmott collection seeks, like
Weatheritt, to tackle the 'theory' of community policing. Smith con-
cludes that community policing 'has made little difference or has not
produced the intended results'.[23] The chapter is valuable in identifying five underlying problems which, Smith argues, account for the
(allegedly) poor results of community policing. These turn out to be
matters which all, in one way or another, relate to politics,
specifically urban politics and the politics of social control. He lists
the fact that, 'police-initiated activity is mostly adversarial: consen-
sus-building activity is hard to plan; policing impinges on different
sections of the community in contrasting ways; decentralization
conflicts with the universal framework of law; formal controls contrast with informal ones, and informal controls are hard to control
formally; the ideal of community cannot cope with the distribution
of resources'.[24] Smith's list gets us further than Weatheritt, but it does
so by speaking directly to the wider conditions in which policy is
framed and operates. It is fundamentally informed by the perception
that policing is always political, and, in its effects, always partisan.

Much of Smith's analysis contains implications about what could
redress the critical problems he highlights (just as this book has
examined how police tackle such problems). Thus, in discussing the
idea that the 'days of community consensus have passed', Smith suggests that many implementation plans have not recognized that communities contain groups with competing interests and 'there needs to
be some machinery which can make it possible for negotiation to
take place where necessary between the different interest groups and
the police'. It surely cannot be impossible to devise such arrangements; indeed, the germs of it being made to work within existing
structures are suggested in my account of the raid on an international
drug smuggling warehouse. Smith's rejoinder would be that this
proves his point that the only planned police work is adversarial and
works against consensus,[25] but the evidence is that local people
excluded drug smugglers from the consensus. Another problem is
that people perceive their local community as very 'local' indeed, so
that community policing needs to be more sensitive to the confined
sense of place held by city dwellers. Given manpower, this can be
tackled and, again, in this book the account of promoting

---

[23] Smith (1987).   [24] Ibid. at 61.   [25] Ibid. at 62.

Neighbourhood Watch in an opulent highrise suggested the role constables play in working through the implications of that jealous version of 'locality'. These are not, then, insurmountable problems of 'philosophy' or 'theory'.

But while these are certainly problems of implementation, they are also problems of politics. The big issue which welds Smith's five problems into one is that community policing walks a tightrope between empowering 'the community' and maintaining the *status quo*. Let us turn to a final chapter from Wilmott's collection to see how. Jon Bright, of the Safe Neighbourhoods Unit, wrote that local organizations, not the police, should take the lead in crime prevention. Based on experience of working with the police in London and elsewhere, Bright argued that community policing, if it was to mean anything distinctive, should rely on solutions and strategies put forward by local residents and be supported by investment in infrastructure (such as restoring porters to housing estates). This was not some radical polemic from an inconvenient outsider; the Safe Neighbourhoods Unit receives official funding and directly provides practical improvements on estates. Nor was Bright's chapter overly in thrall to the wondrous efforts of community police. Indeed, he complains that beats were too large, contacts with residents were unproductive, and community policing had little success with black residents, who still lacked confidence and trust in police.[26] But Bright uses these criticisms to argue that the respective roles of police, other social agencies and the community need to be specified in a planned, locally-attuned way. He does not use the criticisms to dismiss community policing altogether. What he does is to bring the political challenge into the account.

All of this suggests a new research agenda, whose scope takes us outside community policing *per se* and towards systematic study of the benefits and disadvantages of the police institution. The questions are whether the total policing effort is contributing towards achieving the objectives of maintaining order and fostering the control of crime, and whether one approach to policing or another is most successful in achieving them. Any study of one approach cannot do this, yet that is the general nature of police research. Even if it were possible to present all the observations from the fieldwork, and we were to take at literal value all the positive

---

[26] Bright (1987).

assertions of community policing's worth from the interviews while discounting the rest, we would not be able to determine whether a particular style of policing or a particular body of police officers (such as community constables) were achieving worthwhile results in respect of public expenditure and the general purposes of policing. A single programme may be working on its own terms, but we need to determine the measure of its success relative to others. Further, a programme or unit may produce benefits that are simply counteracted by some other programme or unit. Community police may succeed in particular incidents but their efforts may be negated because there are other elements of the institution which exercise predominant influence on the nature of social control. We need to research the institution as a system if we are to pursue *conclusive* evidence of the effects of its parts.

There remain political reasons for the policy maker's measured enthusiasm for community policing and, as the recent history of sector policing (and other areas of criminal justice) suggest, politicians obey other imperatives than research findings. At the 'sloganistic' level, being against 'community policing' would seem to put one in favour of non-communal, sectional policing. Even for the better informed, an awareness of the demerits of relief policing—both in terms of superficial case handling and actual malpractice—must warm one towards an ostensibly more accountable alternative.

But politicians cannot forever excite aspirations that cannot be delivered. If community policing is to square off to political reality it will have to be seen as what the common law long ago promised, a system of enforcement finely attuned to prevailing local standards, those standards being thrashed out and manifest in debate at neighbourhood level. That will not drain community policing of its political volatility. With its promise comes a matter which is genuinely philosophical: how far will we countenance minute variation in the application of law on the strength of such a literal common law approach, when we customarily understand equity to mean the application of universal standards. Are we prepared to use community policing as a form of social engineering to redress the balance which has been skewed in favour of the powerful by the effects of routine policing?

The socio-legal perspective on the history of police tells us that the new police had from the outset a 'civilizing' mission, motivated by the need to ensure the free circulation of commodities, and directed

at overcoming the resistance of the poor.[27] There was fierce resistance to the imposition of legal norms of public order yet anything
less than full enforcement jeopardized the police claim to impartially
enforce the law. Police faced 'the impossible choice of enforcing law
or order',[28] that is, the new bourgeois legal order with its version of
the rights of capital and the duties of labour versus the old norms of
acceptable public behaviour in working class neighbourhoods. The
solution was compromise, with a shift from outright physical confrontation to 'an unwritten system of tacit negotiation' which meant
'turning half a blind eye to the rule book' and 'turning the other half
to a good deal of minor infringement'.[29] Importantly, the change
related not just to the ideological function of the police but to the
emergent split in the working class between the labour aristocracy
('the respectables') and casual labourers ('the roughs'). Interestingly,
McConville and Shepherd's argument that Neighbourhood Watch
has failed because crime is but an intermittent concern is informed
by their observation that 'significant numbers of ordinary people,
including many of the property-owning classes, refuse to accord
"crime" and "criminals" folk-devil status, in some cases because they
see crime as a product of the political economy'.[30]

Over time the compromise solution has been institutionalized in
the division of labour between beat constables, who seek to maintain negotiated order, and paramilitary units like riot police and
regional crime squads, whose brief is to impose statutory order without regard for factors constraining the actions of local police.[31]
Further, 'the more resources allocated to increasing the efficiency of
repressive policing, the more manpower has to be poured into "community relations" to re-stabilize the public image of the force. The
more technologically sophisticated, and hence impersonal, the system
of surveillance, the more homebeat coppers are needed on the
ground.'[32] The whole cycle has to be constantly repeated as new
social groups enter the inner city and 'new contingencies constantly
threaten the always "unstable equilibria" of existing accommoda-
tions'.[33]

The first official instinct when threatened is to apply the paramilitary form, but ironically this undermines the order it was designed

[27] Cohen (1979).   [28] *Ibid.* at 130.   [29] *Ibid.*
[30] McConville and Shepherd (1992) at 226.
[31] Jefferson (1990) at 24.   [32] Cohen (1979) at 133.
[33] Jefferson (1990) at 25.

to uphold. So paramilitarism and community policing progress side-by-side in deadly contradiction. Jefferson also notes an 'internal' irony, that community policing has sought 'to compensate for the unwanted side-effects of the specialization that devalued the all-purpose beat patroller to such an extent that the only alternative was to make traditional, generalist policing itself a specialism'.[34] The question is thus not whether community policing 'works' but what would be the consequence if it were removed because, on criteria insensitive to the 'negotiated order', it worked less well than conventional patrol. The answer may be that the contradiction/compromise would have to be admitted and a new one found, or it may be that we would be left only with repressive policing. To put it bluntly, let us indeed criticize community policing. But before we put the researcher's boot in, let us also pause to consider the alternative. Discussing the interplay between repressive and community policing, McConville and Shepherd perceive an 'essential congruity between policing policies toward "symbolic locations" and the day to day . . . (soft) policing practices of officers on the beat in these areas. Both are based on the need for exceptional and therefore discriminatory policing of the black community.'[35] While their plausible assessment is that policing is thus experienced as contingent and arbitrary, the implication that 'exceptional' (i.e., differential) policing is somehow 'discriminatory' merits further discussion. The implication of their position is that policing should not be attuned to the characteristics of each community but should aspire to some universal standard. Moreover, if the congruity of repressive and 'expressive' policing is to be broken, surely that leaves us with undiluted repression.

Earlier, I discussed Banton's conception of an enhanced, socially-redistributive form of crime prevention. If the 'mediating role' has any substance at a level about the micro-sociology of police–public encounters, the police must move to a more sophisticated understanding of partisanship and sectional interests. Perhaps this is community policing's hidden contribution, not directly to the public but to their own organization. As things stand, sector policing faces large obstacles in converting all frontline policing to a community policing model, and prior to these innovations community police sections have been too small to greatly affect the delivery of police services.

---

[34] Jefferson (1990) at 25.   [35] McConville and Shepherd (1992) at 241.

What community policing has provided is a realism-enhancing, dissenting voice in an organization otherwise disinclined to take the long view or to consider its broader purposes.

In political science, coercive power has both a use in the control of abusive coercion (the function of Leviathan in repressing atavistic struggles) and a role in securing equality. Muir argues that 'the two civilised means of interpersonal control, exchange and exhortation [tend] to magnify natural human inequalities'.[36] In unequal conditions, market exchange does not reduce inequality: the rich use their freedom to get richer, to trade things they have for things in the possession of other 'haves'. The have-nots possess no resources with which to bargain, and are left out of the marketplace. 'Extortionate power can be the great corrective of this tragic condition. It enables the have-nots to get something from the haves for nothing. Coercion can facilitate equality by enabling the dispossessed to accumulate and assume their seats in the marketplace.'[37] Where police act against the crimes of the powerful, and bring calm to the disprivileged regions the policies of the powerful create, then social control is a good. De Tocqueville argued that it was not power that corrupts but the feeling that its exercise is illegitimate.[38] It is not a fault to which police are prone.

---

[36] Muir (1977) at 278.   [37] *Ibid.*   [38] de Tocqueville (1945), section 1.9.

Bibliography

Agar, M. and Hobbs, J. (1985), 'How to Grow Schemata out of Interviews' in J. Dougherty (ed.) *Cognition in Action*, Urbana: University of Illinois Press.

Alderson, J. (1975), 'People, Government and the Police' in J. Brown and G. Howes (eds.) *The Police and the Community*, Farnborough: Saxon House.

Azarya, V. (1985), 'Community', *The Social Science Encyclopedia*, London: Routledge.

Bailey, S. (1982), 'Northumbria Police Community Services Department: Philosophy and Implementation', *Police Officer*, 9, 10–11.

Baker, D. and Donnelly, P. (1986), 'Neighbourhood Criminals and Outsiders in two Communities', *Sociology and Social Research*, 71(1), 59–65.

Banton, M. (1964), *The Policeman in the Community*, London: Tavistock.

—— (1974), 'The Definition of the Police Role', *New Community*, 3(3), 164–71.

Bayley, D. (1982), 'A World Perspective on the Role of the Police in Social Control' in R. Donelan (ed.) *The Maintenance of Order in Society*, Ottawa: Ministry of Supply and Services.

Becker, H. (1967), *The Outsiders*, Glencoe, Ill.: Free Press.

Bennett, T. (1989), 'The Neighbourhood Watch Experiment' in R. Morgan and D. Smith (eds.) *Coming to Terms with Policing*, London: Routledge.

Bennett, T. and Lupton, R. (1992a), 'A National Activity Survey of Police Work', *Howard Journal of Criminal Justice*, 31(3), 200–23.

—— (1992b), 'A National Survey of the Organisation and Use of Community Constables' *British Journal of Criminology*, 32(2), 167–82.

Birch, R. (1982), 'Non-political Solutions to a Grossly Political Problem', *Police Officer*, 9, 6–7.

Bittner, E. (1980), *The Functions of the Police in Modern Society*, Cambridge, MA: Oelgeschlager, Gunn & Hain.

Black, D. (1971), 'The Social Organisation of Arrest', *Stanford Law Review*, 23, 1087–111.

—— (1980), *The Manners and Customs of the Police*, New York: Academic.

Blau, P. and Scott, W. (1963), *Formal Organizations*, London: Routledge.

Brewer, J. (1991a), *Inside the RUC*, Oxford: Clarendon.

—— (1991b), 'Policing in Divided Societies', *Policing and Society*, 1(1), 179–91.

Bright, J. (1987), 'Community Safety, Crime Prevention and the Local Authority' in P. Wilmott (ed.) *Policing and the Community*, London: PSI.

Brogden, M. (1982), *Police: Autonomy and Consent*, London: Academic.

Brown, D. and Iles, S. (1985), 'The Work of Community Constables', London: Home Office.

Brown, M. (1988), *Working the Street: Police Discretion and Dilemmas of Reform*, New York: Russell Sage.

Bucqueroux, B. (1988), 'Executive Session on Community Policing', *Footprints*, Spring/Summer.

Burns-Howell, A. and Jones, J. M. (1982), 'Policing Strategy: Organisational or Victim Needs', unpublished report, Bramshill Police Staff College.

Burrows, J. and Lewis, H. (1988), *Directing Patrol Work*, Home Office Research Study 99, London: HMSO.

Cain, M. (1973), *Society and the Policeman's Role*, London: Routledge.

Chatterton, M. (1979), 'The Supervision of Patrol Work under the Fixed Points System' in S. Holdaway (ed.) *The British Police*, London: Edward Arnold.

—— (1981), 'Practical Coppers, Oarsmen and Administrators: Frontline Supervisory Styles in Police Organisations', unpublished paper presented to ISA Research Committee Conference on the Sociology of Law, Oxford.

Clairmont, D. (1990), *To the Forefront: Community-based Zone Policing in Halifax*, Ottawa: Ministry of Supply and Services.

Clark, C., Drew, P. and Pinch, T. (1989), '(Not so) "Small Talk": Some Verbal Procedures for Managing Agreement and "Rapport" During Selling Interactions', mimeo, Department of Sociology, University of York.

Clarke, R. and Hough, M. (1980), *The Effectiveness of Policing*, Farnborough: Gower.

Cohen, A. (1966), *Deviance and Control*, Englewood Cliffs, NJ: Prentice Hall.

Cohen, P. (1979), 'Policing the Working Class City' in B. Fine *et al.* (eds.) *Capitalism and the Rule of Law*, London: Hutchinson.

Comrie, M. and Kings, E. (1975), *Study of Urban Workloads*, London: Home Office.

Cotterell, R. (1989), *The Politics of Jurisprudence*, London: Butterworth.

Crisp, D. and Newburn, T. (1991), 'Threatening Behaviour and Disorderly Conduct: Policing Low Level Offences under the 1986 Public Order Act', paper presented to British Criminology Conference, University of York.

Critchley, T. (1978), *A History of Police in England and Wales*, London: Constable.

Dalton, G. (1968), 'The Economy as Instituted Process' in E. le Clair and W. Schneider (eds.) *Economic Anthropology*, New York: Holt, Rinehart & Winston.

de Tocqueville, A. (1945), *Democracy in Europe*, New York: Vintage.

Dixon, B. and Stanko, E. (1993), 'Serving the People: Sector Policing and Local Accountability', Uxbridge: Brunel University Centre for Criminal Justice Research.

Donnison, D. *et al.* (1986), *Neighbourhood Watch: Policing the People*, London: Police Foundation.

Eco, U. (1989), *Foucault's Pendulum*, London: Secker and Warburg.

Ekblom, P. and Heal, K. (1982), *The Police Response to Calls from the Public*, Research and Planning Paper 9, London: Home Office.

Evans, P. (1974), *The Police Revolution*, London: Allen and Unwin.

Field, S. and Southgate, P. (1982), *Public Disorder*, London: HMSO.

Fielding, N. (1984), 'Police Socialisation and Police Competence', *British Journal of Sociology*, 35(4), 568–90.

—— (1988a), 'Competence and Culture in the Police', *Sociology*, 22(1), 45–64.

—— (1988b), *Joining Forces*, London: Routledge.

—— (1988c), 'Socialisation of Recruits into the Police Role' in P. Southgate (ed.) *New directions in police training*, London: HMSO, 58–73.

—— (1988d), 'Between Micro and Macro', in N. Fielding (ed.) *Actions and structure*, London: Sage.

—— (1989), 'Police Culture and Police Practice' in M. Weatheritt (ed.) *Police Research: Some Future Prospects*, London: Avebury, 77–88.

—— (1990), 'Mediating the Message: the Co-production of Field Research', *American Behavioral Scientist*, 33(5), 608–20.

—— (1991), *The Police and Social Conflict*, London: Athlone.

Fielding, N. and Fielding, J. (1986), *Linking Data*, Beverly Hills CA: Sage.

Fielding, N., Kemp, C. and Norris, C. (1989), 'Constraints on the Practice of Community Policing' in D. Smith and R. Morgan (eds.) *Coming to Terms with Policing*, London: Routledge.

Fielding, N. and Lee, R. (eds.) (1993), *Using Computers in Qualitative Research*, London: Sage.

Goldstein, H. (1979), 'Improving Policing: a Problem-oriented Approach', *Crime and Delinquency*, XX.

Greene, J. and Decker, S. (1989), 'Police and Community Perceptions of the Community role in Policing: the Philadelphia Experience', *Howard Journal of Criminal Justice*, 28(2), 105–23.

Grimshaw, R. and Jefferson, T. (1987), *Interpreting Policework*, London: Allen and Unwin.

Hibberd, M. (1990), 'Violent Crime and Trouble in Small Shops', in C. Kemp (ed.) *Current Issues in Criminological Research*, Bath: Bristol and Bath Centre for Criminal Justice.

Hogarth, J. (1982), 'Police Accountability', in R. Donelan (ed.) *The Maintenance of Order in Society*, Ottawa: Ministry of Supply and Services.

Holdaway, S. (1983), *Inside the British Police*, Oxford: Basil Blackwell.

Horton, C. (1989), 'Good Practice and Evaluating Policing' in R. Morgan and D. Smith (eds.) *Coming to Terms with Policing*, London: Routledge.

Horton, C. and Smith, D. (1987), *Evaluating Policework*, London: Policy Studies Institute.

Hough, M. (1980), *Uniformed Police Work and Management Technology*, London: Home Office Research Unit.

Irving, B. *et al.* (1986), *Independent Evaluation of an Experiment in Neighbourhood Policing in Notting Hill*, London: Police Foundation.

—— (1989), *Neighbourhood Policing: the Natural History of a Policing Experiment*, London: Police Foundation.

Jackson, H. and Field, S. (1989), 'Race, Community Groups and Service Delivery', London: HMSO.

Jefferson, T. (1990), *The Case against Paramilitary Policing*, Buckingham, Open University Press.

Jefferson, T. and Grimshaw, R. (1984), *Controlling the Constable*, London: Frederick Muller.

Jones, J. M. and Winkler, J. (1982), 'Beyond the Beat: the Facts about Policing in a Riotous City', *Journal of Law and Society*, 9(1), 103–14.

Keith, M. (1988), 'Squaring Circles?: Consultation and "Inner City" Policing', *New Community*, 15(1).

Kelling, G. and Moore, M. (1988), 'From Political Reform to Community: the Evolving Strategy of Police' in J. Greene and S. Mastrofski (eds.) *Community Policing: Rhetoric or Reality*, New York: Praeger.

Knorr-Cetina, K. (1988), 'The Micro-Social order: Towards a Reconception' in N. Fielding (ed.) *Actions and Structure*, London: Sage.

Landry, C. (1991), *Out of Hours*, London: Gulbenkian Foundation.

Lea, J. and Young, J. (1982), 'The Riots in Britain 1981: Urban Violence and Political Marginalisation' in D. Cowell, *et al.* (eds.) *Policing the Riots*, London: Junction Books.

Lubans, V. and Edgar, J. (1979), *Policing by Objectives*, Hartford, CN: Social Development Corp.

Lustgarten, L. (1986), *The Governance of Police*, London: Sweet and Maxwell.

Macdonald, V. N. (1986), *A Study of Leadership and Supervision in Policing*, Ottawa: Canadian Police College.

Maine, H. (1861), *Ancient Law*, London: Dent (1917 edn.).

Manning, P. (1977), *Police Work*, Cambridge MA: MIT Press.

—— (1982a), 'Modern Police Administration, the Rise of Crime-focused Policing and Critical Incident Analysis' in R. Donelan (ed.) *The Maintenance of Order in Society*, Ottawa: Ministry of Supply and Services.

—— (1982b), *The Narc's Game*, Cambridge MA: MIT Press.

—— (1983), 'Queries Concerning the Decision-making Approach to Police Research' in J. Shapland (ed.) *Decision Making in the Legal System*, London: British Psychological Society.

—— (1985), 'Police: Community' in L. Radelet (ed.) *The Police and the Community*, 4/e.

Marshall, G. (1965), *The Police and Government*, London: Methuen.

McBarnet, D. (1981), *Conviction: Law, the State and the Construction of Justice*, London: Macmillan.

McCabe, S. and Wallington, P. (1988), *Police, Public order and Civil Liberties*, London: Routledge.

McConville, M. and Shepherd, D. (1992), *Watching Police, Watching Communities*, London: Routledge.

McLanus, T. (1990), 'Tactics to Target Troubled Neighborhoods', *Footprints*, III (2), 6–7.

—— (1992), 'Officer Wayne Barton: the Pied Piper of Pearl City', *Footprints* V(2), 5–9.

Metropolitan Police (1986), 'Force Appraisal', September.

—— (1991), 'Sector Policing: Guide for Divisional Management Teams'.

—— (1992), 'Corporate Strategy 1992/3–1996/7'.

Muir, W. K., Jnr., (1977), *Police: Streetcorner Politicians*, Chicago: University of Chicago Press.

Murphy, C. (1986), 'Contemporary Models of Urban Policing: a Comparative Analysis', Ottawa: Ministry of the Solicitor General.

—— (1988), 'The Development, Impact and Implications of Community Policing in Canada' in J. Greene and S. Mastrofski (eds.) *Community Policing: Rhetoric or Reality*, New York: Praeger.

NACRO (1984), 'Community Improvement Projects on 12 Inner London Estates', London: NACRO Safe Neighbourhood Unit.

—— (1988), 'Policing Housing Estates', London: NACRO.

Norris, C. (1983), 'Policing Trouble: an Observation Study of Police Patrol Work in Two Police Forces', unpublished doctoral thesis, Department of Sociology, University of Surrey.

Norris, C., Kemp, C. and Fielding, N. (1992), 'Black and Blue: the Influence of Race on being Stopped by the Police', *British Journal of Sociology*, 43(2), 207–23.

Parsons, T. (1937), *The Structure of Social Action*, New York: McGraw Hill.

—— (1951), *The Social System*, New York: McGraw Hill.

Polanyi, K. (1957), 'The Economy as an 'Instituted Process' in K. Polanyi, C. Arensberg and H. Pearson, (eds.) *Trade and Market in the Early Empires*, New York: Free Press.

Pollak, M. (1990), 'The Well-tempered Client', London: Islington Police and Crime Prevention Unit.

Pope, D. (1976), *Community Relations: the Police Response*, London: Runnymede Trust.

Postema, G. (1986), *Bentham and the Common Law Tradition*, Oxford: Oxford University Press.

Pound, R. (1921), *The Spirit of the Common Law*, Francestown, NH: Marshall Jones.

Punch, M. and Naylor, T. (1973), 'The Police: a Social Service', *New Society*, 17 May.

Radcliffe-Brown, E. (1965), *Structure and Function in Primitive Society*, New York: Free Press.

Reuss-Ianni, E. (1982), *Two Cultures of Policing*, London: Transaction.

Royal Commission on the Police (1962), *Final Report*, Cmnd. 1728, London: HMSO.

Rubinstein, J. (1973), *City Police*, New York: Farrar, Straus and Giroux.

Schaffer, E. (1980), *Community Policing*, Aldershot: Croom Helm.

Scissons, E. (1990), *Police Leadership Part II: Organizational Decision-making*, Ottawa: Canadian Police College.

Smith, D. and Gray, J. (1983), *Police and People in London*, London: Policy Studies Institute.

Smith, D. (1987), 'Research, the Community and the Police', in P. Wilmott (ed.) *Policing and the Community*, London: Policy Studies Institute.

—— (1989), 'Evaluating Police Work' in Statistics Users Council, *Law and Order Statistics*, Conference proceedings, 26–38.

Southgate, P. and Ekblom, P. (1984), *Contacts between Police and Public: Findings from the British Crime Survey*, Home Office Research Study 77, London: Home Office.

Southgate, P. (1986), *Police-public Encounters*, Home Office Research Study 90, London: HMSO.

Steedman, C. (1984), *Policing the Victorian Community*, London: Routledge and Kegan Paul.

Tonnies, F. (1955), *Community and Association*, London: Routledge and Kegan Paul.

Trojanowicz, R. (1982), 'An Evaluation of a Neighborhood Foot Patrol Program in Flint, Michigan', East Lansing MI: Michigan State University National Neighborhood Foot Patrol Center.

—— (1986), 'Community Policing: Training Issues', East Lansing MI: Michigan State University National Neighborhood Foot Patrol Center.

—— (1988), 'Serious Threats to the Future of Policing', *Footprints*, II(1), 1–4.

—— (1989), 'Preventing Civil Disturbances: a Community Policing Approach', East Lansing MI: Michigan State University School of Criminal Justice.

Trojanowicz, R. and Bucqueroux, B. (1989), 'What Community Policing can do to Help', *Footprints*, 11(2).

Trojanowicz, R. and Moore, M. (1988), *The Meaning of Community in Community Policing*, East Lansing MI: Michigan State University.

Turner, J. (1988), *A Theory of Social Interaction*, Stanford, CA: Stanford University Press.

Turner, S. (1969), 'Delinquency and Distance' in T. Sellen and M. Wolfgang (eds.) *Delinquency: Selected Studies*, New York: John Wiley and Sons, 11–26.

Waddington, P. (1982), 'What of Community Policing if it's a Community of Criminals', *Police Review*, 62–3.

Weatheritt, M. (1983), 'Community Policing: Does it Work and How do We Know?' in T. Bennett (ed.) *The Future of Policing*, Cropwood Conference series number 15, Cambridge: Institute of Criminology.

—— (1986), *Innovations in Policing*, London: Croom Helm.

—— (1987), 'Community Policing Now' in P. Wilmott (ed.) *Policing and the Community*, London: Policy Studies Institute.

Weinstein, E. (1969), 'The Development of Interpersonal Competence' in D. Goslin (ed.) *Handbook of Socialisation Theory and Research*, Chicago: Rand McNally.

Weinstein, E. and Deutschberger, P. (1964), 'Tasks, Bargains and Identities in Social Interaction', *Social Forces*, 42: 451–6.

Williams, G. H. (1984), *The Law and Politics of Police Discretion*, London: Greenwood Press.

Wilmott, P. 'Introduction' in P. Wilmott (ed.) (1987), *Policing and the Community*, London: Policy Studies Institute.

Wolff Olins Consultants (1988), *A Force for Change: Report on the Corporate Identity of the Metropolitan Police*, London: Olins Consultants.

Wood, C. (1974), 'Lifestyles among West Indians and Social Work Problems', *New Community*, III(3), 249–54.

Worden, R. (1989), 'Situational and Attitudinal Explanations of Police Behaviour', *Law and Society Review*, 23(4), 667–711.

Worden, R. and Brandl, S. (1990), 'Protocol Analysis of Police Decision-making: Toward a Theory of Police Behaviour', *American Journal of Criminal Justice*, XIV(2), 287–318.

Wright Mills C. (1959), *The Sociological Imagination*, Oxford: Oxford University Press.

Young, M. (1986), 'An Anthropology of the Police: Semantic Constructs of Social Order', doctoral thesis, Department of Anthropology, University of Durham.

Index